TWO SIST

BLAKE MORRISON is a poet, no
non-fiction books include *And Whei.*
Father? (1993), which won the J. R. Ackerley Prize and the
Esquire/Volvo/Waterstones Non-Fiction Book Award, *As If*
(1997), about the murder of the toddler James Bulger in
Liverpool in 1993, and a memoir of his mother, *Things My
Mother Never Told Me* (2002). His poetry includes the collections
Dark Glasses (1984), winner of a Somerset Maugham Award,
and *Shingle Street* (2015). He is a regular literary critic for the
Guardian, and the *London Review of Books*.

Praise for *Two Sisters*

'A book at once bold, magnanimous, heart-breaking and
riveting' HOWARD JACOBSON

'Beautiful. Affecting. Erudite' SUSIE ORBACH

'Morrison writes with a reckless respect for the truth'
GUARDIAN

'Pungent, disturbing, entirely unforgettable' *THE TIMES*

'A wonderfully heartfelt and tender thing: delicate and
unstinting and clear-eyed' *OBSERVER*, Book of the Week

'A ground-breaking confessional memoir' BBC Books of 2023

'Harrowing, candid and clear-eyed, unflinchingly honest and
self-critical. Two sad stories. The strangeness of families and the
weight of the past. The guilt of being OK' NICCI GERRARD

'Engrossing' *SPECTATOR*

'A beautiful, brave and brutal memoir that does not shy away
from hard truths' *THE TIMES*

'An acute, wonderfully adroit book, overflowing with sharp
yet compassionate observations about human nature'
THE INDEPENDENT

'A writer of undoubted skill' *NEW STATESMAN*

'True to a complex, many-layered grief' *TLS*

'Few writers can claim to have affected the literary landscape like Blake Morrison . . . *Two Sisters* is not an easy book to read, but it is a bracingly honest one'
MAIL ON SUNDAY, Book of the Week

'Painful, hesitant, honest, agonised, controlled and (especially the latter) full of love' *DAILY MAIL*

'Morrison has a startling gift' *LITERARY REVIEW*

'Affecting . . . it could help those who have lost a sibling'
FINANCIAL TIMES

'Blake Morrison is a writer who tenderly and relentlessly lifts every stone, and the stones beneath, searching for the roots of human feelings and human relations, and revealing them to the reader' LOUISA YOUNG

'Remarkable and heart-breaking' *SHEER LUXE*

Also by Blake Morrison

Dark Glasses
The Ballad of the Yorkshire Ripper
The Yellow House
And When Did You Last See Your Father?
Pendle Witches
As If
Too True
The Justification of Johann Gutenberg
Things My Mother Never Told Me
South of the River
The Last Weekend
A Discoverie of Witches
This Poem
Shingle Street
The Executor

BLAKE MORRISON

two sisters

THE BOROUGH PRESS

The Borough Press
An imprint of HarperCollins*Publishers* Ltd
1 London Bridge Street
London SE1 9GF

www.harpercollins.co.uk

HarperCollins*Publishers*
Macken House,
39/40 Mayor Street Upper,
Dublin 1
D01 C9W8
Ireland

This paperback edition 2024
1

First published in Great Britain by HarperCollins*Publishers* 2023

A catalogue record for this book is available from the British Library

ISBN: 978-0-00-851056-5

Set in Adobe Garamond by Palimpsest Book
Production Limited, Falkirk, Stirlingshire

Printed and bound in the UK using 100% Renewable
Electricity at CPI Group (UK) Ltd

MIX
Paper | Supporting
responsible forestry
FSC™ C007454

This book contains FSC™ certified paper and other controlled
sources to ensure responsible forest management.

For more information visit: www.harpercollins.co.uk/green

For Louise and Liam

'Seeing or hearing the brother, you knew that the sister could not be far off.'

Thomas de Quincey on Charles and Mary Lamb

Nancy Mitford: 'Sisters are a defence against life's cruel circumstances.'
Jessica Mitford: 'Sisters *are* life's cruel circumstances.'

'A sister can be seen as someone who is both ourselves and very much not ourselves – a special kind of double.'

Toni Morrison

'Siblings provide a way of learning to love and hate the same person.'

Juliet Mitchell

'What is this thing you've got about the guy and his sister?'
'It just seemed like an interesting relationship.'

Gore Vidal

1

Early January and I'm with Kathy and our three children at Mum and Dad's house in Yorkshire. We drove up two days ago after spending Christmas at home in London and we'll be heading off again tomorrow. Staying here is more of a squeeze than it used to be in the rectory where my sister Gill and I grew up. Designing and building the new house, in a field at the back of the old house, was Dad's great project when he and Mum retired as GPs, and he's pleased by how it turned out. He has named it Windyridge, after the house his parents owned. There's a big garden, with fine views across the hills towards the Trough of Bowland, and despite the winds that whip through it's warm, which the old house never was. Best of all, Gill is living right next door, with her husband Wynn and their two small children, Liam and Louise. It's what Dad always wanted, to have his children and grandchildren close at hand. Though I've disappointed him by living so far away, his daughter's there on his doorstep: an ideal arrangement.

Perhaps for Gill it's less than ideal. Here she is now, hiding out in Dad's garage at 10.30 in the morning, one hand on the bonnet of his Toyota Corolla to stop her from keeling over, wormy clusters of veins at the corners of her eyes.

I've come through into the garage to get some logs for the fire. An hour ago Wynn dropped Liam and Louise round, on his way to work, saying that Gill was still in bed and would be over later. Here she is. Here but not here. Lurking in the garage.

Come through, I say. It's cold in here.

I brought some gloves for the kids, she says, so they can play outside.

Good thinking, I say.

Gloves for the kids. And here I am, handling Gill with kid gloves, avoiding any comment on her condition. The elephant in the garage.

Yesterday, at our New Year's lunch, she made a bitter, self-accusing remark about how much better Mum and Dad's turkey was than the one she cooked on Christmas Day (subtext: I am a failure, I'm useless at everything). I tried to talk to her afterwards, on the quiet, in the hallway.

What's wrong, Gill? I said.

Nothing.

There must be something.

I might as well top myself, that's all. The kids would rather be here than with me – *Granny and Grandpa's, Granny and Grandpa's, when can we go there, Mum?* Wynn would be better off without me too. He's got everything on a plate as it is – the kids, his meals, his nights out drinking away my money – but he'll have even more if I'm gone. And you, you're never here, what do you care, you've always been their number one, now you can be their *only* one. I've had no life. I don't know what I want, and even if I did I couldn't get it. I haven't the will, I haven't the strength, I might as well top myself.

She went on in this vein for some minutes until Wynn, back from work, walked in on us and she clammed up, went back into the living room, and (despite struggling not to fall asleep) got herself together to do a jigsaw on the floor with Liam. Soon afterwards they all went home together. I imagined the scene back at the house after Wynn and the kids were in bed: Gill helping herself from the Liebfraumilch box in the drinks cabinet or if it was empty looking for one of the other wine boxes secreted about her home – in the doll's house, down the back of the hot-water cistern, behind the Hoover in the cupboard under the stairs. Just a nightcap, she'd tell herself. And if none was to be found, because Wynn has been on one of his purges and removed all the drink he could find, there might be a jar or a jug in the kitchen into which she poured emergency supplies. She's resourceful, my sister. And never more herself than when outwitting those who try to save her from herself.

Now she stands there, swaying in the garage. I move forward to take her arm and steady her but recoil from her wine-dark breath. She has holed up here rather than enter the house, where Mum and Dad will see the state she is in. She knows what they'll say, has heard it all before and isn't in the mood for recriminations.

Why not go home for a bit, Gill? I say. The kids will be fine.

Yeh, she says, no one wants me here, what's the point in staying when . . .

Her words aren't so much slurred as mumbled downwards, to the oil-stained concrete floor, as if too dangerous to say clearly, openly, out loud – words even she's afraid of. I lean forward to catch them, then lean forward to catch her, as she lurches from the bonnet she's been steadying herself on. She's at an angle – the leaning tower of a Pisser, I think, a pun too silly to preserve. Her light-blue eyeshadow has smudged, leaving a blob on her cheek, the one spot of colour in her grey face. Over her shoulder I can see the ordered clutter of Dad's workbench, everything in place yet randomly arranged, garden shears sharing a hook with a roll of wire, tins of nails nestling up against aerosol cans. Only he knows where to find things. My bookshelves at home are the same.

Gill has closed her eyes, shutting out the pain of light. For a moment I see her as she looked in childhood: the same frizzy curls, the turned-up nose, the short, plump body. But the plumpness has moved down and outwards, leaving her with the same fine features and narrow waist but with wide hips and that low centre of gravity certain footballers have – or like a Space Hopper, an inflatable bouncy toy.

What's happened, Gill, I say, suddenly stiff and cold and censorious. Don't you see you're killing yourself.

I'm unhappy. Always have been. That won't ever change.

It can. It will.

Anyway, it's not the drink that's the problem, it's *them* and you.

Me?

They gave you everything and me nothing. You got out, I didn't. You've got a life, I haven't. You turn up here twice a year and then bugger off and never think about us the rest of the time. You can't stand them any more than I can.

I've heard her say all this before, in my head. But it's shocking to hear it spoken out loud.

Let me walk you back to the house and make some black coffee, I say.

I'm fine, just leave me.

It's cold.

You go in then.

Or have a coffee here.

I'm not going in.

We wrangle like this till I agree, all right then, I'll leave her and go inside if she gives me the gloves she has brought over for the children. But when she fishes them from her coat there

4

are only three. She fumbles some more, plumbing the shallows of her pocket as if it were a huge wardrobe in which the glove must be hidden *somewhere*, and keeping at it for an absurdly long time, before conceding, shame-faced, that she must have dropped the missing glove on the way over.

I'll help you look, I say.

OK, she says, suddenly meek.

Retracing her steps, we walk the fifty yards along the drive and through the wooden gate into her garden. There's no sign of the missing glove. By the time we reach her back door she has recovered her angry composure.

You wait here, she says, leaving me on the step, pointedly barring me from entry.

I gaze through the window into the eerily tidy kitchen and playroom, not an alcoholic's house at all, no hint of anyone falling apart, though I know (from Wynn and Mum and Dad) that two small children sometimes run free for hours while their mum lies half comatose in a chair.

How are you doing, Gill? I shout through the door.

Won't be a minute, she shouts back, though it has been several already.

Next to me is a dustbin – the same dustbin, presumably, from which Wynn recently retrieved three wine boxes, twelve bottles of Babycham, two bottles of martini and a bottle of gin, a selection of the booze she'd got through during his absence on a short trip. When I'm up he sometimes shares Gill's drinking stories with me, not in a bid for sympathy but matter-of-factly, because they happened; she's my sister and I might as well know.

Can I help? I shout, and this time I step inside, half expecting Gill to come at me for defying her ban. She is standing helplessly below a high shelf in the hall, reaching up but failing to lay her hands on a large selection of gloves. I spot it at once, a white mitten with the sewn-on patch features – paws, nose, ears – of a rabbit.

I think this might be it, I say, reaching up and pretending for her sake to find it only with difficulty.

Thanks.

Shall we go back then? I say, handing it over, but she's angrier than ever now. I have made her feel small.

You go out, she says, I'm staying.

'You go' would be enough. 'You go out' sounds hostile.

Go on, she says, in case I've missed the hostility, on your way.

I'm guessing that this new surge of vitality – this elated aggression – has something to do with the length of time she spent inside before I joined her. There must be a wine box somewhere and new ones take time to open – it's a fiddly process of tearing the cardboard along perforations before squiggling out the plastic press-bung.

I walk along the hall to the back door.

Get out – out of my house, she says, victorious, to my retreating back. Go on with you.

Now she has won, the tone is less harsh, almost affectionate.

As I turn and stand my ground, she tries to close the door on me, not fiercely but with firm intent.

Don't slam it on me, I say, you'll only be sorry when you remember this later.

When you've sobered up, I mean. But she doesn't rise to this, or fall for it, just presses the door against my right foot, the last thing keeping me there.

Go on, get out, she says, with the same resolve.

All right, see you later, I say, removing my foot from the door and heading off down the garden path, the white rabbit mitten in my hand.

2

If you're reading this, my sister is dead. I may be dead too, but that's beside the point, for you if not for me. Many years ago I resolved not to write about her while she was alive, or rather not to publish anything that I had written. She – Gill – had walk-on parts, like a film extra, in two memoirs I published about our parents.* That's all it was: the odd look-in or passing mention. There was plenty to be said but not yet. Even if she had given me *carte blanche*, the page would have stayed blank. You can't write an honest memoir when the subject is alive. At any rate I can't. Death is the only permission.

After those books about Mum and Dad came out, I was sometimes asked if I had another memoir in me. No, I'd reply,

---

*In my memoirs about them, I used the terms 'my parents', 'my father' and 'my mother'. Fair enough, perhaps, because the book was subjective, an interpretation of them from my point of view, not Gill's. Even when drafting this book, I found myself instinctively saying 'my parents'. Now it feels wrong, as if I were wresting them away from Gill, whose parents they were too. In a book where I write about her, there's all the more reason to make redress. 'Our' sounds too formal, though. So in general I'm adopting a usage that seems more acceptable in a family memoir than it did two decades ago: Mum and Dad.

I write fiction these days because I've run out of family. Once or twice I answered even more facetiously: I don't know if I've another memoir in me but my sister's quaking in her boots. There's an assumption that to write honestly about someone is an act of aggression; that's the gallery I was playing to. But I felt no aggression towards Gill – didn't then and don't now. She's gone, that's all, and though there's no retrieving her I'd like to make sense of who she was and what she became. It wasn't just that she changed over time. She could change from day to day. Drink made it worse but the origins went deeper. You never knew which you'd get, the kind and loving Gill or her doppelgänger. Two sisters.

I had another sister as well. Josie's a smaller part of the story I'm telling. A half-sister, whereas Gill was full (and often full on). A baby sister proudly held up to Gill and me, as we stood at a hospital window, on the day that she was born, but whose relation to us was never acknowledged. A sister I didn't know *was* my sister until eight months before she died.

Two sisters, both younger than I am and both dead. It's painful to think about that and tempting to let them be. But I want to understand why their lives took the direction they did – and why they died, self-destructively, before their time. I know there's no simple answer; that I'm writing from the limited perspective of a brother (or half-brother); that my memories are fragmented and unreliable. Still, I can't not make the effort. With Gill, I can't *help* making it. What she went through, and what her family went through, many others have gone through too. My hope is that telling her story will prompt recognition; perhaps the solace of commonality too. And that means being honest. The ethics of writing about real people are problematic. Candour can seem disrespectful. But when you grow up with a lie, as my sisters did, it's important to be truthful. Soft-pedalling would be cowardly. And the truth isn't malicious. I'm here to commemorate them, not expose.

It may be that I've another more selfish purpose: self-exoneration. When you're newly bereaved, and the death of the person you're mourning strikes you as preventable, guilt is impossible to avoid. Why didn't you meet more, speak more, tell them you loved them (assuming you did)? If you had, might you have saved them? My sisters' deaths left me feeling neglectful. And when I turned to books for comfort or commonality, I found neglect there too. I hoped to find an author whose writing about a sister (real or imagined) could articulate my thoughts and feelings, whose insights could help me see things I'd missed, whose words could stand in for mine. Low as I was, even the greatest book might have failed to reach me. But I hadn't expected the choice to be so limited. Why did so few books explore brother–sister relationships? In particular why did so few male authors write about sisters? Did their sisters not matter to them – or the relationship in general not matter enough to merit enquiry? Brothers writing about brothers; sisters writing about sisters; sisters writing about brothers – there were many examples of those. But brothers writing about sisters? Very few.

The sibling relationship is usually the first we have with someone of our own generation. Barring misadventure it's also the relationship that lasts longest – longer than the relationship with parents, or with a partner, or with one's kids. So why is its place in literature so modest? Perhaps it's the tradition of the writer as isolated genius, or family escapee, that deters mention of siblings – 'the powerful concentration on one's own person-ality, the act of an artist's indefatigable and invincible will' as Vladimir Nabokov puts it. In his memoir *Speak, Memory*, Nabokov offers just a couple of pages on his two brothers;

though one of them, Sergei, was only ten months his junior, he dismisses him as 'a mere shadow in the background of my richest and most detailed recollections'. Still, that's more acknowledgement than he gives his sisters, who merit only a passing reference and that so inaccurate that they 'angrily remonstrated' with him when the memoir appeared.

If asymmetry defines a child's relationship with its parents (the parents holding the power), the sibling relationship is meant to be more even and commensurate.* It's also a relationship that can't be dissolved; you can fall out with a sibling but not legally divorce or disown them. (A few friends I've talked to, who have bad relationships with their siblings, wish they could.) Yet there's nothing new about its low profile, whether in literature or psychoanalysis. Valerie Sanders, writing about the Victorian period in her book *The Brother-Sister Culture in Nineteenth-Century Literature*, reports that 'None of the great names in the field has much to say about sibling relationships . . . There is no sense in any of the major male autobiographers of the period that relationships with brothers or sisters were at all significant.'

By the same token, because a sibling isn't (or shouldn't be) a lover or spouse, there's not the same expectation of intensity. There may be tension. But passion? It's felt to be a lesser relationship, a hangover from childhood and adolescence, not the stuff of grown-up narrative.† As J. R. Ackerley put it, about his

---

* In her book *Siblings* (2003) Juliet Mitchell suggests that 'we have suppressed the importance of siblings', arguing that horizontal (sibling) relationships have been insufficiently considered, not least by psychoanalysts, because of a Freudian preoccupation with vertical ones (parent–child).

† An extreme version of this prejudice can be found in the American poet Robert Bly's book *The Sibling Society*, which uses 'sibling' as a

sister Nancy: 'She was my sister only, my only sister, but my sister only . . . I am only her brother, her only brother, but only that.'

It's not just that relatively few male authors have written about their sisters; it's that when they do, their efforts are overlooked. Thomas Hardy's poems of 1912–13, on the death of his wife Emma, are very well known. But how many people know the elegy he wrote for his sister Mary when she died of emphysema in November 1915? The eldest of his sisters, she was, he told a friend, 'almost my only companion in childhood' and 'the one with the keenest literary tastes and instincts':

> The fire advances along the log
>> Of the tree we felled,
> Which bloomed and bore striped apples by the peck
>> Till its last hour of bearing knelled.

---

synonym for adolescent. Sibling society, as he defines it, is a society hostile to authority and hierarchy; where the wisdom of elders is denied; where verticality (deference to those above you, protectiveness to those below) has been replaced by horizontality (the belief we're all equal and therefore owe nothing to each other); where gender differences are dismantled; where 'we are all fish swimming in a tank of half-adults'. I bought the book hoping to find something about siblings but Bly uses the word merely to denounce the selfishness, shallowness, irresponsibility and incivility he associates with adolescence. I was similarly frustrated by Juliet Flower MacCannell's *The Regime of the Brother*: a feminist psychoanalytical study of the shift from monarchy (or autocracy) to democracy after the Enlightenment, and the failure of that shift to bring freedom and equality to women, it has, despite its title, nothing to say about brothers.

The fork that first my hand would reach
   And then my foot
In climbings upward inch by inch, lies now
   Sawn, sapless, darkening with soot.

Where the bark chars is where, one year,
   It was pruned, and bled –
Then overgrew the wound. But now, at last,
   Its growings all have stagnated.

My fellow-climber rises dim
   From her chilly grave –
Just as she was, her foot near mine on the bending limb,
   Laughing, her young brown hand awave.

Completed at speed (Hardy published it within a month of Mary's death) and old-fashioned in idiom ('peck', 'knelled', 'awave'), it's not as successful a poem as those he wrote about Emma. Still, its commemoration of their closeness in childhood ('her foot near mine') is touching, and the image of Mary re-emerging from the grave with her 'young brown hand' is reminiscent of how he pictures Emma as a 'voiceless ghost' suddenly 'Facing round about me everywhere,/With your nut-coloured hair'. It's symptomatic that I missed the poem when I read Hardy's Collected. I'm part of a culture that treats sibling relationships as inconsequential.

Finding it after Gill's death spurred me on to look for other examples of writing about siblings. I read obsessively, not just from guilt, but to understand how brothers have traditionally thought and felt about sisters – and to look at mine through the lens of books. Perhaps it's daft to use books in that way. But I've spent my life among them: where else would I go? And the genre – sib-lit – turned out to be less narrow than I'd first thought. That's why this is a memoir full of quotations – a commonplace book or cento. Why its narrative is interspersed with anecdotes about famous (and infamous) brother–sister relationships. And why it has footnotes.*

Some of the brothers I came across were cruel to their sisters, others gentle and protective. Either way, I couldn't help measuring myself against them. I've never pined for a brother; the books in which brothers feature, whether novels or biographies, reminded me why. Still, I was grateful for my immersion in sib-lit. Even at its gloomiest, it helped me get my bearings.

That said, the authors I read were helpful only up to a point. They hadn't written about *my* sister – or sister*s*. Only I could do that. I had letters and diaries to draw on; relatives whose memories I could check against mine; photos to remind me of episodes I'd half forgotten. And where there were gaps or obstructions, I was forced to surmise. That's not quite the same as fictionalising, since the protagonists were people I knew in real life. But it did involve some speculation, just as it would for any biographer. This isn't a biography but it's closer to biography than it is to fiction. It's life writing. And as with most life writing, the trigger for it was death.

There's my trigger warning. Some of what's here is discomfiting. I'm sorry that's the case. But I'd be lying to pretend otherwise. And my aim is to tell the truth.

---

*As well as their intrinsic fascination and relevance, the examples of notable brothers and sisters I came across were a relief from the story I had to tell. For any reader inclined to skip these, chapters 5, 8, 10, 12, 14, 17, 19, 21 and 23 are less directly concerned with Gill and Josie. Footnotes can be skipped too, of course – they often are.

3

'I believe I should count the fact of having had a sister, younger than myself but close to me in age, as one of my pieces of good luck.'

Simone de Beauvoir, *All Said and Done*

There's a photo of me as a toddler trying to climb inside my sister's pram. From the rear, I could be a girl: I'm wearing frilly bottoms, with straps across my back holding them up, like a swimsuit. My feet are in the spokes of the pram's back wheel and my hands grip the side. Gill's lying on a pillow, the hood of the pram folded behind her. It's a sunny day and we're in the garden. My efforts to climb in must be shaking the pram; the expression on Gill's face isn't happy. In fact she looks to be crying.

At the time Dad was a keen photographer, or doting parent, and he took two more photos straight after this one. In the first, I'm sitting in the pram, at the handle end, holding out a bottle to Gill; in the second I'm lying on top of her, my mouth wide open as if to sing a lullaby or (in the way of parents with their newborns) to *ooh* and *aah* at her. In these photos she has stopped crying. She doesn't even seem to mind me invading her space.

There's no mistaking from the photos that I'm bigger than she is but the difference isn't huge. The gap between us was just sixteen months; the pram had been mine till a few weeks before. Mum and Dad had taken their time before starting a family. But having started, they moved fast to complete it. First a boy, then a girl: that would do nicely. It had worked for Dad, who'd always been close to his younger sister Mary. And it suited Mum, who as the nineteenth child of twenty was reacting against her populous Irish-Catholic upbringing. Father, mother, two kids, two dogs and two cars – that was the model they went for. With the advantage that the kids were close in age and could keep each other company: share games, share toys, even share a pram.

Was I climbing into the pram out of jealousy? I don't remember resenting my sister's arrival or suffering the trauma of non-uniqueness. But then I wouldn't, would I? Psychoanalytic theory suggests I must have done. 'The sibling is *par excellence* someone who threatens the subject's existence,' Juliet Mitchell says, and Louise Glück bears witness to this in her poem 'Paradise': 'I was the firstborn./Believe me, you never heal,/You never forget the ache in your side,/The place where something was taken away/ To make another person.' Then again, I was a boy, and boys had primacy. A brother might have been a rival. But why feel threatened by a younger sister? What danger did she pose to my omnipotence? I could afford to be nice rather than compelled to slap her down. She wasn't Goldilocks taking my things. Let her have the pram. I was old enough to have a pushchair.

There's a name for children born close together: Irish twins. We weren't quite that but Mum was Irish and two of her siblings had been born just eleven months apart. George Eliot has a sonnet sequence, 'Brother and Sister', which celebrates this kind of early-childhood proximity where 'the one so near the other is'. Any gaps are minor, 'a Like unlike', 'the self-same world enlarged for each/By loving difference of girl and boy'. The closeness can't last forever but 'the twin habit of that early time' outweighs the pain of later separation.* A *like unlike* says it well: Gill and I were of a piece but different; in the self-same world but worlds apart.

Nabokov said of his brother Sergei: 'We seldom played together, he was indifferent to most of the things I was fond of.' Did Gill and I play together? We must have. Yet I can't recall it. Most of early childhood gets forgotten anyway, but even in the memories that have stuck joint play doesn't feature. While I raced my Dinky cars round the billiard table, Gill was giving tea parties to her dolls, each of us on our own planet, the separate universe of Girl and Boy. Did she mind? Did I? Not really. I wanted to be me; she wanted to be her. Though encouraged to share, we had different interests. Decades before I became one, I sometimes thought of myself as an only child.

*

* If the poem sounds saccharine, there's a reason. Eliot published it in 1869, a couple of years before *Middlemarch*, while brooding on her relationship with her brother Isaac, to whom she'd once been close but who disowned her when she began living with the 'licentious' (i.e. married) George Henry Lewes. Her tender, Wordsworthian celebration of their childhood years is craven in its appeal to him to remember the good times and in its assurance that, if she had her time again, she wouldn't change a thing: 'were another childhood-world my share,/I would be born a little sister there.' She hoped the poem might make Isaac relent. But it was eight more years before he did – not because the poem belatedly won him round but because, after Lewes's death, she married John Cross and became, in Isaac's mind, respectable.

In the long run, sixteen months is a small gap but not when you're a child. Henry James recounts in his memoir *A Small Boy and Others* how his brother William 'had gained such an advantage in his sixteen months' experience of the world before mine began that I never for all the time of childhood in the least caught up with him or overtook him . . . We were never in the same schoolroom, in the same game, scarce even in step together or in the same phase at the same time; when our phases overlapped, that is, it was only for a moment – he was clean out before I had got well in.' The behind-ness did Henry no harm. It may even have contributed to his becoming a novelist – rather than try to catch up with his hyper-active brother, he sat and watched, developing observational skills he might not otherwise have had.

Gill was watchful too. It's one of the ironies of what happened later. Even now I can sense her stare – the keenness of her eyes as they take in the world.

She was a bonny baby, everyone said, cherubic almost – pink-cheeked and with lovely blonde curls. She also cried a lot as a toddler. No big deal, Mum and Dad said, she'll soon grow out of it – tantrums were just the flipside of laughter. 'I'se such a good little girl – sometimes!' said the girl in the Mabel Lucie Attwell picture in our bathroom. A Longfellow rhyme said much the same: 'There was a little girl,/Who had a little curl,/Right in the middle of her forehead./When she was good,/She was very good indeed,/But when she was bad she was horrid.'

Gill wasn't horrid, only distressed. When asked what the matter was, she couldn't account for it. She had tears but no words. And that made her difficult to console.

Like George Eliot's Maggie Tulliver, she was gifted with the 'superior power of misery'. Her fits of unhappiness made the rest of us unhappy. She wasn't *left* to cry but it seemed an age before she stopped.*

There were family outings. Card and board games. Weekly swimming lessons at the baths in Nelson. Sledging in winter, on the field at the back of our house. Later came a ski-ing trip to Scotland, for which we were kitted out in matching sickly-yellow waterproof jackets – not just Gill and me, but Mum and Dad as well. The swish family Morrison. Parents and children, not to be told apart.

The house was spacious, and Gill and I sometimes felt isolated, as if in lockdown during a pandemic. There wasn't much socialising outside school: no sleepovers, few invitations to tea. Maybe our parents' status, as doctors, was intimidating to other kids' parents. Or the house was: an old rectory, with outbuildings, at the top of the village. At any rate most of the asking back was to ours and often enough we'd be told that the child in question – Stephen or Jeffrey or Christine – wasn't able to come.

Birthday parties were the exception: a thrilling escape from

---

* George Eliot is angry with those who treat childhood tears as insignificant: 'We have all of us sobbed so piteously, standing with tiny bare legs above our little socks, when we lost sight of our mother or nurse in some strange place . . . Every one of those keen moments has left its trace and lives in us still, but such traces have blended themselves irrevocably with the firmer texture of our youth and manhood; and so it comes that we can look on at the troubles of our children with a smiling disbelief in the reality of their pain . . . Surely if we could recall that early bitterness, and the dim guesses, the strangely perspectiveless conception of life that gave the bitterness its intensity, we should not pooh-pooh the griefs of our children.'

just-us-two. There were fancy-dress parties as well; Gill won when she went as a film star and came second as a squaw. The games were always the same – Pass the Parcel, Postman's Knock, Musical Chairs, Musical Bumps, Musical Statues, Apple Bobbing – but no less fun for that. A lot of concealment was involved: Hide and Seek, Hunt the Thimble. A fair bit of blindness too: Pin the Tail on the Donkey, for example, and Blind Man's Bluff. The latter was unnerving: with a scarf over your eyes – no peeping! – you'd be twirled in all directions. Gill laughed as she played, unaware that one day there'd be no bluffing about it.*

Vladimir Nabokov, in *Speak, Memory*, on the parenting he and his brother Sergei had, said: 'I was the coddled one; he the witness of coddling.' Did Gill feel uncoddled? Or that she somehow mattered less, because she was a girl? Recalling her childhood in Egypt, the novelist Nawal El Saadawi describes how when her father sat out on their balcony looking at the stars, only her brother would be allowed to join him. Female relatives subscribed to these double standards too: when her grandmother gave money to the children at Eid, the boys would receive twice as much as the girls. 'God has told us that a girl is worth half a boy,' she explained.†

Dad would never have stopped Gill looking at the stars with

---

*The game is also known as 'Blind Man's Buff' – 'buff' meaning the push you give to the person in the blindfold to confuse them about their whereabouts. But to us it was always 'bluff' since a lot of cheating went on regarding how little, or how much, you could see.

† Female collusion with the patriarchy proved uglier still when, at six, like every other girl in the village, Nawal was circumcised, and four women held her down during the procedure.

him. For the most part we were treated equally, 'share and share alike, the cardinal point of justice driven home to [us] with vicious exactitude' (E. L. Doctorow, *The Book of Daniel*), with the result that there was no bad feeling between us.* Still, there were double standards. And though she didn't protest when Dad and I were allowed larger helpings at mealtimes, some part of her must have been objecting. Why were we allowed more – whether of food, fun or freedom – just because we were men? 'Our basket held a store/Baked for us only, and I thought with joy/That I should have my share, though he had more,/Because he was the elder and a boy.' (George Eliot, 'Brother and Sister')

Mum was a GP at a time when, in the provinces at least, it was unusual for middle-class wives to work outside the home. A succession of women were hired as live-in housekeepers: first Austrian Rosa, then long-nosed Lennie, then a woman who quit after walking in on Dad while he sat on the toilet. Their job was to clean, cook and take phone messages for the doctor(s), not to be au pairs or nannies. As children tended to be in those days, we were left to our own devices.

As the second youngest in a large family, Mum was used to detached mothering. Her mother had gone to church every day, praying to the virgin Mary; *she* went out to work every day, healing the sick and delivering babies. I took her absence for granted. Gill found it harder. I'd had sixteen months of

---

* 'We loved each other with a perfect Fondness,' a character called Camilla says of her childhood relationship with her brother Valentine in Sarah Fielding's *The Adventures of David Simple*, 'there was no Partiality shewn to either of us; nor were we told, if we did not do right, the other should be loved best, in order to teach us to *envy*, and consequently to *hate* each other.'

exclusive attention before she was born. She never had Mum to herself.

Gill began school a year after I did. The school was tiny, with a total of eighteen pupils at its peak and at times as few as fourteen. There were three of us in my year (all boys) and four in Gill's (three girls and a boy). The head teacher, the *only* teacher, was a kindly silver-haired woman called Miss Todd, who had to teach five-year-olds at the same time as teaching ten-year-olds, all in the one room. There'd be sums, reading, art and craftwork (with raffia), plus stories to finish the day. I can't recall any outings; there weren't the resources, or the transport, to take us to libraries, museums, galleries, theatres or cinemas. The only escape was for nature walks, up Cam Lane.

A busy road ran through the village. To make our route to school safer and shorter, Dad knocked a hole in the wall beyond the vegetable garden, and fitted a small gate, allowing access across the village green. I like to think I took Gill's hand as we walked there. But I may have thought it too cissy. Once we reached school, we went our own ways.*

At school Gill was shy and quick to take offence. Because pupil numbers were so small, friendship was a competitive

---

*Scout, on being taken to school for the first time by her brother in Harper Lee's *To Kill a Mockingbird*:

When we slowed to a walk at the edge of the school yard, Jem was careful to explain that during school hours I was not to bother him . . .

'You mean we can't play any more?' I asked.

'We'll do like we always do at home,' he said, 'but you'll see – school's different.'

business; if you were excluded by your year group you'd be on your own. It happened to me as well as Gill but the girls were more adept at exclusion games. As if to arm herself against rejection, Gill would be acerbic and make things worse for herself. She was wary of girls who found life easier than she did, because they were pretty or clever or adept with a skipping rope or could run fast. Her jealousy would sometimes spill out. The one girl she could rely on was Christine, who lived across the road.

I've no memories of bullying Gill and she didn't accuse me of doing so. But I did once run her over. I'd been given a pedal car as a Christmas present, the same one I'd been given the previous Christmas – white, with a red seat, silver radiator grille and a long bonnet – but with a small petrol engine, taken from a lawnmower, fitted in the back. I drove it in a circuit round the house. The engine's only flaw was a tendency to overheat. If it stalled I'd have to wait an hour before I could restart it. That's my excuse.

Gill was standing on the gravel path behind Granny's cottage as I came round the corner. Look out, I shouted, still some distance away and not going very fast. She saw me coming but didn't move. I slowed and tried to avoid her but the path was narrow and if I'd stopped the engine would have stalled. As I went by, the left front wheel caught her ankle. She may have screamed but any cries were drowned by the noise of the engine. I knew I'd hit her but carried on. She wasn't there on the next lap. Now I did stop. What on earth were you doing? Mum shouted as she comforted Gill in the kitchen. Her ankle was only bruised but (as Mum said and Dad angrily reiterated when he got home) it could have been a lot worse. I was threatened with a driving ban and confiscation of the car.

Of course I apologised to Gill. But my chief feeling was indignation: she'd seen me coming – why hadn't she moved? Why was she so *stupid*?

'Stupid' was a routine insult. Any kid at school might use it of another. But Gill was on the receiving end more than most. She would even use it of herself: I know I'm stupid but . . . Mum and Dad rightly denied that she was stupid. She's bright, possibly *too* bright, Dad would later say, with an over-active mind. She anticipates things two moves ahead. That she failed to anticipate me running into her with the pedal car was hardly her fault. Wouldn't any normal driver have stopped? It might not have been malicious of me but it was selfish, thoughtless and – yes – stupid.

What did Gill get as a Christmas present while I was getting a car? A doll's house? A rocking horse? Something girly anyway. I don't remember her playing with my Dinky cars, or wanting to drive my pedal car, though I wasn't possessive and wouldn't have minded. Sexism ruled, with toys as with most things. And boys had priority.

It wasn't just our parents. The whole culture worked that way. Even nursery rhymes played a part. There was 'Jack and Jill', all the more resonant since my sister was a Gill:

> Jack and Jill went up the hill
> To fetch a pail of water.
> Jack fell down and broke his crown,
> And Jill came tumbling after.

The boy leads the way – first to be named, first to fall down the hill. But at least Jill gets a mention. In the second stanza she disappears completely. He'll be OK but whatever happened to her?

Up Jack got, and home did trot,
As fast as he could caper,
He went to bed to mend his head,
With vinegar and brown paper.

The nursery rhymes we learned, and the songs we heard on Uncle Mac's weekly radio programme on the Home Service, reinforced the idea of gender division ('I'm a pink toothbrush, you're a blue toothbrush') and featured mostly male protagonists: Tubby the Tuba, the Billy Goats Gruff, Little Jack Horner ('What a good boy am I'), Georgie Porgie (kisser of nameless girls), Tommy Steele's Little White Bull. The most saccharine was a lullaby Mum liked to sing:

Little man you're cryin', I know why you're blue
Someone took your kiddy-car away
Better go to sleep now
Little man you've had a busy day . . .

Johnny won your marbles, tell you what we'll do
Dad will get you new ones right away
Better go to sleep now
Little man you've had a busy day . . .

Perhaps there was an equivalent, girl-focused lullaby for Gill. But if so I can't remember it.

4

When Gill was six or seven, Mum and Dad became friends with a couple called Sam and Beaty, who ran a local pub* – Auntie Beaty and Uncle Sam as Gill and I were encouraged to call them. Children weren't allowed in pubs back then, so when we went as a family, on Sunday lunchtimes, Gill and I would be left to sit on a bench outside, or in the car, with orangeade and crisps to tide us over. The pub closed at two but Mum and Dad sometimes lingered past three. I sensed he was keener than she was on the new friendship. He also went to the pub most nights. If there were rumours I was too young for them to reach me and wouldn't have understood them if they had. But Dad wasn't good at dissembling and his increased pub-going can't have escaped people's notice. Nor that it was Beaty on whom he lavished his attention.

The bigger shift was when he started taking Beaty out: every Monday evening he'd pick her up and take her somewhere, usually to a club to drink and dance. Beaty was in low spirits – stressed by the long hours at the pub and depressed by her

---

*In an earlier memoir, in order not to identify them, I said it was the bar of a golf club. Now they're dead I can be more truthful, though I'm sticking to their invented names.

and Sam's failure to conceive a child. Open as she was, she'd discussed these problems with Mum, a good listener as well as a GP. Her knowledge of Beaty's problems made it easier for Dad to persuade her that the Monday outings were a good idea – a way to 'cheer Beaty up'. How was Sam won round? Even the weakest or most easy-going of men might have objected to the arrangement, if only because of the failure it implied on his part: shouldn't he have been the one to cheer his wife up? But Sam was tied to the bar and hadn't the freedom to take her out. I can imagine Dad reminding him of that and persuading him that Beaty needed a break – that her nerves were strained, that Monday nights being quiet he didn't need her help at the bar, that since Kim had agreed surely he could do the same. Or perhaps it was Beaty (off her own bat or under pressure from Dad) who argued the case on their behalf, with the further guilt-inducing suggestion that her nerves were strained in part because of her failure to conceive.

There may have been some fiction to make the arrangement more palatable to Sam – an implication, or more than, that they'd be meeting people they knew, that this wasn't just a twosome. Obviously they couldn't pretend that Kim would be going with them, because Sam could check. Mum wouldn't have played ball anyway. To be browbeaten into accepting her husband's freedom to go out with another woman was one thing; to lie to save his and Beaty's skin was a step too far.

Whatever the case, Sam accepted the arrangement.

Dad's father Ernest died in November 1958. I'd just had my eighth birthday and was taken to see him lying in his open coffin – a move designed to remove my fear of death, which partly worked (he looked so peaceful in there) but was traumatising just the same: the waxy flesh, silence and immovability haunted me for years. Beaty's daughter, Josephine, was born in October 1959, eleven months later. The dates lend some credence to what Mum told me in a rare moment of candour after Dad's death – that Dad's grief was a key factor in the commencement or acceleration of his relationship with Beaty; that it wasn't just Beaty who needed cheering up; that in the desolate months after losing his father so suddenly (a coronary) and early (at the age of sixty-eight) he had gone off the rails; that Beaty's company had been a comfort to him when he 'wasn't himself'.

That winter he was in need of warmth. Did he not get enough of it from Mum? She'd lost her parents, within a few months of each other, over a decade before. How sympathetic had he been then? Insufficiently, at a guess. Or maybe she wasn't grief-struck by the loss, having been independent from an early age: first convent boarding school, then medical training in Dublin, then hospital work in wartime England – there'd been years of loosening ties before her parents died. It was different for Arthur, she knew that. But he still had his mother, didn't he? As well as a wife and two children. Whereas she'd given up so much, surrendering her name, nation and religion (Agnes, Ireland and Catholicism) in order to be with him. Don't talk to me about loss, she might have said, to stop him maundering. I'm sure she didn't say it – bore with him, was kind, let him have his late nights out God knows where – but couldn't help thinking it.

Grief as an excuse for infidelity? There are worse ones. It's common for the newly bereaved to feel desperate for sex. I felt it myself, keenly, in the weeks after Dad died. Like father like son.

Miserable in their different ways, Dad and Beaty cheered each other up by making love. Furtively. Probably in his car. It can't have been at her place, where Sam was always around, or ours, where even if Mum was out working, and Gill and I were at school, there'd be a housekeeper. The story of them going to a club may have been a lie. After a time they may have started going to a hotel instead. But what sort of hotel in those days would have let out its rooms for a few hours to a couple? In London, yes. But in the provinces? In the 1950s? And it *would* only have been for a few hours. They couldn't stay overnight. Dad had morning surgery. And there were appearances to keep up as well as the forbearance of their partners. The Monday excursions were risky enough – patients of his, or customers of hers, might spot them together, and draw conclusions – but no one could say for sure the relationship was illicit. The scandal would only come if they were seen leaving a hotel, or returning home, on a Tuesday morning.

I'm assuming, because she got pregnant, that it happened more than once. But if the time of the month was propitious, a single lapse – desire overwhelming them, caution thrown to the winds – would have been enough for Beaty to conceive. That's what happens in Victorian novels, why not in life? Then again Dad did once own up (when I pressed him, with filial impertinence, many years later) to being infatuated with Beaty 'for months' – 'for years', Mum corrected him. And I can remember his delight in her. For a time it may have been platonic – nothing more transgressive than a kiss. But at some point she gave in and let him make love to her.

Gave in . . . let him: passive though I'm making her sound, I can't help thinking of it that way. Everything I know about her tells me that she would have felt duty-bound to resist, to remind him it was wrong, that they were married to other people, that she'd feel awful betraying Sam and Kim. But when Dad wanted something – everyone agreed about this – there was no stopping him. I don't mean he'd have forced himself on Beaty; he wasn't violent or even especially strong. But he was persuasive. She wouldn't be the first woman to consent to sex while feeling she ought to say No. She loved him. Part of her must have thought, What the hell. Or OK then. Or simply, passionately, Yes.

Did they continue having sex after she conceived? The love affair – the infatuation or (another word he used of it) obsession – went on for much of my childhood. I can remember them taking us out for drives while Mum worked and how they'd park in a spot where we could play and they be left alone in the car. But after a time the sex may have stopped. First passion, then the pregnancy shock, then the dilemma what to do next, and afterwards the curtailment of sex. Either their outraged partners kicked up. Or they imposed a ban on themselves, because of the horror of what had happened.

Horror? They came to think of the unborn child as a blessing. But at first, as they agonised over what to do, horror was surely the reaction.

Did Dad suggest an abortion? It would certainly have been discussed. Did he urge it? Perhaps. He'd two children already and wasn't looking to have a third, least of all one born outside marriage. A year or two before, Mum had a miscarriage – late enough to know the baby was a boy – and the thought of that third child, which *had* been wanted but didn't come to pass, or to term, was a sadness to him and all the more so to her. Which made Beaty's pregnancy all the more awkward; repugnant even.

The abortion wouldn't have been difficult to arrange. He was a doctor, with contacts. As an obstetrician Mum had even more contacts. But Beaty had always wanted a child. And – no less crucial – she was a Catholic.

Oh, the irony: another Catholic! Despite his family's anti-Catholicism, to which Dad wholeheartedly subscribed, he'd not only married a Catholic but chosen one as his lover. A different kind of woman – worldly, secular, unwilling to imperil her marriage – might have agreed to an abortion. Not Beaty. No way, she'd have said, it's a crime to destroy a foetus. And he, reluctantly, despite all the trouble there'd be, accepted it. It was her right, her body and her choice.

Besides, reluctance was only part of it. He loved Beaty. And he loved her with more passion than he loved Mum – perhaps not with more passion than he'd felt for Mum in the early days, before she *was* a mum, but with more passion than he felt now, fifteen years on. A child born of passion is a wonderful thing, he and Beaty would have agreed. Had he been calmer, or less of a sentimentalist, he might have seen it differently. But he'd lost his father only a few months before and he wasn't in a calm or pragmatic state of mind. He might have reasoned – optimist as he was – that all would turn out for the best. Play their cards right and the arrival of a baby need not be a matter of shame. Whereas to Beaty, an abortion would have been worse than shameful – a sin in the eyes of God. Once reconciled to the idea, Dad endorsed it. Not that he could say it to anyone except her, but a child born of their love would be marvellous.

Another scenario sometimes comes to mind. That so desperate was her longing for a baby, she initiated the affair. That she used her sex appeal – Beaty was certainly sexy – to draw him in. That she picked him out from her other customers at the bar as the perfect sperm donor: a middle-class professional, healthy, sociable, with good genes. That they might not even have known each other all that well, let alone been in love, when they first, or for the one-and-only time, had sex.

I think the chances of this are remote. Beaty wasn't the calculating kind. And if she couldn't get pregnant by Sam, why expect to get pregnant by Arthur?

It's more likely she assumed she *wouldn't* get pregnant. That she'd been made to think – men being men, and Sam being more assertively male than most – that she was the one with a fertility problem and that it was safe to have sex with Arthur. She'd have thought it wrong. And her seeming inability to have a child would have been a sadness. But if they were going to do it, there'd be no need for contraception, which as a Catholic she wasn't keen on anyway.

Two things I can't believe: that she lied to him, 'tricked him into it', by pretending to be infertile when she knew she wasn't; or that she told him she wanted a child and he volunteered to inseminate her.

The shame for Beaty – and in 1950s provincial England shame was as ubiquitous as warm beer – would have been a child born out of wedlock. But she was married. And if the child could be passed off as Sam's, it would be a child born *in* wedlock. To quote Milton, in *Samson Agonistes*: 'I prayed for children and thought barrenness in wedlock a reproach'.

Wedlock: an unfortunate word for the state of matrimony, implying as it does restriction, confinement, imprisonment – a door closed on the wider world. My *OED* tells me that 'wedlock' can also be used as a synonym for wife, as though the onus of keeping a marriage going – of keeping it locked – falls on the woman. A spouse can be *wedlocked* and a would-be spouse *wedlockable*. But the villain is a *wedlock-breaker*: a man or woman who prises open the locks in order to grab the loot of freedom and enjoy the riches of adultery.

*

Decades later, after Beaty died, her daughter Josephine asked Sam, possibly not for the first time, Am I yours? Yes you are, he replied.

If everyone enmeshed in the secret agreed on this as the official version, he would have had to say it – even then, when the other three were dead. But it's not implausible that Sam believed it. He and Beaty had tried to have a child for years, without success. But they wouldn't be the first couple to whom a child was born in such circumstances or – in more recent times – after having a previous child by IVF. And because he so badly wanted Josie to be his, it's possible he deluded himself – and when he told her 'Yes, you are' wasn't wilfully lying, or tactfully protecting her, but speaking what he thought of as the truth.

Yes, it's possible. But on balance, I think he knew she wasn't his. Perhaps not when she was conceived or as a baby, but as time went on and her resemblance to Arthur became hard to miss.

Equally, as the one who brought her up, she *was* his. Sam might not have fathered Josie but he was her father.

If he knew, how did he react when Beaty first told him she was pregnant?

Sam was a large man: *burly* is the word that comes to mind. And as a publican, he knew how to look after himself; there were sometimes drunk and difficult customers to deal with, and always the risk that they would turn violent. The job wasn't for cissies; you had to be big, tough, an enforcer.

My father was small – 5 foot 7 inches he liked to say, though 5 foot 6 was nearer the mark. I imagine the scene. The news having just been broken to Sam, and Sam wanting to break something in return – if not Beaty's nose, then Arthur's neck.

He was tied to work seven days a week, manning the bar, changing barrels, washing the glasses, restocking the shelves, watching the till, doing accounts, with only Beaty and the occasional part-timer to help him. And as a man with a public position to maintain – the position of publican – he'd no desire to confront Arthur at either of their workplaces. The only opportunity was after hours, when Arthur stayed on drinking late, as he often did. Perhaps Sam invited him to stay on, 'for a quiet word', the import of which was understood between them. Or perhaps he tricked him into staying on, by cheerily announcing a lock-in – a lock-in for only one customer, a lock-in during which he could punish him for the breaking of wedlock.

I've a memory of Sam taking a swing at Dad. On one of those Sunday lunchtimes at the pub, when Gill and I were sometimes allowed into the kitchen, behind the scenes. Though it might be a false memory, I can see the swing clearly, and can locate where it happened, in the doorway between the bar and the kitchen. If so, Sam failed to connect; I don't remember Dad having a black eye or bruised cheek. But the image remains: the swing, the miss, raised voices, Sam grabbing Dad's jacket by the lapels and shaking him, while Beaty and my mother fluster round them and tell Sam not to be stupid, till he lets Dad go, and turns away, and the moment passes.

If I did see the swing, I must have asked why it happened – if not at the time, then later, alone with Mum, at home. The question probably surprised her; she hadn't noticed me noticing; as far as she knew, I was playing elsewhere. Oh *that*, she said. Sam sometimes loses his temper, that's all, especially when he's under pressure and has had too much to drink; every publican drinks too much, it's an occupational hazard, your father just happened to be standing there, there was nothing to it, nothing serious, more play-acting than a quarrel, a bit of larking about that got out of hand; just forget about it, you weren't meant to be there, when you're an adult you'll understand, it's really nothing to worry about – all right?

Yes, I think a punch was thrown, and that Dad ducked it, but that it wasn't when Sam first learned – or suspected – that his wife was having an affair and that the baby growing inside her was Arthur's. The punch came later, in the second or third trimester. Up till that point, Sam had kept his anger under control. Arthur was a valued customer, a man people looked up to, a doctor; and he'd been helpful, financially and practically, in helping Sam's business. Beaty was high-strung, and whatever he felt about the pregnancy he didn't want her losing the baby – she'd be devastated, and hell to live with. So for a time Sam swallowed his pride. Until it welled up again, as rage. Arthur had cuckolded him. He didn't deserve to get away with it. His friendliness towards Sam was patronising, and his loans and offers of help were demeaning. He treated the pub as if he owned the place – as if he'd rights in it as well as rights in Beaty. There was much to resent and finally the resentment boiled over. He took a swing – only the once, as far as I know, though there may have been other times when I wasn't there to witness it, or to imagine witnessing it in retrospect.

Another reason for trusting my memory of that punch is that Sam (I now know) had a history of violence. Beaty alluded to it in a letter to me years later. 'We'd only been married a few weeks when he split my bottom lip in moody anger.' She apologised for complaining ('I'm sorry to be saying nasty things about him') but the gist was that his grumpiness and insensitivity, along with the occasional outburst of violence, had driven her to take refuge – and (so she implied) sent her into the arms of

Dad. Jealousy and anger at the affair may have made things worse, but Sam's violence continued long after the affair had stopped: 'When he was made redundant at fifty-seven he seemed to snap – and three times used me as a punchbag. The third time he knocked me unconscious against the oh so sharp edge of my mother's music cabinet and split my head open. My then GP said next time it would be the police. Oh Blake, can you imagine the disgrace?'

Did Sam's punch or the imminent birth lead to a summit of four, a what-the-hell's-to-be-done crisis meeting? A tense but civilised discussion over coffee in Sam and Beaty's kitchen that ended with them arriving at a joint policy and swearing each other to secrecy: *no one must ever know the child is Arthur's*? It's a possible scenario. But I can imagine two threesomes in conversation just as easily – Arthur–Beaty–Sam and Arthur–Beaty–Kim. Easier still is to imagine each married couple having it out in private, and the subject never being raised with the other couple.

All I do know is that when, in a moment of adolescent pique and arrogance, I asked Mum and Dad about Josie's paternity (late one night, on holiday in Abersoch, after they'd prevented me from sharing a bed with my girlfriend of some years, and she had gone off to bed alone), they both seemed unshocked – equally so – and responded in concert with a denial. It was as though they were issuing a rehearsed joint statement; as though this was an accusation they'd long been expecting, or had met before, which they dealt with by reading from the same script. Mum didn't burst into tears or show strong emotion of any kind. Her expression was one of mild amusement: the very idea!

*

More extraordinary than Mum's tolerance of the affair was the fact that she delivered Beaty's baby. She often delivered her patients' babies but to deliver the child of her husband's mistress can't have been easy. She did the job, though; professional as she was, of course she did. And after Josie was born, once Sam – busy as ever with the pub – had been and gone from the hospital, Dad took us with him to visit. Gill and I stayed outside while he went in. Then a nurse held the baby up for us at the window. No one said, 'There's your baby sister.' But we'd never been taken to see a new baby before and never would be again. We knew it was special.

We saw a lot of Josie during her infancy. Was Gill aware of having a rival? Did she feel less loved than Josie? She was seven when Josie was born. It's not as if they were close in age and therefore competing. Still, if I noticed Dad's preoccupation with Josie, it surely must have registered with Gill, at least subliminally.

Josie was a beautiful child – blonde, smiling, affectionate. Dad was always taking photos of her. The photos came back in a Kodak wallet with a smiling girl in a swimsuit on the front – a girl who looked just like the girl in the photos inside.

Gill had once been photogenic, too. But over time that cuteness had gone. Mine too. We were a dull chubby pair, outclassed by Josie. Not yet teenagers, we'd already lost our looks. Josie was the one with the glow.

Like me, Gill must have seen that Mum, for a time, was unhappy. But how could she help when she didn't know the reason? Even if she had known, she wouldn't have understood. Had she been older, she and Mum might have comforted each other. Both were feeling a sense of abandonment: the man they loved most in the world had turned his attention to another woman and another girl. He still behaved as if he loved them. But not with the passion they were used to. Not with the exclusivity that helped them feel good about themselves.

A beautiful mistress and a beautiful daughter – no wonder Dad was happy with life. What could have been catastrophic – a public shaming, divorce, etc – was a triumph. He'd got away with it.

'Never put it in writing,' he liked to say. Before he married, wooing Mum while a doctor in the RAF, he *did* put it in writing: what he felt about her, what he thought about life, sex, religion, politics, medicine, how he hoped they would marry when the war was over. But with Beaty he was circumspect. There were no love letters that their spouses could intercept. Or none that survived.

It was the same with Josie. Nowhere did he acknowledge her as his child. No words betrayed the secret. Only – eventually – his DNA.

I once walked in on Beaty when she was breastfeeding Josie in our bathroom. Sorry, I said, and turned to go. It's fine, pet, I'm only giving her my milk, she said, and – happy to be watched or to initiate me in one of nature's wonders – gestured for me to sit down. There was nothing to be ashamed of, after all.

I stared, fascinated. In Beaty's eyes, I was just a child. But at ten I'd begun to be interested in women's breasts, and here was a glorious, unlooked-for opportunity to see one. The bathroom was warm, the milk smell intoxicating. I was too young to know about sex, and this was nothing to do with sex, but there was something deeply sensual about the atmosphere.

Years later, when I did know about sex, the memory came

back. How Beaty had let me see her naked breasts. Not in the way she'd let Dad see them. Not to touch, only to look at. Even so. In my own fashion, I'd shared his excitement.

It was 1960 or 61 when I saw Beaty's breasts, so you could say the 60s had arrived – that in her lack of physical constraint, she represented some new freedom. But Josie, no less than Gill and I, was a child of the 50s. And whatever Beaty's lack of inhibition about breastfeeding, her affair with Dad was a 50s affair – shameful and clandestine. Free love, open marriage, wife-swapping, car keys in a bowl: none of that had reached Yorkshire, or not the rural, middle-class part of it to which we belonged.

And yet there was something unconventional, to say the least, about Beaty's absorption into our family. She and Josie came over every weekend, and sometimes at teatime during the week, and went away on holiday with us too – leaving Sam behind to work and possibly fester.

Meanwhile Gill was no longer 'Daddy's little girl'. She was Daddy's bigger girl. The little one was Josie.

5

In the charged atmosphere at home, in the company of friends, Gill and I took up Doctors and Nurses – a game that involved a little dressing up and a lot of undressing. Perhaps we'd have done so anyway; it's natural for children to explore each other's bodies. (Or so we believed;* today's children may have been told otherwise.) Our parents were half aware of what we got up to but didn't seem to mind. And the game was consensual, if not quite egalitarian (the girls had to fight to be doctors, the boys hated being nurses). We played it with schoolfriends like Irving and Christine, and with our cousins Edward and Jane. I don't remember much touching but there was a lot of

---

*So Laurie Lee believed too. In *Cider with Rosie* he presents 'sex games' as innocent, with girls often taking the initiative. Before Rosie makes her 'cidrous' adolescent advances to him, there's ten-year-old Jo, who when asked, as if by a doctor, 'What seems to be the trouble?', promptly undresses: 'Her body was pale and milk-green on the grass, like a birch leaf lying in water . . .' The adults in the book accept these activities because they too used to engage in them: 'Sooner or later one was always caught out, but the thing was as readily forgotten; very little in the village was either secret or shocking, we merely repeated ourselves . . . if anyone saw us they laughed their heads off – and there were no magistrates to define us as obscene.'

examining: *so that's what a he or she looks like naked*. We were imitating Mum and Dad as medics; the mimicry was of hospitals, not sex, about which we were still in the dark. Later, aged twelve, at grammar school, when a boy first told me how men and women did it, I refused to believe him.

The games were played in threes and fours so I'm troubled by a memory of Gill and me wandering away from Mum and Dad, and from the tartan rug we'd spread out for a picnic, and her rejecting my suggestion of a game of Doctors and Nurses. The refusal wasn't like her. What caused it? The fact it was just the two of us, when others had always been present before? A new protectiveness towards and sense of privacy about her body? It's unlikely she'd reached puberty; more likely we were eight or nine. And it's not that we did anything. No, Gill simply decided that Doctors and Nurses had run its course – children though we were, it was time to put away childish things.

Or had the game lost its innocence for other reasons? In later life, when she'd been drinking, she sometimes spoke of having been abused. She didn't say how or by whom or at what age. Nor did she specify what kind of abuse – whether molestation, a beating, emotional bullying or neglect. And when she sobered up she'd retract the accusation or deny she'd ever made it. But *in vino veritas* and all that. I sometimes wonder if those childish pursuits preyed on her mind because something else – something not-childish – happened to her then or later.

It's equally possible she gave Doctors and Nurses as little thought as she did Postman's Knock or Cowboys and Indians. I don't remember any of our playmates overstepping the mark. And there was no kissing or frisson between the two of us. We were proof, if anything, of the truth of the Westermarck effect, named after the Finnish anthropologist Edvard Westermarck and also known as reverse sexual imprinting – the theory that it's unnatural for people who live in close domestic proximity during their early years to be sexually attracted to each other. We knew one another too well.

Melanie Klein considered sexual relationships between children to be 'the rule in early childhood' and for their continuation into puberty to be 'much more frequent . . . than is usually supposed.' Another study by Victor G. Cicirelli suggests that 'Normal sexual curiosity, exploration, and experimentation among siblings in childhood and adolescence can be distinguished from sexual exploitation or sexually abusive behaviour.' Can sexual experimentation with a sibling *in adolescence* be described as 'normal'? It's almost certainly coercive and – even in rare supposedly consensual cases – psychologically damaging. Research suggests that, of the two sexes, the damage to a girl is greater.

Perhaps the real damage comes when there's a significant age gap between the participants – when a predatory teenager or adult (usually male) exploits the innocence of a younger child or sibling. Though we were old enough to know that Doctors and Nurses was vaguely naughty, no one *really* old, twelve or thirteen say, ever took part; nor was it a game that Gill and I played with our little half-sister Josie. That would have seemed silly and wrong.

Few parents today would allow their kids the freedom we had; some would be horrified by how we used it. Times change and we change with them. In my grief since Gill's death I've been re-examining childhood memories, in search of things that might have damaged her. But when I picture us playing Doctors and Nurses she's as happily engaged as everyone else

– only tiring of the game, as we all did, when it went on too long.

More to the point, I can't spot a predator. There's no lurking teenager or adult. No paedophile waiting to exploit the age gap between them and Gill.

Virginia Woolf's account of being sexually abused by her half-brother, Gerald, is shocking; in part, because she was six and he eighteen:

> There was a slab outside the dining room door for standing dishes upon. Once when I was very small Gerald Duckworth lifted me onto this, and as I sat there he began to explore my body. I can remember the feel of his hand going under my clothes; going firmly and steadily lower and lower. I remember how I hoped that he would stop; how I stiffened and wriggled as his hand approached my private parts too. I remember resenting, disliking it – what is the word for so dumb and mixed a feeling? It must have been strong, since I still recall it. This seems to show that a feeling about certain parts of the body; how they must not be touched; how it is wrong to allow them to be touched; must be instinctive.*

---

*Woolf recalled the episode again, in a letter to a friend, just a few weeks before her death in 1941. It's interesting that she was in her late forties before committing the memory to paper. The essay in which she describes it, 'Sketch of the Past', is, in part, about the 'horror' of recovering buried memories and how it's only as one gets older that one can blunt 'the sledge-hammer force of the blow . . . by putting it into words . . . By doing so I take away the pain . . . [and] put the severed parts together.' It's as if when Gerald touched her 'private parts' they became 'severed parts', and the only way she could heal the trauma was through writing.

Virginia's older half-brother George abused her as well, over several years, when she was in her late teens and he in his thirties. They would return from evenings out in London society and he'd help her undress, then fondle her: as she put it, he 'flung himself on my bed, and took me in his arms . . . cuddling and kissing and otherwise embracing me'. In what 'wise' or fashion she doesn't specify, but a letter to Vanessa alludes to 'George's malefactions' and in another, to her friend Ethel Smyth, he's referred to as 'my seducing half-brother'.

Perhaps the abuse was 'more emotional than penetrative', her wisest biographer Hermione Lee suggests, 'but Virginia Woolf herself thought that what had been done to her was very damaging.'*

I'm digressing. Nothing in our Doctors and Nurses games resembled Virginia Woolf's experience. But I've a reason for straying into the subject of incest. In the literature of brothers and sisters *as written by men*, it's the theme that turns up most often: from Byblis and Caunus in Ovid's *Metamorphoses* to Amnon and Tamar in the Bible, from Jacobean playwrights to Romantic poets, from Defoe's *Moll Flanders* and Tolstoy's *War and Peace* through twentieth-century novels (Nabokov's *Ada*,

---

* Remarkably, she recounted George's behaviour to a London audience, while he was still alive. An earlier draft of her talk says, less accusingly, that he 'taught us all that can be known of sex in theory from the early days': *in theory* doesn't suggest a hands-on seducer. Moreover, the memoir she was writing in the years before her death omits all mention of George's abuse, as if it didn't affect her as Gerald's had. On the other hand, it may have affected her so deeply she couldn't bring herself to speak of it again. A diary entry by Ottoline Morrell records a conversation when Virginia confided that he used to 'paw her all over: she said "He sent me mad"'.

Ian McEwan's *The Cement Garden*, Jay McInerney's *Model Behaviour*) to the present day. Chateaubriand, Thomas Mann, Klaus Mann,* Lawrence Durrell, Graham Greene, John Irving, James Ellroy . . . the list is long. Transgression is alluring to authors; as Shelley put it, incest 'like many other *incorrect* things [is] a very poetical circumstance.' He wrote about it (before being forced to censor) in his poem *The Revolt of Islam*. Byron explored it too, first in poetry then in reality with his half-sister Augusta.

As St Augustine observed, where would we be without incest? 'As there were no human beings except those who had been born of these two [Adam and Eve], men took their sisters for wives – an act which was as certainly dictated by necessity in those ancient days as it was later condemned by the prohibitions of religion'. In the ruling dynasties of Ancient Egypt, marriage between brothers and sisters followed the example of the divinities Isis and Osiris and was thought to keep the bloodline pure; hence the recent DNA results showing that Tutankhamun was the product of the relationship between Akhenaten and his sister. Several early European heroes – Cú Chulainn, Mordred, Roland – have been portrayed as the product of incest. And many authors have allowed their characters to

---

*The Manns are an odd case. Klaus's play *Siblings* describes itself as being inspired by Cocteau's *Les Enfants Terribles* but the more obvious connection is with his father Thomas's story 'The Blood of the Walsungs' in which a brother and sister, Siegmund and Sieglinde, lose themselves in 'mutual caresses' and a 'tumult of passion' before and after a performance of Wagner's *Die Walküre* (which features a brother and sister with the same names). In *Siblings*, Paul and Elizabeth are 'bound together in everything', bringing death and destruction to those around them; the play ends with the siblings lying in bed together on the point of death and 'touching each other – at last'.

challenge the taboo. In John Ford's *'Tis Pity She's a Whore*, Giovanni argues that incest is natural, not a vice:

> Shall a peevish sound,
> A customary form, from man to man,
> Of brother and sister, be a bar
> 'Twixt my perpetual happiness and me?
> Say that we had one father, say one woman
> (Curse to my joys!) gave us both life and birth;
> Are we not, therefore, each to other bound
> So much the more by nature? By the links
> Of blood, of reason?

By this rationale, incest is the ultimate version of arranged marriage, the union of two people from the same background. 'Nearness in birth and blood, doth but persuade/A nearer nearness in affection' Giovanni tells his sister Annabella, and she's easily persuaded, having long fancied him as much as he does her. All goes ecstatically till she falls pregnant, is married off and her new husband belatedly discovers the truth – at which point, the moral order reasserts itself and the play ends in a bloodbath.

In Ovid's *Metamorphoses*, the tragedy of Byblis is to fall in love with her twin brother Caunus: 'the one thing we have in common is the thing which keeps us apart.' Convincing herself it's best to be honest, she writes Caunus a letter that's self-pitying but slyly persuasive: 'Let old men keep the laws . . . A love that scorns prudence is in keeping with our years.' Angry and disgusted, Caunus flees the country to escape her. She follows him in vain, and, consumed by her own tears, becomes a fountain.

Twincest is also a motif in Graham Greene's *England Made*

Me. 'She might have been waiting for her lover,' it begins, but Kate Farrant, 'his elder by half an hour', is waiting for her brother Anthony in Stockholm, where she has a job lined up for him with the wealthy industrialist Erik Krogh. Though they don't go to bed together, their attraction to each other is palpable. 'I love you,' Kate repeatedly tells him. 'It's just family affection,' he replies, but later realises 'with astonishment and pain that he had been wrong just now, that this after all was love . . . Nobody, he thought, can put it over her on looks'. Their love is obvious even to outsiders: '"Is that your sister?" "Yes." "I don't believe you. You're in love with her." "Yes." "You naughty boy."' When Anthony begins a sexual relationship with another woman, Kate can't bear it: 'She bitterly envied lovers their more complete alliance.' And when she agrees to marry Krogh, Anthony protests. In the end, despite his love for Kate, his sexual desire for another woman wins out and he decides to return to England – but is murdered by one of Krogh's henchmen before he leaves.

Not all incestuous unions end badly. Nor does tackling the taboo necessarily land an author in trouble. Where *Lolita*, with its paedophiliac narrator Humbert Humbert, was banned in the UK and France when originally published and still causes controversy today, there was no furore about the incest in *Ada*. The sex Ada has with her brother Van begins when she's twelve and he fourteen. True, to start with they think they're merely cousins, not siblings. But it's a lifelong love affair and there are no regrets when they look back. Nor does Nabokov downplay the eroticism of their first sexual encounters:

> Ada went on all fours . . . He groped for and cupped
> her hot little slew from behind then frantically scrambled
> into a boy's sandcastle-moulding position; but she turned

over, naively ready to embrace him the way Juliet is recommended to receive her Romeo. She was right. For the first time in their love story, the blessing, the genius of lyrical speech descended upon the rough lad, he murmured and moaned . . . When he grew too loud, she shushed, shushingly breathing into his mouth, and now her four limbs were frankly around him as if she had been love-making for years.

Perhaps the most surprising contributor to the theme is Gore Vidal, in his book *Two Sisters*. Intriguingly subtitled 'A Memoir in the Form of a Novel', the plot, such as it is, hinges on the bisexual narrator V's obsession with the beautiful twins Eric and Erika: he loves but never sleeps with the brother, and cares little for but impregnates the sister ('Erika was my consolation prize' he says of their one-night stand). Or so it seems: what he learns in middle age, through access to Eric's youthful notebook, is that brother and sister were lovers. The child he thought was his was Eric's.

'Curious that incest which was such a major theme in the nineteenth century figures hardly at all in our literature,' V reflects in *Two Sisters*. Bizarrely, he attributes this to modern housing arrangements, where with families 'jammed together in small apartments' all sense of mystery is lost, whereas in 'earlier, less crowded times' romance between family members could blossom. He's doubly wrong here. Crowded family arrangements make incest *more* likely. And there's been no let-up in the appearance of incest as a literary theme.

I've come a long way from Gill. All these books about incestuous adult liaisons have nothing to do with our infant closeness or those games of Doctors and Nurses. But I think they prove my point – a depressing but unsurprising one. When male authors write about brother–sister relationships, incest is invariably the theme.*

---

*A qualification: it's not only male novelists who have written about sibling incest. As well as Iris Murdoch's *A Severed Head*, Penelope Lively's *Moon Tiger*, Donna Tartt's *The Secret History* and Sylvia Townsend Warner's extraordinary story 'A Love Match', there's Ivy Compton-Burnett's *Brothers and Sisters*, which explores its impact on two generations. When the main protagonists, a married couple called Christian and Sophie, discover that they had the same father, the shock is so great that they both die and their adult children are left feeling 'horribly besmirched'. The novel oozes repulsion at the idea of marriage and child-bearing in general, which may be no coincidence: all seven of Ivy Compton-Burnett's sisters remained unmarried, as did she, and none of the twelve siblings had children. Nevertheless, despite a passing suggestion that 'in some countries it has been normal for children of the same father to marry', there's no question that she sees incest as morally unspeakable – a view women authors tend to express more forcibly than male ones.

6

There were fewer books in the house than you'd expect in a middle-class home: Mum wasn't much of a reader, Dad even less so, and both had busy jobs. But we did have some childhood staples: Enid Blyton and Beatrix Potter, *Black Beauty* and *Heidi*. Fairy-tales, too, including a selection of the Brothers Grimm. 'Hansel and Gretel' was the one I kept returning to – not for its scary bits but for its model of sibling togetherness: this was how a brother and sister ought to be, looking out for each other, joining forces against wicked adults. It's Gretel who saves Hansel at the end of the story, by pushing the witch into the oven and rushing to free him. But until that moment, Hansel is the one in charge. It's he who stays calm when they overhear their parents planning to abandon them ('Gretel wept bitter tears, and said to Hansel, "Now all is over with us." "Be quiet, Gretel," said Hansel, "do not distress yourself, I will soon find a way to help us."') It's he who lays down the pebbles that – shining like silver coins in the moonlight – lead them safely home from the forest. It's he who takes command after they've been abandoned for a second time and they come to the gingerbread house ('"I will eat a bit of the roof, and you, Gretel, can eat some of the window"'). And it's he who temporarily outwits the witch, when she tests how oven-ready he is, by holding out a chicken bone

49

rather than his finger. It's not only because he's older that Hansel takes the lead but because he's a boy.* It's not only because she's younger that Gretel keeps bursting into tears but because she's a girl. The moral is clear. Sisters are vulnerable and brothers should use their loaf (as Hansel literally does) to protect them.

One day when she was about eight, a heavy wardrobe fell on Gill. I was playing in my bedroom, along the corridor from hers, and heard the crash but didn't realise what it was. Mum, in the kitchen, knew at once and rushed up the stairs, screaming as she ran. I'd never heard her scream before; the noise worried me more than the crash. By the time I worked out what was happening, and followed her into Gill's bedroom, she'd already lifted the wardrobe so that Gill could crawl free. Apart from the shock and a few bruises, she was OK. Mum was less OK, blaming herself for parental inattention to dangerous furniture. 'That flaming wardrobe,' she said, cuddling Gill close. 'It could have killed you.'

Misrememberings. In an exercise I wrote at primary school at the age of ten, I describe 'My Bedroom': the arched window overlooking the village with little triangular windows each side; the yellow curtains; the pictures I've put up, of vintage cars, footballers, trains and birds. 'The beds have brown covers (Gillian has a bed in the room as well),' I write. Below, there's a floor plan showing my bed to the left, facing a chest of drawers, and hers to the right, facing a wardrobe. Was this the

---

*George Eliot's sonnet sequence shows a similar balance of power: 'He was the elder . . ./And I the girl that puppy-like now ran,/Now lagged behind my brother's larger tread.'

wardrobe that fell on her? If so I can't have heard it from my bedroom along the corridor, because our bedroom was one and the same.

'My bedroom', I call it, not 'Our bedroom'. I'll let myself off on that one, since 'My Bedroom' was the title of the exercise. But I'm struck that Gill's presence is acknowledged only in parenthesis and that I end the piece with the words: 'I like my bedroom, because I can be by myself to think.'

'By myself' suggests she didn't share it after all. Perhaps the bed *had* been hers (a matching single) but she'd moved out by then. When did she get her own bedroom? Gill would remember but she's not around to ask.

The cuddle Gill got when the wardrobe fell on her was special. Could she have done with more of them? Mum wasn't as tactile as most mums. But that was her nature: we took it on board. Perhaps the problem, if there was a problem, came later, in Gill's teenage years, when mothers and daughters often achieve a new level of intimacy, however fraught – with confidences shared and battles fought, as the daughter moves towards womanhood. It may be Gill and Mum did have that kind of relationship, in private, away from male ears and eyes. But everything I know about them suggests not – that Mum was too self-contained to be a confidante and Gill too self-occluding to confide.

Dad was more effusive than Mum – tactile but also volatile. We knew he loved us but his tempers made us worry that we'd driven his love away. I'm speaking for Gill here because she can't. And it may be that I'm speaking out of turn. Still, when we looked back as adults, our stories about Dad coincided: how exhilarating but domineering he was; how he both spoiled and scared us; how the motto we most associated with him was 'I may not be right but I'm never wrong.'*

In his spare time, when he wasn't 'on call', Dad went through different phases. One year his passion was golf, the next gardening. Another year he bought a Nikon camera. Till then all he'd taken were black-and-white baby photos. Now he worked in colour. The results were sumptuous, more Mediterranean than Yorkshire Dales.

The booklet that came with the Nikon showed a series of photographic stunts, which he recruited us to perform. In one photo, he has me crouching in the foreground, hands out, palms upward, with a diminutive Gill, a mini-me, balancing on them. It's a trick of perspective – she's standing in the distance on a hump of grass. But we look like we're acrobats who have discovered how to shrink the human form. I hold my sister in the palm of my hand.

Extraordinary how potent cheap photo stunts can be. But there was a kind of magic to our childhood. A glamour even. Or so it seems to me as I sit over old photos, welling up like D. H. Lawrence in his poem 'Piano':

---

* Children with an overbearing parent can fail to thrive – weak saplings in the shadow of a giant trunk. Or, when they grow up, go off the rails. The Thatcher twins, Mark and Carol, were born a year after Gill. 'My God, they look like rabbits, put them back,' Denis Thatcher said when he first saw them. Fated to be conspicuous, they went on to humiliate themselves in middle age, Carol by getting sacked from the BBC's *The One Show* when she refused to apologise ('I stand by what I said') for using a racist term about the French tennis player Wilfred-Jo Tsonga, Mark through a series of financial scandals. Had their mother been less formidable and their father more emotionally available, would they have turned out differently? Come to that, might the country have been different too?

The glamour
Of childish days is upon me, my manhood is cast
Down in the flood of remembrance, I weep like a
    child for the past.

Our two-week summer holidays were spent by the sea – in Caernarvonshire, Galloway, Anglesey and, once, Kerry, where Mum had been born. Early-morning swim, breakfast, walk, lunch, boat ride or golf round, pub, dinner, card game, bed: that was the typical pattern. It rained a lot and the wind blew cold along the strand. The sauna we once had in Scotland, with the heat-surge from a wooden ladleful of water, was a welcome exception.

When Gill was nine, we went abroad for the first time, to Majorca. It was the May half-term and already hot there – to us, used to damp Pennine weather, improbably so. Gill and I spent hours at the hotel pool. Back home, at Nelson Baths, there was a rule against running and jumping. Not here. We took turns racing along the side and hurling ourselves in. One morning I noticed that a group of Germans on their sunbeds were laughing each time Gill plunged in. She had put on weight lately and her costume sagged round her waist. When she ran the fat wobbled and when she hit the water she made a big splash. With each run and splash, the Germans' laughter grew more raucous. Indignant – how dare they laugh at my sister! – I took her by the hand and led her away. Bemused, she hadn't been aware of the laughter. I didn't enlighten her. But there would be no more fun at her expense.*

---

*Miss Bartlett in E. M. Forster's *A Room with a View*: 'Oh for your brother! He is young, but I know that his sister's insult would rouse in him a very lion.'

Maybe the memory has stuck because it shows me in a favourable light, acting protectively towards my sister. Or maybe it's there as an emblem of other times when Gill was teased. Or is it because I felt embarrassed by her? It was nasty of the Germans to mock, but how could she open herself up to ridicule like that and not notice?*

There's a photo of us arriving back at Manchester Airport from that holiday. Dad must have rushed ahead to take it. I too have rushed ahead, down the steps and five yards across the tarmac. I'm walking forwards but with my head turned back towards the plane (BEA written on the side, a Union Jack under the cockpit) where the rest of the family are disembarking: first Gill, then Mum, then Granny (widowed eighteen months before). There's a hold-up behind Gill, because she's clutching her new Spanish doll under her right arm while steadying herself with her left hand on the rail of the steps. The flight crew are standing at the foot of the steps, ready to help. It's a photo, not a cine film, but Gill's descent seems to be happening in slow motion. And though I can't read the expression on my face, because my

---

* Fiction offers many examples of brothers avenging an insult to their sisters, including Nicholas Nickleby flying to the rescue of his sister Kate when she is pestered by the odious Sir Mulberry Hawk. The most precocious piece of fraternal gallantry I've come across is that of the five-year-old Gregor von Rezzori, as described in his memoir *The Snows of Yesteryear*. When a slightly older boy snatches his nine-year-old sister's black, red and gold bow, then spits on and tramples it, he thwacks the boy over the head with a toy sabre till it bleeds profusely: 'I showed myself worthy of my future role as a grown-up: a knight, entrusted with protecting the frail and vulnerable weaker sex.' Sadly, he was helpless to save his sister when she was diagnosed with lymphoma and died aged twenty-one.

head's turned away, I'd guess it's a look of impatience. Why so slow, Gill? Get a move on!

Impatience is a fault of mine. But perhaps I'm not the only one to have missed something here: that the reason for Gill's slowness on the steps may have been that she couldn't see them as clearly as the rest of us did; that she was developing eyesight problems which wouldn't be detected till many years later.

That Spanish doll had a lasting place in her heart. Her friend Christine remembered seeing her with it and feeling jealous. If ever friends and family went on holiday abroad, Gill would ask if they could bring a doll back for her.*

Though I put a stop to the Germans' laughter, did I also, thereafter, stop feeling protective towards Gill? I'm asking because of the contrast between what I did that day and what I failed to do a few years later, in my teens. We were in Abersoch, where my parents had recently bought a 'chalet' (or large caravan) overlooking the beach. Someone had asked us to the yacht club and over drinks Gill and I were invited to go sailing. As Mum and Dad watched from the balcony, we stood on a wooden jetty while the dinghy came alongside. The water was choppy and we waited for the boat to steady itself. Eventually it did and I scrambled aboard. Gill hesitated before sticking a leg out. As she did, the boat slid away a little. She lunged forwards to grab the side. The gap between boat and jetty widened. Her left foot was on the jetty, her right foot in the water and her

---

*This may have been a common phenomenon at the time. In her memoir *Motherwell*, Deborah Orr recalls her mother 'asking people to bring back a doll' whenever they went on holiday: 'Before long, the Scottish and Welsh dolls were joined by several from Spain and a couple from Holland . . . There were eventually about seventy.'

two hands either side of the rowlocks. 'Blake!' she screamed, before the boat bobbled back towards the jetty and someone – not me – leaned over and pulled her aboard. It was over in an instant but her left shoe and sock were wet. She'd been scared and I'd done nothing. I'd been too embarrassed – by her clumsiness, her panic, and the fact of her being my sister – to help. As if she was nothing to do with me.

She enjoyed herself on the boat ride, the mishap soon forgotten. Not by Dad, though. When I went to the yacht club gents on our return, he followed, pushed me up against the wall and raised a fist to my cheek. Corporal punishment wasn't his style but for a moment I thought he would hit me. What the hell was I doing? How could I just sit there while my sister nearly fell in the water? By God, if ever he saw me behave like that again, he'd . . .

I was a teenager, acutely self-conscious and easily embarrassed. That's why I hadn't acted. But Dad was right. I'd been a shit, saving my blushes rather than saving my sister.

I'm getting ahead of myself here but by the time we were teenagers the dynamic between Gill and me had changed, perhaps because she reached puberty first. I was young for my age, with an undescended testicle, poor bowel control and puppy fat. Gill was smaller but her head of curls made her look bigger. Older, too. Hardened. Battle-scarred. More accustomed to pain.

Pain? The early years in any life are formative, some would say all-defining: the child is mother to the woman. But was Gill's childhood especially painful? Not in her view. Were she around, she'd tick me off for suggesting as much. *I've good memories of childhood. If it had been bad, I wouldn't have had two children of my own.* There were things that might have damaged her: the teasing at school, the wardrobe falling on her, the slow poison of patriarchy. And the combination of an enigmatic mother, overbearing father and self-absorbed brother might not have been ideal. But I mustn't let the bad stuff overwhelm the good or project my present sadness onto the past. I've been looking for moments – and more than moments – when things went wrong for Gill. But she would deny they did go wrong. *If you're searching for reasons why I turned to drink, you're barking up the wrong tree.**

She's right. I've been misremembering. Or un-remembering. *De*-remembering. I've erased how much fun Gill was, the practical jokes she played, her enthusiasm for clothes, pop music, dogs, cats, ballet, comedy sketches. And I've erased all the times we played together: the dens we built, the ruined greenhouse we pretended was a pirate ship, the dressing up as a prince and princess.† I get out the photos again, Dad's dotingly plentiful photos. Here we are, side by side, outside a tent in the back garden. In the swimming pool he built from old petrol cans and a blue plastic sheet. On a Welsh beach with buckets and spades. At the top of a water slide, me with my knees bent ready to go, Gill – her elasticated swimsuit pushed down to her waist – holding the rail behind me. Here we are, alarmingly, beside the family car (an orange Metropolitan convertible) with

---

* 'My childhood was easier than most, and I ended up drinking anyway,' Leslie Jamison writes in her book *The Recovering: Intoxication and Its Aftermath*.

† Prince Charles was born two years before me, Princess Anne two years before Gill, and we sometimes recast ourselves as them. When I look at childhood photos of them together – he with dark hair in short trousers and a pullover, she with blonde curls in a frilly dress – it's easy to see why. Older brother, younger sister (just as we were) grinning for the camera (just as we did) while in 50s clothes (just as we wore): royals and plebs are interchangeable.

Gill dressed as a bride (white dress and white veil) and me sitting at the wheel, as if ready to depart on our honeymoon.

So many photos. So much evidence of our shared pursuits. We turned out very differently. Why? Then again, why not? Siblings do often turn out very differently. We also had plenty in common, including nostalgia for our early years. Whenever I'm tempted to think of us as opposites, I remind myself of the similarities.

There's an idea that unhappy children grow up to be unhappy adults. Now I'm coming round to the opposite view, that a happy childhood can make adulthood unhappy, the bar having been raised too high. It's watching a cine film that does it (the sixty-year-old reels preserved on a memory stick). There's Gill toddling in the dunes, running on the beach, carrying a bucket of seawater, holding Mum's hand, as contentedly tubby as I am – indeed, she is the cuter and the more captured on film, all smiles in fact, her starring role in a forty-three-minute picture show shattering this idea I've carried round for years that I purloined a portion of happiness intended for her or was dealt the luckier hand.

I even distrust my memories of her crying. All children cry. And all siblings think their younger siblings are crybabies. Gill probably cried no more than I did.

Do I contradict myself? Very well then, I contradict myself. Or Gill contradicts me, as she sits looking over my shoulder. *You've let what happened later colour your memories of childhood. Nothing terrible happened. I wasn't unhappy or traumatised. Even if I had been, it wouldn't explain me.*

*

---

*I take her point. But adult dysfunction *is* often attributable to childhood trauma. If Edward St Aubyn's Patrick Melrose hadn't been raped by his father and neglected by his mother, would he have become a heroin addict?

In our last couple of years at primary school, Gill and I began riding lessons in nearby Carleton. I'd have preferred to be riding a bike but Mum and Dad wouldn't allow it: the road through the village was too fast, they said. I stopped complaining when Simon, who was Gill's age, was knocked off his bike by a speeding car, spent months in hospital with a head injury, and came out wan and strange. Awful for him but a vindication for Mum and Dad.

I was thirty before I learned to ride a bike. I don't think Gill ever did.

Ponies were thought to be OK, though. We were both on leading reins to start with, and even when allowed to ride 'on our own', in a group of a dozen or so riders, were closely patrolled, with no opportunity to canter, let alone gallop. I found it frustrating. Perhaps Gill did too. She wasn't as mad about ponies as the other girls, the ones who stuck around all day, mucking out stables and grooming their favourite mount.

The riding instructors in Anglesey, where we holidayed one summer, were more relaxed – cavalier even. We were given free rein and when our ponies hit the beach we couldn't stop them: the mile-long gallop along the strand was thrilling. The teenage son of our godparents was staying with us and fell for one of the riding instructors. Gill and I were spellbound watching them hug and kiss. There's a photo of us in swimsuits, sprawling in their arms, infatuated by their infatuation – so this was love, euphoric as a mile-long gallop.

Inspired by our sudden enthusiasm, Dad bought us a pony. The farmer who sold her described her as frisky and that became her name. We took turns with her at the riding school. The other ponies picked on her, bumping and biting, which made us feel picked on too – the kids too posh to make do with the riding-school ponies. Frisky later had a foal: Kinty. There's a photo of us stroking her muzzle, Gill in red trousers and a sky-blue cardigan, an upended silver pail on the ground. We look entranced.

The entrancement didn't last. When Gill was eleven, everything changed. The ponies went back to the farm they'd come from. And Gill departed too. Our riding days were over – and so was the childhood we'd shared.

7

'School parted us; we never found again
That childish world where our two spirits mingled.'
George Eliot, 'Brother and Sister'

Three of us took the eleven-plus in my year. Stephen and I passed and went to the grammar school; Jeffrey failed and went to the secondary modern. I remember the shock of those results; the three of us were friends, we'd worked and played together for six years, I'd never noticed any difference between us. Our separation seemed so arbitrary and was; three years on, his abilities reappraised, Jeffrey was offered a place at grammar school.* Success and failure were part of the system there too, with streaming. But the cruellest division came at eleven: pass and you got to study Latin; fail and you felt a reject.

My reward for passing was to be sent on holiday to the south of France, where friends of Mum and Dad were staying in a beachside hotel with their two boys. Gill remained at home, with promises that she'd be given a similar treat after *her* eleven-plus.

---

*My memory was that he joined us there but I'm told he declined the offer. A nice riposte: if the grammar school didn't want him at eleven, then sod them, they weren't having him at fourteen.

I can't remember where she went or who with, just the upset when her result came through.

Mum and Dad blamed her failure on the disruptions at primary school. Miss Todd, the previous head teacher – in effect the *only* teacher – had retired and Mrs Hartley, her eventual replacement, had no experience of running a village school. Standards had slipped. Preparations for the exam were inadequate. Gill's friend Christine also failed. There was, my parents told Gill, no disgrace in failing. She mustn't think of herself as stupid. But their disappointment was palpable. And so was hers. We were siblings. Things should be the same for us both. It was so unfair.[*]

Whether from snobbery or awkwardness (it was the school where most of their patients' kids went), Mum and Dad didn't want Gill going to the secondary modern. As doctors, they could afford to go private. With no suitable day school in the area, they looked into boarding schools. The most promising of them, St Anne's, was in Windermere, a two-hour drive away. The Lake District had good associations: we'd been many times, to swim, camp and watch Donald Campbell try to break the

---

[*] Charles Dickens in *Great Expectations*: 'In the little world in which children have their existence, whoever brings them up, there is nothing so perceived and so finely felt as injustice.' In Dickens's case, the injustice was being sent off to work in a factory at twelve while his sister Fanny (two years older than he was) went to the Royal Academy of Music on a scholarship. That this was a reversal of standard practice – the girl, not the boy, being the one to receive an education – may have made it all the harder for him. To see her win a silver medal for her music and feel himself to be 'beyond the reach of all such honourable emulation and success', was devastating: 'the tears ran down my face . . . I had never suffered so much before.'

world speed record on Coniston Water. When we drove up to
vet the school, the mood was optimistic. Rather than denoting
failure, Gill's eleven-plus result had opened up an opportunity
– the chance to attend a better school than the one she'd have
gone to had she passed.

St Anne's was celebrating its centenary that year, having
begun life in 1863 on the promenade in Lytham St Anne's
(hence the name), before the lease on the building ran out and
it moved to Windermere. The headmistress – Miss Vera
Crampton, 'Muff' to the girls – had been there since 1928, as
though to make good the school's promise of stability. The
grounds seemed pleasant enough. And with a total of 270
pupils, including the juniors in Elleray House, the school wasn't
so big that Gill would feel lost. The main building, Browhead,
was horribly gloomy, with dark wood panelling and black-and-
white reproductions of droopy Pre-Raphaelite paintings, and
two bleak notices, 'Do Not Talk' and 'Do Not Run'. There
was little sign of intellectual pursuits being encouraged – a
solitary newspaper (the *Telegraph*) and magazine (the *Illustrated
London News*) were pinned up in the corridor – and the headmistress looked every bit her age. But there weren't many
alternatives: it was already June and Gill would be starting in
September. No entrance exam was required; a place was offered
and accepted.

The only question was what to do about me: if Gill was off
to boarding school, surely I should go too. The obvious place,
much nearer than Windermere, was Giggleswick, where Russell
Harty, soon to become Mum's favourite television presenter, had
been teaching a few years before. We toured the grounds and
had half an hour with the headmaster. My reluctance must have
been obvious: since I was happy where I was, he asked, why
move me? His reaction disarmed Mum and Dad, as did the

strength of my resistance. It was agreed I could stay at home, while Gill was sent away.

The hope was that she would flourish in a new environment – flourish personally, that is, with academic achievement a secondary consideration. Mum had been to university, in Dublin; Dad too, in Manchester. They'd be pleased if their children followed suit but it wasn't of vital importance, not in my case and even less so in Gill's. The attitude to education taken by Maggie Tulliver's father in *The Mill on the Floss* – 'a woman's no business wi' being so clever; it'll turn to trouble' – still persisted in some quarters, or backwaters, including our village. A middle-class girl might become a secretary or teacher, a working-class girl a shop assistant, but by her early twenties she'd be married and starting a family. Mum and Dad had more aspirations for Gill than that. But their main concern was that she be happy – and mix with girls who were 'nice', not rough. That privately educated, middle-class girls can be rough hadn't occurred to them.

There's a photo of Gill carrying a suitcase, on the front steps of our house. She's wearing her new uniform: white blouse, navy gymslip, grey socks and black pumps. Smiling broadly, she looks ready for the adventure – not a hint of apprehension or nerves.

Throughout the summer, Mum and Dad had been talking up the benefits of St Anne's. There'd be more girls to make friends with than there'd been at primary school. The facilities were far superior, too: think of all the games she could play – hockey, netball, tennis – and the range of lessons, and the beauty of the Lakeland setting. She might feel a little homesick at first but that would wear off. There were exeat days when we'd visit, and it would be half-term before she knew it. Come next year's summer holidays, she'd probably be invited to stay with other girls or would invite them to stay with her. Christine had no such opportunity; life was unfair like that; not everyone's parents could afford boarding school. She should make the most of it. Things were going to be great.

They looked less great when she arrived. There were ten of them in her dorm, most of whom had come up through the junior school and knew each other already. The facilities were more austere than she'd imagined: the bedside cabinet was hers but the wardrobe and chest of drawers were shared. For someone shy and self-conscious, getting undressed for bed in front of other girls was a trial. Any giggling made her uncomfortable, as if it were aimed at her. The night-time sobbing from nearby beds might have made her feel less alone. But it only compounded her misery.

Routine was strict. The day started at 7.15, with breakfast at 8, lessons all morning, lunch ('dinner') at 1.10, tea at 4 (bread, jam and a slice of cake), a light supper at 6, bed at 7.30 and lights out at 8.15. There were baths twice a week, nail-cutting every Monday, and a hairwash every other Saturday (you were given a time-slot for that, and hoped it was early, before the hot water ran out). The schedule kept girls busily occupied. But it still left time to brood.[*]

Like me at eleven, Gill was plump. And like me she was teased for it and lost weight. The teasing wasn't the only cause of her weight loss. There was also the unpalatability of the food. Breakfast was porridge – or greasy fried bread, tinned tomatoes, scrambled egg out of a packet, and Wonderloaf white bread and

---

[*] Some of the details here and elsewhere in this chapter are drawn from what Gill told me or wrote in letters, and some from conversations with and material lent to me by Jennifer Potter: see p.74.

margarine. Lunch was mince or an awful stew (mostly gristle) or maybe fish fingers, with soggy vegetables and mashed potatoes (out of a packet), followed by spotted dick or jam tart – all served up by a seedy cook called Jack, who had his favourites (Gill wasn't among them). The one good meal was Christmas dinner, when there'd also be a party at which you were assigned a partner and had to parade together round the school singing 'John Brown's Body'.

Despite the general moaning about the food, some girls ate heartily, offsetting the grease and stodginess by playing games. And on Sundays everyone walked a mile in crocodile fashion to church. The weekends meant free time, aside from prep and some achingly boring Saturday entertainments, such as piano recitals or slideshows of foreign parts. Weekends were when Gill felt loneliest, though weekdays after teatime were also a challenge. You were allowed to change out of your scratchy winter uniform into mufti. But if you were alone – and Gill was too often alone – the freedom was oppressive.

There was other stuff she found difficult. Being the last one to get picked at rounders, for example, not because she was bad at it but because she was new. Or morning assembly: on Fridays, girls were given neatness marks for being untidy or order marks for being disorderly, and Muff would read out the names of offenders; alternatively, you might be called up to sign the Honourable Mention book, because you'd gained 90 per cent marks. Both were horrifying prospects to Gill. All she wanted was to pass unnoticed. To make a friend or two and feel less homesick. Not to have to face a sea of girls.

I knew how she felt. At school, I kept my head down, avoiding attention. We were like toddlers who think that covering their eyes makes them invisible.

*

I don't remember missing her when she went off to St Anne's. We'd already had a year at different schools. Perhaps I even exulted a little in my new status (or renewed status) as the Only Child at Home. I'd the run of the house and our parents' exclusive attention.

Mum and Dad worried if they'd done the right thing, but Mum had been a boarder at the Loreto Convent in Killarney and had flourished there. Give Gill a term or two and she'd surely do the same.

The signs weren't encouraging. We would visit twice a term on exeat days, have lunch in a hotel by the lake or a picnic on the fells, then drive back. There'd be tears as we left but Mum and Dad thought that natural, and in her weekly letters home Gill put a brave face on things. To Granny – Dad's mother, who lived next door to us – she was less circumspect. 'I miss everybody terribly as I am so homesick,' she wrote, at the start of her second term, 'but the funny thing is I have not cried once – until writing this letter.' Dad later reproached himself for not writing to her; he relied on phone calls instead. When she complained about being teased by other girls, he told her not to get upset but to tease them back. 'I will try to remember the points you told me,' she wrote to him in a note marked 'To Daddy – PRIVATE' and reported that the other girls hadn't been so nasty recently, apart from her namesake Gillie.

Later the bullying got worse again. She'd change for PE or hockey, and when she came back, find her uniform had disappeared – that sort of thing. Perhaps she complained to the teachers, and they pooh-poohed it: no bullying ever occurred at St Anne's. More likely she held her tongue.

*

In her absence, I grew closer to Mum. And adopted a way of talking to her – intimate, gossipy, emotionally analytical – I thought of as feminine. I was trying to fill the hole that Gill had left. It was also partly a reaction against Dad; as a shy teenager, I found his confidence emasculating; if someone had to be outnumbered, now we were three, let it be him. There's a photo of me aged twelve or thirteen, dressed up in a grass skirt, pink hairband and bikini top. I look pretty comfortable. Indeed there's the unmistakable impression of someone fancying himself – of fancying himself as herself. Sometimes I'd stand naked in front of a full-length mirror, with my balls and penis tucked between my thighs – under and behind them, that is, just the V of my pubic hair showing, as though to make myself a girl.

Not that I was the only female companion for Mum. There was always a housekeeper. And at weekends there'd be Beaty and Josie. Stuck in a dorm with girls she didn't like or who she felt didn't like her, Gill struggled with that. Whatever her resentment of me, I'd not be hanging about her bedroom. Whereas Josie might be: opening her doll's house, riding her rocking horse, playing with her jewellery.

Mum struggled too. Josie's presence was a reminder of Dad's infidelity. And when she saw how he looked at Beaty, she guessed he was unfaithful still.

Few women I've talked to can understand why she stayed with him. Still, times were different then, and wives less likely to divorce philandering husbands. And for Mum to have left Dad would have been an admission that her marriage had failed – as some back in Killorglin had predicted it would when they heard that she was marrying an Englishman. It was better to stick it out – stay put and stay wed. And since she was staying, it made sense not to sever the relationship with Beaty. If she did, people would know why.

She'd always had periods of depression and now they got worse. At one point she took herself off with a suitcase, with no explanation of where she was going. But she was back within the week to stick it out. I don't remember her ever rowing with Dad, then or later. She'd be silent sometimes. She also had terrible migraines. But that was as bad as it got.

It wasn't just stoicism. She'd grown up with secrets. There was her older sister Chris, for instance, who'd been sent away after falling pregnant as a teenager, whose child was put up for adoption, and who was later married, as a virgin, to a man who knew nothing about the child. Whatever you say, you say nothing: Mum had been raised on that principle. It helped her to conspire in the fiction of Josie's paternity – and to treat her and Beaty as family.

There was another factor: she *liked* Beaty. She liked her because she was fun. She liked her because she used to work as a nurse and Mum enjoyed the company of nurses. She liked her because she was a fellow Catholic, albeit (for the most part) a more dutiful one. And she liked her because she saw her as a victim – a woman who deserved better than the surly man to whom she was married. Perhaps, perversely, she even liked her because, she, Beaty, loved Arthur – they had that in common.

And there was something else. She knew she was smarter than Beaty, better educated, more together. And she knew Arthur knew it too. He was in it for the sex but had no intention of running off with Beaty. He'd made that clear – he wouldn't leave his marriage and if Mum tried to leave with the kids he'd fight to stop her. It was strange to feel that assurance when your husband was fucking someone else. But she had it. Of course she felt more than a little contemptuous of Dad. If he'd been more sensitive, he would have anticipated how she'd feel about him being unfaithful, and if he'd been less full of himself he wouldn't have been unfaithful in the first place. But Mum no longer felt a sense of abandonment. At some level, she didn't even feel betrayed.

It wasn't just weakness that made her accept Beaty and Josie into her life. But she still found it hard to see her husband doting on his younger daughter, when his older daughter – *their* daughter – was no longer at home.

By Gill's second year, boys were an increasing presence at St Anne's. Not that they were admitted as pupils (though young ones would be a few years later), but they loomed large in conversation. There was particular excitement when letters were handed out after lunch. It was one thing to idolise a pop star but to have a boy actually write to you was massive – an upping of your status and source of jealousy among your peers. Even girls in Gill's year were getting such letters, or pretending to, or telling stories about boyfriends back home.

When asked if there were boys she had a crush on, Gill shrugged. There was no one in our village she fancied or who fancied her. And Robin Gibb of the Bee Gees didn't count. All she had was an older brother. This might have worked in her favour, but when I was spotted one exeat day, and she was quizzed about me afterwards, she found the attention annoying, as if she was being teased.

Our visits to St Anne's are documented in family photos. There's Gill crossing the stepping stones of a wintry Lakeland stream in a grey coat, red shoes, white socks and white hairband; posed with Mum next to two classmates and *their* mums, the girls in thin-striped blue-and-white dresses and dark-blue blazers; posed again in the same outfit with Mum and Dad, in front of their latest convertible (a drophead Triumph Herald). It must have been me who took the last one: it's high summer and Dad's on crutches, having snapped his Achilles tendon while showing off on a diving board. He's grinning – they're all grinning, as if St Anne's is a fine old school and Gill's having a marvellous time there.

That summer – the Achilles tendon summer – we spent a week with Beaty and Josie in a caravan in Scotland. Dad had his leg in plaster, which might have deterred him from going near the sea. Instead he tied a large plastic fertiliser bag to his leg, trusting it to be waterproof, and waded in; when it leaked, he had to go to hospital for a new plaster to be fitted. The caravan wasn't big but we all crammed in. There are photos of Josie in a swimsuit lying at the edge of the water or being taught to swim by Dad. The resemblance between them is unmistakable. Uncle Arthur, she called him, while Mum was Auntie Kim.

I don't remember any tension. Photos of Gill from that time show her happy and absorbed: head down addressing a golf ball; thigh-deep in sea as she clambers aboard an inflatable; perched below a concrete wall, at the edge of a beach, with two tennis rackets, a football, a putter and a hula-hoop spread out on the sand. She wasn't crazy about sport but Dad encouraged her: the family that played together stayed together.

What she did love was fashion. She'd moved on from dressing up her dolls to picking out nice dresses for herself in magazines. In the rare moments Mum had the time, they'd go shopping. Her prize outfit that summer was a white, knee-length floral dress, which she wore with white socks, white gloves and (her curls tucked under its rim) a white hat like an upturned saucepan. If only there'd been more chances to wear it before

September came, when she was forced to ditch it for her scratchy winter uniform.

The longer she spent at St Anne's, the more she missed home.

She missed the nature walks up Cam Lane and the wild flowers – speedwell, ragged robin, foxgloves.

She missed Nikki, the long-haired dachshund we'd acquired, with his floppy ears and caramel fur.

She missed her record player.

She missed the warmth of York stone on her bare feet on a summer evening.

She missed Dad snoring in front of the television.

She missed sitting by the tree in the middle of the village – the love tree, everyone called it.

She missed the stocks on the green, into which adults said we'd be put if we misbehaved.

She missed hearing the X43 bus to Manchester come through.

She missed the tractor in the field out back.

She missed the posters in her bedroom.

She missed playing with Christine.

She missed the holly tree outside the bathroom window, where an owl once perched.

She missed warming her back against the Aga.

She missed the dung-and-straw smell of the stables.

She missed lying in bed as long as she liked on weekends.

She missed muesli.

She missed Malham Cove, Kilnsey Crag, Ilkley Moor, Nelson Baths, the double humpback bridge at East Marton.

She missed Mum kissing her goodnight.

Meanwhile there was Gillie to contend with, her namesake and nemesis. What does Nemesis look like? In Greek mythology she's a winged goddess with a sword or dagger bringing retribution to those guilty of hubris. Gill wasn't guilty of hubris. And Gillie – a verbal rather than physical enforcer – didn't carry a sword. Was she tall, blonde, advanced for her age? I can't picture her, though it's possible I saw her on exeat days and she must be there in the annual school photos. Clearly she was popular, articulate, a natural leader. Heaven help you if you weren't on her side. But the bullying was nuanced. If you complained about her to a teacher, it sounded pathetic: 'she stared at me, Miss', 'she keeps whispering about me, Miss', 'she makes up tales about me, Miss'. There may have been others she picked on but Gill felt singled out. Another girl, finding her crying, consoled her that 'Gillie doesn't mean it' and urged her, as Dad did, to 'pay no attention'. But attention was paid. Gill took it personally; it *was* personal. Gillie had found her weak spot and inserted a blade.

I'm guessing some of this because Gill didn't like to talk about it. Once home, any pain she'd endured while away wasn't for discussion. But the pain was visible, despite her efforts to hide it. And at school she went on being wounded.[*]

She stuck it out at St Anne's for another six months, till writing a letter of such misery that Dad, on receiving it, walked out of his morning surgery, drove up to the Lakes, collected all her

---

[*] 'Everybody in the world seemed so hard and unkind to Maggie; there was no indulgence, no fondness, such as she imagined when she fashioned the world afresh in her own thoughts. In books there were people who were always agreeable or tender, and delighted to do things that made one happy . . . The world outside the books was not a happy one . . . And if life had no love in it, what else was there for Maggie? . . . There is no hopelessness so sad as that of early youth, when the soul is made up of wants and has no long memories.' (George Eliot, *The Mill on the Floss*)

things and brought her home. Other families might have analysed what had gone wrong; other brothers might have asked more questions. But Gill had no wish to look back. She'd a gift for changing the subject or blocking things out. Her three and a half years at St Anne's are mostly a blank to me. Perhaps, through force of will or PTSD, they were a blank to her as well. I know she was bullied and that a girl called Gillie was responsible. And that St Anne's damaged her self-esteem. Going away at all was a mistake: she felt banished, as though exiled for her eleven-plus failure. But the school itself also played a part. It didn't pick up how unhappy she was. It failed in its duty of care.

What little I do know of St Anne's I owe to the writer Jennifer Potter, who was there around the same time as Gill. I hoped her experiences might shed light on Gill's. But Jennifer was one of the school's achievers (captain of the hockey team, deputy head girl, winner of prizes), made good friends there, and stayed on till the sixth form. There was more freedom higher up the school: she remembers a fancy-dress competition, for instance, when she stood inside a large cardboard box painted with dials while her friend Sandra Burrell danced round her dressed in the gym mistress's tracksuit and how nobody guessed what they were meant to represent (radioactivity). And in the fifth form, she and Sandra created a play about Christine Keeler: the atmosphere in the audience was electric. Gill, three years behind Jennifer, would have been in her second year at the time. Would she have understood the play, I wondered? Did she know all about sex by then?

Despite good memories of the school, Jennifer describes St Anne's as Victorian and repressive. And poor academically – the kind of place middle-class parents in the north sent daughters who'd failed their eleven-plus (well, yes) and where most girls left after doing O levels. In Jennifer's year, only she and a couple of others went on to university. A copy of the school magazine for 1970 cites just one girl doing so, while six went to teacher training colleges and five to train as nurses.

'It's the narrowness I remember most,' Jennifer told me. The majority of girls' schools at the time were narrow too. I think of a line from Larkin: 'I suppose it's not the place's fault'. And perhaps it's not St Anne's fault that things went wrong for Gill. I shouldn't think of it as Lowood School in *Jane Eyre* or the school on which Lowood was based, in Cowan Bridge, where Charlotte Brontë's sister Maria fell ill and died. Jennifer has no memories of bullying at St Anne's. Even the nicknames girls had were surname-derived, rather than malicious. Sandra's was 'Barrel' and Jennifer's was 'Potty'. What was Gill's? Probably Morry, same as mine at grammar school.

Thanks to Jennifer, who loaned them to me, I've been looking through copies of the school magazine, *The Stannite*, in search of any mention of Gill. I scan the various awards: the Royal Schools of Music exams, the Royal Drawing Society exams, the Royal Life Saving Society exams, the school singing and Christmas card competitions, the Speech Day prizes, the gymnastic stripes. I scan the netball, rounders and hockey reports, and the lists of games captains for each form, and the winners of the Sports Day races (flat race, high jump, long jump, potato race, sack race, crab race, egg and spoon). I scan all the school societies – Photographic, Dramatic, Debating, Music and Arts. I check the authorship of all the poems and prose pieces. There's nothing. I didn't think there would be but the absence is no less painful. It's as if Gill didn't exist.

And now she doesn't.

The only bright spot, if you can call it that, is a couple of photos. One shows a line of boarders standing sideways to the camera, each with her hands round the waist of the girl in front, as though doing the conga. The curly-haired girl in the middle, taller than those around her, looks very like Gill. In the other photo the girls are in two rows, those at the front seated, those behind them standing. The curly-haired girl is there in the middle again, at the back. Gill? It looks like her. But both photos are of Elleray girls, which means that Gill, at twelve, must have been boarding at Elleray, where the juniors were housed. If most of the rest of her class boarded at Browhead, that must have added to her feelings of isolation, even inferiority.

Then again, it might not be her at all. I'm looking because I miss her. But she's missing.

8

Sisters do go missing. They go missing in horrible ways, abducted, murdered, forcibly married, 'disappeared' for causing trouble to the powers that be. And sometimes they go missing by choice, to escape their families or – as we'll discover later in this story – because they've fallen out of love with life. But for now I'm thinking of a gentler kind of erasure – of sisters who slip under the radar, of whom little or nothing is known, whose place in the historical record has been excised. Blame patriarchy. Blame the men who thought them of no consequence. Or accept that blame doesn't come into it – that the past is a foreign country (and that some foreign countries still inhabit the past): they do things differently there.

More specifically, I'm thinking of sisters who play a vital role in the lives and legacy of their brothers but aren't known about or given credit. It's true some sisters prefer to stay in the wings, offstage. But they deserve acknowledgement all the same. I can't be the only person who knows little or nothing about the following five women, to whom their brothers – all writers – were indebted in one way or another.

Anna Maria Levi

Primo Levi's sister Anna Maria was born eighteen months after him. According to his biographer, Carole Angier, 'he waited impatiently for her to grow up, so that he could talk to her . . . As brother and sister grew older, they grew closer, until they seemed to be able to communicate without speaking. They invented a private language which not even their parents could understand . . . Each was the other's closest confidant, partner and spiritual ally'. He told his first biographer Flora Vincenti that this was no mere sibling affection but 'a spiritual affinity, which expressed itself in solidarity and profound understanding' and which 'helped him to overcome the obstacles of his extreme introversion'. Though younger, Anna Maria was the more confident, outgoing and attractive, and acted as his protector as well as helping his development as a writer.

It was through a letter smuggled to her from Auschwitz in July 1945 that the Levi family learned that Primo, against the odds, was still alive eighteen months after being incarcerated. The following year, after reading extracts from it, she played a key role in encouraging him to submit the typescript of *If This is a Man* to publishers. To his dismay, it was turned down by all of them, including Einaudi, where two of the editors who rejected it, Natalia Ginsburg and Cesare Pavese, were writers he greatly admired. A chemist by profession, unsure whether his writing had any merit, Primo might have given up at that point. But Anna Maria persisted on his behalf, showing the typescript to a fellow partisan, Sandro Garrone, who then took her to see Franco Antonicelli, a publisher who had brought the works of Joyce and Kafka to Italy before the war and who had just re-opened for business. Antonicelli accepted the book and Primo's career as a writer was launched.

At the end of his life, when he was suffering from depression and, he said, feeling worse than he had in Auschwitz, Anna Maria put him in touch with a psychoanalyst, in the hope that might save him. It was too late. Six weeks later he killed himself.

Eileen Joyce

In his frustration at the interminably delayed publication of *Dubliners*, James Joyce's rows with his wife Nora could get heated. During one of these, in 1911, he stuffed the manuscript of his work in progress, *A Portrait of the Artist as a Young Man*, into a lighted stove in their flat in Trieste. It was rescued by his sister Eileen, who burned her fingers in the process. She would later claim 500 pages were lost before she could retrieve them; whatever the number, those she saved were seemingly legible. 'There are pages here I could never have re-written,' Joyce told her. Next day, in guilt and gratitude, he bought her a pair of mittens.

Joyce had three brothers and six sisters. Google 'Joyce's sisters', though, and what you'll get is a series of entries on 'The Sisters', the opening story of *Dubliners*, in which, despite the title, the two sisters (elderly siblings of a dying priest) play only a minor part. As the eldest child in the family, and later an exile, Joyce wasn't close to most of his sisters. Eileen, seven years his junior, was the exception, following him to Trieste in 1910 where she helped look after his two children, Lucia and Giorgio. She had a fine voice and Joyce composed music for her to sing.

Eileen met her Czech husband Frantisek Schaurek while he was taking English lessons from Joyce, who later acted as best man at the wedding, borrowing a dress suit for the occasion. For a time the married couple lived in Prague where their daughters were born – the first, Bozena Berta, was named after

Beatrice and Bertha, the two lead female characters in Joyce's play *Exiles*, the second, Eleonora, after Nora.

In 1926, Schaurek committed suicide after embezzling money from the bank where he worked. Eileen was in Dublin at the time and when she got back to Trieste she refused to believe her husband was dead; the corpse had to be exhumed to convince her. She returned to Ireland permanently in 1928 but maintained close contact not only with Joyce but with Lucia, who by then was showing signs of mental illness. In 1935, Joyce summoned her to Paris, where she looked after Lucia for three months. Later, Lucia lived with her in Dublin.

In short, Joyce was doubly indebted to Eileen: for saving his manuscript and for a time, until she was eventually committed to a mental institution, for saving Lucia.

Henriette Renan

Who? Till recently I hadn't heard of her brother either. But Ernest Renan's *Life of Jesus*, the idea for which came from Henriette, was one of the best-selling books of the nineteenth century. And as a philologist, theologian, political philosopher and memoirist he was read by many key literary figures of the late-nineteenth and early-twentieth centuries, including Proust, Joyce and Edith Wharton. More troublingly, his racist, colonialist and anti-democratic ideas helped to inspire Mussolini. Henriette can't be blamed for those, because they belong to his later work and she was dead by then. In fact it was her death in 1861, during a trip they took together to Syria and Palestine, that spurred him to complete his *Life of Jesus*, which he dedicated to her: 'Do you remember . . . those long days in Ghazir, in which, alone with you, I wrote these pages, inspired by the places we had visited together? Silent at my side, you read and copied each sheet as soon as I had written it, while the sea, the villages, the ravines and the mountains were spread at our feet. When the overwhelming light had given way to a vast army of stars, your shrewd and subtle questions, your discreet doubts, led me back to the sublime object of our common thoughts. One day you told me you would love this book – because we composed it together.'

If Ernest sounds pious, it's understandable: he and Henriette fell ill on that trip at the same time; when he recovered consciousness he was told she had died two days before ('but for the fatal swoon that seized me on the Sunday night, I do believe my kisses and the sound of my voice would have kept life in her for a few hours more – long enough, perhaps, to have saved her in the end'). How much of his *Life of Jesus* she had a hand in isn't clear. But if she hadn't accompanied him to the Middle East it wouldn't have existed: 'without her help,' he said, 'I certainly could not have carried through my self-imposed task.' She had been editing his work since his twenties ('her invaluable criticism would discover shades of negligence in style which might otherwise have escaped me') and his indebtedness to her went back to their childhood in Brittany. After their father's death when she was seventeen and Ernest five, Henriette became the family breadwinner, first as a teacher in Paris, then as a governess in Poland. Her earnings didn't just go to pay off their father's debts. They helped to fund Ernest's education in a Paris seminary. Her own faith had lapsed and though she didn't discourage his ambition to be a priest she was pleased when he continued his studies instead. To help him out, she sent him 1200 francs, which he said 'saved me from being overwhelmed by task-work which would have broken me down'.

Returning from Poland, she lived with him in Paris, where they edited several journals together. Their dynamic was an inversion of gender stereotypes: 'with you analysis is the first thing,' he told her, 'with me that only comes after the initial judgement made by the heart.' In the September following her death, he privately published a little book about her – one hundred copies only, for distribution among friends: 'So modest and retiring was my sister, so great her aversion to this clamorous world, that I should have thought I saw her rising from the grave to reproach me if I had given those pages to the public.' It became his justification for omitting her from his memoirs twenty years later. Or an excuse, as his fame and self-regard grew, to present himself as a solitary genius.

Maria Chekhova

Though he wrote a play about three sisters, Chekhov had only one, Maria. But she did the work of three, not only in his lifetime but during the fifty-three years she outlived him. A portrait of him hung in her bedroom: even as a young woman she was in thrall to him ('she's afraid of you and looks at you with such humble and sincere eyes,' Aleksandr, the eldest of their four brothers, told him). By the age of twenty-nine she had received three marriage proposals but, on Anton's advice, turned them all down. She was 'one of those rare, incomprehensible women' who did not want to marry, he said, and she agreed that she'd never really been in love.

While Anton worked as a doctor, wrote and travelled, Maria (Masha as everyone called her) taught in schools in Moscow, ran the family estate and looked after their parents. He could be stingy about giving her the money she needed but when his plays were put on in Moscow and St Petersburg she bathed in his limelight: 'You've always been the person closest and dearest to me,' she told him. Though she opposed his marriage to the actress Olga Knipper towards the end of his life, when he was suffering from TB, it wasn't so much from jealousy or dislike of Olga but from fear for his health. For the same reason, she opposed Olga taking him on a trip to Germany three years later. Within weeks he was dead.

In his will he left Maria his house in Yalta, his money and all future income from his plays. Because it hadn't been properly witnessed, the will was declared invalid but Olga didn't contest it and gave Maria all she needed from her and Anton's joint account. Maria duly gave up school-teaching and devoted herself to preserving Chekhov's name through the management of his archive. She donated his personal belongings to a museum established in their birthplace, Taganrog, and opened a museum at the house she'd inherited from him in Yalta. Through the Stalinist era, she placed the collected works of Lenin on Anton's bookshelves and put up portraits of Gorky (a Soviet favourite) in the Yalta house; during the German occupation, the Gorkys were replaced by Gerhart Hauptmanns: whatever the regime, she found a way to protect her brother's reputation. She died in 1957 at the age of ninety-four.

Sarah Fielding

As an author in her own right, whose novels – the first of them, *The Adventures of David Simple*, in particular – were popular during her lifetime, Sarah Fielding is a different case from the other four. But her books tend to be looked at, if at all, for the light they shed on those written by her brother Henry. And that would dismay Henry's great rival, Samuel Richardson, who thought Sarah the more talented sibling: 'What a knowledge of the human heart! Well might a critical judge of writing say, as he did to me, that your late brother's knowledge of it was not (fine writer as he was) comparable to yours.* His was but as the knowledge of the outside of a clockwork machine, while yours was that of all the finer springs and movements of the inside.'

Sarah was born three years after Henry and grew up in very different circumstances. After their mother died when she was seven, their father quickly remarried and a bitter legal dispute began over the children's custody and inheritance – she and her younger siblings moved in with their maternal grandmother while Henry went to Eton. (Feckless fathers, avaricious step-mothers and inheritance scams became recurrent themes in Sarah's writing.) Though well educated, with a good knowledge of Latin and Greek, she wasn't well off, which was why, as an unmarried woman in need of an income, she took up writing. Having anonymously contributed a letter ('From Leonora to Horatio') to her brother's novel *Joseph Andrews* and a chapter (a narrative about Anne Boleyn) for his next book, *Miscellanies*, she published *The Adventures of David Simple* anonymously as 'the Work of a Woman and her first Essay; which, to the good-natured and candid Reader will, it is hoped, be a sufficient Apology for the many Inaccuracies he will find in the Style, and other Faults of the Composition.' Continuing in the same self-deprecating vein, Sarah suggested that 'the best Excuse that can be Made for a Woman's venturing to write at all, is that which really produced this Book: Distress in her Circumstances: which she could not so well remove by any other Means in her Power.'

Within two months of publication, the book went into a second edition, and for this Henry wrote a preface, in part to dispel the rumours that the novel was his: 'In Reality, two or three Hints which arose on the reading it, and some little Direction as to the Conduct of the second Volume, much the

---

*The critic is thought to have been Samuel Johnson.

greater Part of which I never saw till in Print, were all the Aid she received from me. Indeed I believe there are few Books in the World so absolutely the Author's own as this.' As if to distance himself still further, he pointed to 'grammatical and other Errors in style in the first Impression, which my Absence from Town prevented my correcting'. Over 600 changes were made to the second edition, some of them fussy amendments, others florid additions more characteristic of his prose than of Sarah's, and one a reference to Don Quixote that has no basis in the original but which serves to emphasise the picaresque genre in which brother and sister were working. Henry's insistence on the novel's 'Imperfections' and his amazement that a young woman 'so unacquainted with the World' should know so much about human nature are reminiscent of Charlotte Brontë's condescending preface to Emily's *Wuthering Heights*. How Sarah felt about his condescension isn't known; not too badly, perhaps, as she allowed Henry to contribute half a dozen letters and another preface to her epistolary follow-up, *Familiar Letters*, three years later. She would at least have been grateful for the affection Henry expressed to 'one so nearly and dearly allied to me, in the highest Friendship as well as Relation' and for his tribute to her novel's 'deep and profound Discernment of all the Mazes, Windings and Labyrinths, which perplex the Heart of Man'.

In the same year the novel was published, Henry's wife died and Sarah came to live with him in London, acting as his housekeeper for the next three years. Henry wrote of her, at the time, as 'the Woman in the world whom I like best', and she moved out only when he married his cook, Mary, who'd fallen pregnant by him. (In doing the decent thing and marrying 'beneath' him, Henry became an object of ridicule in polite society.) Moving back to the country, Sarah published several more books, including *The Cry*, a novel she wrote jointly with her friend Jane Collier; collaboration was a far more common practice then than it is now, and Sarah already had some experience of it with Henry. But none of her later books was as commercially successful as her first. Poverty and illness cast a shadow on her last years; she died at the age of fifty-seven, fourteen years after her brother.

David Simple is a more vulnerable fictional hero than Henry's Tom Jones or Joseph Andrews, and in her confrontation of patriarchy and capitalism Sarah's tone is less comic than her brother's. But they approached fiction in a similar spirit, as a means to expose hypocrisy. And each depended on the other for support. As a character in Sarah's novel *The Governess* puts it, 'my good Mamma bid me to remember how much my Brother's superior Strength might assist me in his being my Protector; and that I ought in return to use my utmost Endeavours to oblige him; and that then we should be mutual Assistants to each other throughout Life.'

Did their intimacy extend beyond books? Henry Fielding's biographers, Martin and Ruthe Battestin, suggest it might have, if only in childhood. One of the witnesses in the legal battle over the Fielding children's inheritance and upbringing testified that Henry 'was guilty of committing some indecent actions with his sister Beatrice', eight years his junior. And the Battestins speculate that he may have behaved similarly with Sarah, since sibling incest is a theme that recurs in her *David Simple* and his *Joseph Andrews*. In the former, incest is a charge falsely made against the innocent Camilla and Valentine by their wicked stepmother; in the latter it's a revelation that threatens to kibosh the wedding of Joseph to his beloved Fanny (who've grown up not knowing each other), before it turns out they're not siblings after all. The Battestins make a good deal of Henry and Sarah's fascination with incest.

But there's no evidence that it happened between them – any more than it happens between their characters.

Feminist scholars have rightly argued that Sarah Fielding's novels deserve to be better known. And although biographies of Chekhov, Joyce, Primo Levi and Ernest Renan make passing mention of their sisters, otherwise a single portrait or handful of photos are all that remain of these women. I keep looking at the images online. It's a displacement activity, I know. Gill's the person I'm searching for. Rather than accept she's missing, I think that if I look for long enough she'll eventually, somehow, turn up.

9

A lot had happened at home in the years Gill was away. A new live-in housekeeper had arrived, Pat,* who at eighteen was only four years older than I was and who kept me company in ways not intended by Mum and Dad. She'd been with us for over a year while Gill was away, which Gill must have found hard: Josie might have visited but Pat *lived* with us, had her own bedroom, was made to feel part of the family – a usurping, substitute daughter. Now that Gill was back, Pat and I no longer had the house to ourselves when Mum and Dad were out. Her presence inhibited us. The kissing, and the more-than-kissing, had to stop.

Dad would later complain that Gill had learned nothing at St Anne's. But she was offered a place at Skipton Girls' High School all the same – the school she'd have gone to if she'd passed her eleven-plus. She liked to say that getting a place there was surprising, given how 'stupid' she was. But it wasn't

---

*In my memoirs about Mum and Dad, I called her Sandra, in order to spare her blushes. But she complained about the name-change – why had I bothered? Was I ashamed of her? – so I'm restoring her to herself here.

Dad's string-pulling that did it. She sat an exam and the result was good enough to get her in.

There's a photo of her on our front doorstep on her first day. It's a replica of the one taken when she started boarding school. But instead of a suitcase, she's carrying a satchel. And her expression isn't exuberant or optimistic. It's apprehensive. Chastened even.

The virtue of the high school was that the day ended at 3.30 – no more lonely nights away from home. Every Thursday we watched *Top of the Pops* together. Gill had more time for solo performers and romantic ballads than I did but mostly our tastes coincided: the Who, the Kinks, the Animals, the Doors, the Yardbirds, Procol Harum, Manfred Mann and (it went without saying) the Stones and the Beatles. We were intrigued by the people in the studio audience, some no older than us – were they friends of the programme-makers or could anyone go? Most were terrible dancers; a few simply stood and gawped. The performers could be lacklustre too, miming so badly they seemed not to know their own lyrics. By contrast, the black American groups – mostly on the Motown label – were high-energy: the Supremes, Marvin Gaye, the Four Tops, Martha and the Vandellas, Smokey Robinson, and – most exciting of all, a boy barely older than we were – Stevie Wonder. In one of his songs, Stevie uses the words 'uptight' and 'out of sight' as positives. It's a strange idiom. To Stevie, blind since birth and wearing dark glasses, *everything* was out of sight.

As well as soaps (*Z-Cars, Coronation Street, Emergency Ward 10*) and quiz shows (*Double Your Money* with Hughie Green, *Take Your Pick!* with Michael Miles), we'd a fondness for comedy:

Hancock's Half Hour, *Steptoe and Son* and *The Rag Trade*. The last was set in a clothing business in London, Fenner's Fashions, and starred Barbara Windsor, Miriam Karlin and Sheila Hancock as the seamstresses. Did the banter and sorority inspire Gill to think the rag trade the right line of work for her, much as the BBC's *The Wednesday Play* and *Theatre 625* series got me interested in writing? She was only eleven when *The Rag Trade* ended and might have developed the interest in dressmaking anyway. But it was after watching it that she asked for a sewing machine for Christmas.

We were seeing less of Beaty and Josie by then. Dad still drank at Sam's pub but went to others too, including the Bull at Broughton. The Sunday family sessions had dwindled and with Josie now at primary school Beaty no longer brought her over during the week. But the friendship persisted – maybe the affair too. And after Mum and Dad bought the chalet in Abersoch, Beaty and Josie often came to stay with us.

They stayed on their own sometimes, too. On one occasion, Dad's sister Mary turned up with her daughter Jane, expecting the place to be empty, only to find Beaty and Josie there. Mary had guessed about Beaty's relationship with Dad – maybe through Granny, who lived next door to us and reported how often Beaty and Josie used to come round. Her disapproval – how did Mum put up with the affair? – added to her annoyance: either she'd not been told that Beaty and Josie would be using the chalet or had been misinformed about when they'd be vacating it. An awkward interlude followed, while Beaty and Josie packed their bags. Had it been anyone else, Mary would have laughed off the miscommunication and encouraged the little girls to play together (Jane was just a couple of years older than Josie). She might even have said, 'Why not stay another night, if that's what you were expecting? There's room for us all.' Instead she sat, arms folded, on the terrace, making clear that she resented someone like Beaty – not family – being allowed to use the chalet at all. Others might tolerate her brother's mistress but she'd not be doing the same.

Sam sometimes joined Beaty and Josie in Abersoch, but he avoided lying out on sunbeds on the terrace, an activity (or non-activity) the rest of us went in for whether or not it was sunny. More often he'd drop them off then pick them up again a few days later. He couldn't leave the pub: that was the excuse. But later, when he worked for a brewery company, he still didn't join us on holiday. For him it wouldn't have been a holiday. Too much false jollity. All that effort of keeping up pretences.

Even in later years, when the two couples did sometimes spend time together, Sam was the odd one out. I've a photo Dad took of Mum and Beaty standing in a pub car park, Beaty with an umbrella, Mum with her left arm outstretched, both smiling. At the edge of the picture there's Sam, just his sleeve and trouser leg showing, as if he's skedaddled from the photo, or as if Dad has intentionally or inadvertently left him out.

Gill loved summer holidays in Abersoch. Back in Skipton, the high school was proving less fun. She was still very withdrawn, as though fearful of another Gillie emerging. Auntie Sheila, one of Mum's younger sisters, warned her to 'trust no one and be careful when making friends'. It was bleak advice but, after the St Anne's experience, she followed it.

Her favourite subjects were the non-academic ones, the so-called softer options – Home Economics, for example. At home she made frocks and blouses on her new sewing machine. Christine, from primary school, remained her closest friend. She got on with Pat too and sometimes went out with her – unless Pat had a new boyfriend and was unavailable.

As for me, I'd my own set of friends and if Mum and Dad pushed me to take Gill along when I went out for the night I would resist. I wasn't my sister's keeper, was I? I could drop her somewhere if that helped (at seventeen I was driving a car) but I didn't want her tagging along. I don't remember her asking to join me anyway. We were teenagers now, busily going our separate ways.*

The pressure from Mum and Dad was understandable: an older brother looking out for his sister – what could be more natural? But there was more to it than that, an idea that Gill needed looking *after*. Men were the stronger sex. Though cleverer than Dad, Mum kow-towed to him. And Gill was taught to look up to me, which meant looking down on herself.

Perhaps the sexism damaged me as well. My single-sex grammar school reinforced the notion that boys were superior: we might have romantic feelings for girls but they weren't our equals. Some of the authors I discovered at university – Germaine Greer, Kate Millett, Andrea Dworkin – changed my ideas. But

---

* 'There were certain needs and expectations for life that could not properly be filled by your brother or sister. That was normal. And she must have come to feel, as he did, bored or unfairly burdened by the habits of a relationship that were drying up into sentimental gestures. And added to that was what he supposed was the normal inevitable loathing for the people who look like you and smell the same as you. That experience of total dissatisfaction with the closely related: who are not smart enough, good-looking enough, cool enough to get through a day without boring you or shaming you.' (E. L. Doctorow, *The Book of Daniel*)

till then I took male dominance for granted. Girls seemed to accept it too – whether it was asking for a date or kissing in the cinema, boys had to take the initiative.

Gill was no feminist but she'd a habit of biting things back, as though she had something she needed to say, if only she could work out what it was. Later in life, drink loosened her tongue, with accusations of mistreatment from men: father, boyfriends, husband. I got off comparatively lightly because I'd moved away. But to Gill, in her cups, even that – my defection from home – only proved what a bastard I was.

I've an old shoebox stuffed with teenage correspondence: letters addressed to the Crofters, the band I was part of (on drums) before we folded after two gigs; anonymous Valentines probably sent by male friends as a joke; effusive amorous notes matching effusions of mine (thankfully lost but sometimes quoted back at me). I'd hoped to find something from Gill. But she was back home by then. Why would she write to me?

In with the letters is a small green pocket diary I kept at sixteen, with 'A Dodgson & Son, Lane Ends Garage, Earby' on the cover – a diary Dad was given as a valued customer. The entries are in tiny handwriting and block capitals. Gill gets two mentions early on: first because she has German measles, then because I'm grateful to her for hinting the girl I was going out with wasn't as keen on me as I was on her (sure enough, she broke up with me straight after). After that Gill goes missing as I take up with Jillian, my first serious romance, made all the more romantic when she tells me, a couple of weeks into our relationship, that she'll soon be moving to Australia. There's a lot about our ups and downs – meeting outside school or in the park, going for walks by the canal, seeing films, sneaking into empty rooms to kiss and touch each other. Otherwise the diary is banal: homework, football results (Burnley's or the team I played for on Sundays), the setting up with my friend Stephen of a village youth club. I talk about seeing Josie at weekends; she'd have been seven then. The only other reference to Gill is about her first communion, in the village church where we sang in the choir. Intriguingly I call her Gillian, which in my handwriting (some of it in pencil) isn't easily distinguished from Jillian (who later shortened herself to Jill). I express no surprise at having a sister and a girlfriend with the same name.

Teenage boys aren't usually interested in their younger sisters so perhaps there's nothing odd about Gill's relative absence. She was just a backdrop to my own dramas. Reassuringly there were few dramas of her own. She might not have been very happy at the high school but she was home again, where she belonged.

(The references to church in the diary came as a surprise. In my memory, I'd given up going at fourteen, shortly after I was 'confirmed', a rite of passage that seemed more Catholic than C of E. Gill was confirmed two years later but neither of us was religious: church was an excuse to see our friends, whose presence in the choir was why we'd joined it. Confirmation de-confirmed us. The ghoulish, servile ritual of holy communion – the bended knee at the altar rail, the wafer on the tongue, the sip of acrid wine from the metal cup – made me an atheist and Gill, I'm pretty sure, an agnostic.)

Gill approved of Jill and colluded with our relationship – indeed she literally looked out for us when Dad was prowling round trying to catch us up to no good. (Did he patrol so fanatically because he was worried what had happened to him would happen to me? That I'd get Jill pregnant?) Gill and Jill weren't in the same year group but they got on. Later – many years later – they'd get on even better.

I'd met Jill before Gill met her; there was no question of me stealing my sister's friend. With a later girlfriend, Jane, it was more of an issue. 'I have had two long half-hour conversations with Gillian on the phone,' she wrote in a letter, 'with no offer of a word with you . . . she sounded very morose.' Jane wondered if this 'was a gentle hint that you prefer not to communicate with me again' but thought it more likely that Gill felt 'left out'. She apologised for 'causing trouble' between us.

The trouble soon blew over. But as far as Gill was concerned she had prior rights in Jane and wasn't going to let her speak to me.*

*

---

*A prime example of trouble between siblings over romantic relationships comes in Italo Svevo's novel *As a Man Grows Older*. When the main protagonist Emilio Brentani embarks on a relationship with the beautiful, fickle Angiolina, his loyal sister Amalia is first worried, then excited ('love had entered the house . . . brother and sister were embarking on the same adventure'), then horribly jealous: 'She hated that unknown woman who had stolen away her companion and her only comfort.' A hopeless infatuation of her own compounds the unhappiness. Emilio finally breaks off the relationship with Angiolina, but not before Amalia becomes delirious and dies: 'Death! It was the first time he had imagined Amalia dying . . . he saw himself alone, overwhelmed by remorse because he had not profited by the happiness which up to that moment had been his for the asking, the happiness of devoting his life to someone who needed his care and self-sacrifice. With Amalia every hope of comfort vanished . . . Oh, if only he had known that his life contained such a precious mission as to guard and cherish this life which was entrusted solely to him, he would never have felt the need of approaching Angiolina.'

Jill's departure was a sweet sorrow. Each week we'd exchange elegiac airmails. And once a fatter envelope came, with photos of Jill's life Down Under: one showed her in profile, with her hair up, pouring a glass of gin, the sun glinting off the silver optic. I returned to it obsessively, imagining the occasion, a barbecue at her house where she'd get to know the neighbours, among whom, surely, there'd be a handsome boy about her age . . . Today, I'd have found out on Facebook or Instagram, but with letters it was hard to tell what, if anything, she was hiding. Gradually our letter-writing dwindled, then stopped. She didn't say she was seeing anyone but I assumed she must be. I could hardly complain – I'd begun doing the same. What other way to get over our tragedy?

Gill didn't interfere. She liked Jill but knew she'd not be returning soon.

I was writing bad poems, inept imitations of everyone from Hopkins to Brian Patten and all of them self-pitying melodramas (a broken heart, loneliness, the cruel adult world). The one instance of me writing prose – set down in a French composition exercise book – had to do with Gill. I'd come home from playing football to find that Dad had left for Manchester. Gill had phoned, very upset, asking to be picked up; she'd gone to hear one of her favourite pop stars, Scott Walker, then fallen ill. Mum's upset seemed excessive. Was there more to this? Had Gill been raped or something? On their return, Dad was stony-faced and Gill tearful. Later, she told me she'd had some kind of 'blackout' during which she'd been arrested for shoplifting; the police had called Dad; she'd escaped with a caution but it had all been a nightmare.

Later still, with Gill asleep, I tried to talk about it to Mum and Dad. If Gill had been stealing, was she unhappy or depressed? Was it some compulsion disorder, like kleptomania. Might it help for her to see a counsellor or psychiatrist? Impatient with my theorising, Dad said there was no need: he and Mum were doctors, weren't they; the problem was they'd spoilt us both and we'd no sense of responsibility, a problem made worse for Gill because she couldn't express herself. My account describes how 'dismally' the conversation ended – how 'when you really want to say something important you can't, when for most of your life you go round saying things you're not really bothered about saying at all'. It's horribly melodramatic, as if I'm the one deserving of pity – the misunderstood son in a dysfunctional family.

I'd been in trouble myself the year before, when – at the end of a summer night in Abersoch – two schoolfriends and I were caught smashing a couple of roadside reflector plates and making off with a traffic bollard; we were charged with larceny and criminal damage. In the subsequent court case, thanks to our craven letters of apology (dictated by Dad), the efforts of a local solicitor (funded by Dad) and our status as grammar school boys, we were cleared of larceny and given a token fine for the damage. But the result was me having a criminal record, whereas Gill had escaped with a caution. Why were Mum and Dad so much more distraught by what she had done? Because I'd been with friends, half drunk and in high spirits, whereas Gill had acted alone? Because our offence was spontaneous and hers (they thought) more calculated? Or was it simply double standards, the idea that *stealing was less permissible for girls*?

There's another thought, now I look back: had I somehow set an example? Did Gill see me as inspiringly rebellious, contemptuous of property law since property is theft? Did she feel authorised to follow suit?*

In her memoir *A Girl's Story*, Annie Ernaux recounts how she and a friend, another French au pair working in London, graduated from stealing sweets in corner shops to nicking bikinis from Selfridges. She describes the anxiety beforehand, the adrenalin rush of the act, then the elation of getting away with it.[†] They stopped after her friend was caught one day. Gill must have felt something similar – the thrill of the illicit, the frisson of transgression – till a store detective intervened.

---

* 'Individuals with an offending sibling close in age are at elevated risk of offending,' a 2017 Dutch research paper found, adding that 'a child may observe criminal behaviour by his or her sibling(s), learn from it, and eventually show criminal behaviour him- or her-self'. Examples of siblings committing crimes together are less common, and in the case of same-sex siblings almost unknown, but there have been a few brutal exceptions. In 2004 Kenneth and Kari Allen, a brother and sister from Indianapolis, killed their mother, grandmother and grandfather with a hammer before dismembering their bodies, encasing them in concrete and burying them in a basement. In 2014, Sabrina and Kenneth Cummins, a brother and sister from County Kildare, strangled a mentally disabled man with a leather belt, suffocated him with a plastic bag and tried to poison him with cleaning fluids. And in April 2016, a fifteen-year-old girl and her ten-year-old brother suffocated and stabbed their six-year-old brother, then buried him in a shallow grave.

† 'The moment of the hit, when the hand makes the object disappear into a pocket or a bag, is charged with an acute consciousness of self, of the danger of being oneself at that moment, which lasts until the falsely casual exit from the shop with that burning thing in one's possession. After that, nothing can surpass the jubilation, outside, at fifty metres' remove for safety, of having yet again defied fear, attained a peak of personal achievement whose proof, whose trophy we carry off, in our hand, or in a bag, or on our bodies.' (Annie Ernaux, *A Girl's Story*)

Perhaps, like Ernaux, she had an accomplice. None was mentioned at the time but, now I think of it, the Manchester story doesn't hang together. Would Gill really have been allowed to go on her own to a gig in Manchester, a two-hour bus ride away, aged fifteen? A friend must have gone with her. If so, the friend must have been with her in the shop.

Unlike Annie Ernaux and her friend, Gill didn't stop. After the Manchester episode, there were a couple more let-offs before she was charged with stealing from a girl's purse after a badminton class at the local gym. The court case was in Skipton and, to Mum and Dad's consternation, word of it got round. Perhaps they'd been right to worry about Gill. But wrong to dismiss the idea of counselling. If this was more than teenage rebellion, counselling might have helped.

Still, stealing was commonplace in our peer group. At a party Gill and I threw in the Abersoch chalet a couple of years later, many of our LPs and singles went missing; there'd been a few gatecrashers and we blamed them but it could have been someone we knew. Most teenagers nicked stuff because they lacked stuff. The difference was that Gill *did* have stuff. Whatever her motive – loneliness, misery, jealousy, attention-seeking, self-hatred – it wasn't need.

Was it the morning after that same party when Gill opened the door to my bedroom in Abersoch and, seeing a second head on the pillow, quickly retreated? We didn't talk about it afterwards; I'd been pretending to sleep; she'd been leaving for work. I was in my late teens; it can't have surprised her that I had a sex life. But we didn't discuss it.

Had Gill not gone to boarding school, might we have been closer and hung out together more? Might she have gone on dates with my friends? Might we have shared the humiliations of teenage courtship? And talked about sex? And felt better for that? Maybe. That summer would have been a good time, with both of us doing holiday jobs, away from Mum and Dad. But at the end of it I went off to university and the moment passed.

10

My choice of Eng Lit as a degree was a disappointment to Mum and Dad, who'd have liked me to read medicine, become a GP and take over the family practice. It was also a veering away from Gill, who'd no more interest in studying literature than I had in dressmaking. As younger children, along with our cousins, we'd performed to the family at Christmas – songs, skits and comedy sketches – and made some recordings on tape. But by our teens we'd stopped collaborating. When I wrote a poem, I kept it to myself rather than seeking her opinion; when she chose a pattern for a dress, she didn't ask me what I thought of it. Making a poem or a dress was a solitary activity, not stuff we could do together.

The gap widened as we got older. That's how it is for most brothers and sisters. But there have been some notable exceptions – cases of mutual support and artistic (or scientific) collaboration. I don't imagine, when I read about them, that Gill and I might have been the same. I don't even envy them, since there's often something unhealthy about the relationship, if only its inequity: the brother as creator, the sister as muse, scribe, secretary, manager, cleaner, housekeeper, gatekeeper, accountant, executor, archivist, eternal dogsbody behind the scenes. Still, their stories are fascinating.

Dorothy and William Wordsworth

> . . . Where'er my footsteps turned,
> Her Voice was like a hidden Bird that sang;
> The thought of her was like a flash of light
> Or an unseen companionship, a breath
> Of fragrance independent of the wind.

The most celebrated of all sibling partnerships, its intensity stemmed from their separation as children; as Dorothy put it in a letter to a friend, 'We have been endeared to each other by early misfortune'. After their parents' deaths, when she was six, Dorothy was farmed out to various relatives. When she and William met in Halifax in 1794 – she twenty-two, he a year older (and recently returned from France, where he had left behind his pregnant lover Annette Vallon) – they were comparative strangers. Falling on each other for emotional support and intellectual companionship – 'Two of a scatter'd brood that could not bear/To live in loneliness' – they set off for the Lakes (as Frances Wilson's *The Ballad of Dorothy Wordsworth* puts it) 'in the manner of an elopement'. Once settled there, they walked, read poetry and planned a future when they need never be separated again.

In 'To My Sister', from the *Lyrical Ballads*, William urges Dorothy to 'Put on with speed your woodland dress' and join him outdoors. In 'Lines . . . above Tintern Abbey' she turns up as his 'dear, dear Friend . . . dear, dear Sister'. In *The Prelude* she's the 'companion' who helps him find his true vocation:

> She in the midst of all, preserved me still
> A Poet, made me seek beneath that name,
> And that alone, my office upon earth.

Just as William needed Dorothy to find 'my true self' ('She gave me eyes, she gave me ears'), so Dorothy wrote that 'Fraternal love has been the building up of my being, the light of my path'. 'I am willing to allow that half the virtues with which I fancy him endowed are the creation of my own love,' she wrote to a friend, 'but surely I may be excused!'

As his secretary or amanuensis, she was charged with copying out his poems – no easy task since he liked to compose while out walking. 'Mr Wordsworth went bumming and booing about,' one local recalled, 'and she, Miss Dorothy, kept close behint him, and she picked up the bits as he let 'em fall, and tak 'em down, and put 'em on paper for him.' In later years she also corrected his proofs. More importantly, she read her diaries aloud to him, with observations he could make use of in his poems. In an entry for January 1798, she wrote of a sky 'spread over with continuous cloud', of how the moon could 'chequer the earth with shadows' and of the sky as a 'black-blue vault'; his poem 'A Night-Piece' has the sky 'Overcast/With a continuous cloud', with the moon 'chequering the ground' and sailing 'in a black-blue vault'. In the presence of nature, Dorothy said, she sometimes fancied herself 'more than half a poet', and her descriptions could outdo his: 'The moon shone like herrings on the water', 'The moon rose, large and dull, like an ill-cleaned brass plate'. Though she wrote them 'to please William' and didn't expect them to be published, her journals are a glorious achievement in their own right.

Because of their closeness, rumours of incest followed the Wordsworths, probably without foundation, though some of Dorothy's fervent diary outbursts make you wonder: 'Oh, the Darling! Here is one of his bitten apples! I can hardly find it in my heart to throw it into the fire.' 'The fire flutters & the

watch ticks I hear nothing save the Breathing of my Beloved'.*
Just as Annette Vallon was supplanted by Dorothy, so Dorothy
was supplanted when William married Mary. But the intimacy
endured (she even joined the happy couple on their honeymoon).
And in respect of William's poetry, it was the sister, not the
mistress or the wife, who had the deepest influence.

Charles and Mary Lamb

> Her behaviour to her brother was like that of an admiring
> disciple; her eyes seldom absent from his face. Even when
> apparently engrossed in conversation with others, she
> would, by supplying some word for which he was at a loss,
> even when talking in a distant part of the room, show how
> closely her mind waited upon his.
>
> (A contemporary account of Mary Lamb, quoted in
> Sarah Burton, *A Double Life*)

Mary Lamb was born eleven years before her brother Charles
and survived him by twelve. She nurtured him in childhood;
he cared for her in adulthood; she enjoyed dominion over him
as a boy, 'whom I could control and correct at my own pleasure';

---

* In her book *The Brother–Sister Culture in Nineteenth-Century Literature*,
Valerie Sanders gives several examples of the extravagant language
siblings used in Romantic and Victorian times. Thomas Macaulay, to
his sister Hannah after their sister Margaret was married: 'you alone
are now left to me. Whom have I on earth but thee?' Benjamin Disraeli:
'I wish to live only for my sister.' It's true that these pale in comparison
to what William said to Dorothy in a letter: 'Oh, my dear, dear sister,
with what rapture I shall again meet you . . . So eager is my desire to
see you that all obstacles vanish. I see you in a moment running or
rather flying to my arms.' But to be fair to William, he wrote this to
her after an absence of several years.

he became her 'lord & master' when she began to suffer nervous breakdowns. The strain of nursing her family – her paralysed mother, senile father, geriatric aunt and convalescent elder brother John – exacerbated these breakdowns. And they reached a pitch, or nadir, one evening in September 1796, during preparations for dinner, when Mary stabbed her mother through the heart with a kitchen knife. Rather than being arrested for murder, she was taken to the Islington madhouse; at the time, those deemed insane were not put on trial for their crimes. Within six weeks she was considered mentally fit for release. In the meantime Charles dedicated a set of poems to 'the author's best friend and sister, with all a brother's fondness'. The compassion shown to Mary by Charles, their friends and the state was remarkable.* No one acting as she did could hope for such treatment today.

Charles's kindness towards Mary may also have stemmed partly from guilt: he'd been out when she killed their mother and 'was at hand only with time enough to snatch the knife out of her grasp'. More importantly he *identified* with her. A year before the murder he too spent six weeks in a madhouse in Hoxton, writing to Coleridge, 'I am got somewhat rational now, and don't bite anyone. But mad I was'. Even in later years Thomas Carlyle, for one, thought him to be 'in some considerable degree insane'. Madness didn't stop him writing: while in Hoxton he wrote a sonnet for Mary, ticking her off for being too kind a critic ('My verse, which thou to praise were o'er

*A brother could learn from Charles. Or indeed from Mary, who advised a friend whose mother 'had gone out of her mind' to 'be certain that she is treated with *tenderness*. I lay a stress upon this, because it is a thing of which people in her state are uncommonly susceptible & which hardly any one is at all aware of, a hired nurse *never*, even though in all other respects they are a good kind of people.'

inclined/Too highly, and with a partial eye to see/No blemish') and ticking himself off for failing to 'repay/But ill the mighty debt of love I owe,/Mary, to thee, my sister and my friend.'

Two years after the murder, Mary was returned to Charles's custody and remained there till he died: 'We house together, old bachelor and maid, in a sort of double singleness', he wrote. Many visitors dined with them, including Dorothy and William Wordsworth. Having guests stay overnight was more problematic, Charles decided: the stress might result in Mary having further breakdowns. She did often relapse and spend periods back in the Hoxton asylum, leaving him feeling like 'a widowed thing'. Her condition, he thought, meant the two of them were 'marked'. One woman, the actress Fanny Kelly, turned down his proposal of marriage because (so she told her sister Lydia) 'I could not give my assent to a proposal which would bring me into that atmosphere of sad mental uncertainty which surrounds his domestic life.' Mary felt guilty on his behalf and worried that their intimacy was destroying them both: 'Our love for each other has been the torment of our lives.' Charles disagreed: 'I could be nowhere happier than under the same roof as her.'

Though they lived together as childless singletons, they were fond of children and never happier than when harping back to their own childhood. Perhaps it was this that prompted William and Mary Godwin to invite them to write something for their Juvenile Library series. The resulting book, *Tales from Shakespeare* – with Charles working on the tragedies, Mary on the comedies, and William Blake among the artists who illustrated it – was a great success. A collection of tales, *Mrs Leicester's School* (seven written by Mary, three by Charles), added to their financial security, going through nine editions over the next few years. 'Boys are generally permitted the use of their father's libraries at a much earlier age than girls are,' Mary observed, and she aimed to correct that by writing 'chiefly' for girls, even if that meant their brothers helping them with difficult passages and 'carefully selecting what is proper for a young sister's ears'.

Mary's mental health remained variable and the pressure of caring for her may have contributed to Charles's heavy drinking. His 1813 essay 'Confessions of a Drunkard', published anonymously, shows how out of hand it got. It's not known whether Mary contributed to its composition or to any of the essays he published under the pseudonym Elia. But there's no question that they were a team – two vulnerable adults whose collaboration made them stronger, two children growing old together.*

Felix and Fanny Mendelssohn

Fanny was four years older than Felix and as children they both received piano lessons from the same tutor, who declared that 'she plays like a man' (no praise could have been higher). Goethe thought the siblings 'equally gifted' but their father

---

*The idea of an unmarried brother and sister growing old together in the same house would strike most of us today as unhealthy. It was once far more common and to Dickens's Nicholas Nickleby seemed entirely desirable. 'Rich or poor, old or young,' he tells his sister Kate late on in the novel, 'we shall ever be the same to each other, and in that our comfort lies. What if we have but one home? It can never be a solitary one to you and me. What if we were to remain so true to these first impressions as to form no others? It is but one more link to the strong chain that binds us together.' Luckily, they don't have to put it to the test: within thirty pages of this effusion, they're both married.

Henry James and his sister Alice weren't lifelong companions under the same roof but they did live together for a while after their parents' deaths: 'My sister and I make an harmonious little menage, and I feel a good deal as if we were married,' he reported.

discouraged Fanny's ambitions: 'Music will perhaps become his [Felix's] profession, while for *you* it can and must only be an ornament, never the root of your being and doing'. For many years she contented herself with the role of mentor to Felix. 'I have watched the progress of his talent step by step,' she wrote when he was thirteen, 'and may say I have contributed to his development. I have always been his only musical adviser, and he never writes down a thought before submitting it to my judgment. For instance, I have known his operas by heart before a note was written!' He would submit pieces for her approval and rework them according to her suggestions. She was similarly dependent on him: 'Don't forget that you're my right hand and my eyesight, and without you, therefore, I can't proceed with my music'. In later years she missed her role as his Minerva or muse, 'sadly recall[ing] the time when I used to know his music from its birth'. But she continued to be involved: when, in his absence, she attended rehearsals in Berlin for his oratorio *St Paul* she was fierce in ensuring that it was performed as he would have wished – or as *she* wished: 'in my role as advisor, I was able to avert great disaster for the noble apostle.'

When she complained that motherhood was getting in the way of her music, he consoled her that if he had 'a baby to nurse' he wouldn't be writing scores either: 'you certainly have sufficient genius to compose'. She had no such faith in herself and accused him of disliking her recent work: 'Did I really do it better in the old days, or were you merely easier to satisfy?' He apologised for giving that impression – 'My nature was always to be a screech-owl, and to belong to the savage tribe of brothers' – and assured her of his continuing admiration: 'You know well how I love all your productions, and some are especially dear to my heart.'

Dear as they were to him, he published some of these productions as if they were his, on the grounds that her privacy, or womanhood, needed protecting. She didn't object but eventually, in her thirties, began to think about publishing a collection of songs under her own name. Felix was against the idea. 'Fanny, as I know her, has neither enthusiasm nor calling for authorship,' he told their mother. 'She is too much a *Frau*, as is proper, raises Sebastian and cares for her home, and thinks neither of the public nor the musical world, nor even of music, except when she has fulfilled her primary occupation. Allowing her music to appear in print would just stir her up in that.' Despite his opposition Fanny went ahead, awkwardly breaking the news to him in a letter: 'I'm no *femme libre* . . . I trust you will in no way be bothered by it, since, as you can see, I've proceeded completely on my own in order to spare you any possible unpleasant moment.' He was slow to write back but in the end gave her his 'professional blessing . . . may you know only the joys of authorship and nothing of its misery'. 'I know that he is not quite satisfied in his heart of hearts,' she told a friend, 'but I am glad he has said a kind word to me about it.'

Publishing a selection of her *Lieder* boosted Fanny. But the pleasure of recognition was short-lived. She died after suffering a stroke while rehearsing one of Felix's cantatas. He outlived her by only six months.

In recent years, with the release of previously unknown compositions, Fanny's reputation has risen. With 400 pieces to her name, she's no longer regarded as her brother's sidekick but as the most important female composer of the nineteenth century. Her music may be indebted to Felix's but so is his to her: as one recent biographer puts it, they were 'like musical twins, who had uncanny abilities to intuit each other's musical thoughts, inspirations and frustrations.'

William and Caroline Herschel

Who participated in the toils of Sir William Herschel? Who braved with him the inclemency of the weather? Who shared his privations? A female. Who was she? His sister. Miss Herschel it was who acted by night as his amanuensis; she it was whose pen conveyed to paper his observations as they issued from his lips; she it was who noted the right ascensions and polar distances of the objects observed; she it was who, having passed the night near the instrument, took the rough manuscript to her cottage at dawn and produced a fair copy of the night's work on the following morning; she it was who planned the labours of each successive night; she it was who reduced every observation, made every calculation; she it was who arranged everything in systematic order; and she it was who helped him to obtain his imperishable name . . . Many of the nebulae in Sir William Herschel's catalogues were detected by her during these hours of enjoyment. Indeed in looking at the joint labours of these extraordinary personages, we scarcely know whether most to admire the intellectual power of the brother or the unconquerable industry of the sister.

The address given when Caroline Herschel was awarded the Gold medal of the Royal Astronomical Society is laudatory yet condescending: the brother's the brainbox (inspiration), the sister his dogged apprentice (perspiration). As a tribute to someone who discovered eight comets it's less than generous. But the putdown would have come as no surprise to Caroline, who colluded in constructing an image of herself as the Cinderella of astronomy, the innocent heroine who achieved fairy-tale success thanks to the princely brilliance of her brother. 'I am nothing,' she wrote in her memoirs, 'I have done nothing; all I am, all I know, I owe to my brother. I am only the tool which he shaped to his use – a well-trained puppy-dog would have done as much . . . I did what he commanded me.'

As a girl, Caroline was schooled to cook, clean and sew, while her brothers were trained to have musical careers. But she learned to read and write, and at the age of twenty-two left Germany for England, to join William (older than her by twelve years) and another brother, Alexander, who were making a living as musicians and music tutors in Bath. As a sideline, William had developed an interest in astronomy and began to make telescopes. In 1781 he discovered Uranus, the first person to find a new planet since the Ancient World. A change of career followed: he was made Astronomer Royal and moved with Caroline first to Datchet then Slough. She became his assistant, 'spending the starlit nights on a grass-plot covered by dew or hoar-frost' as she swept the sky for nebulae. Accidents with the equipment were frequent – on one occasion she was badly injured when 'an iron hook, such as butchers use for hanging meat' became embedded in her thigh – but she persisted. In 1786 she discovered her first comet. The convention had been for women's contributions to science to go unacknowledged. William insisted she be given credit. She was modest when making her case nonetheless: 'In consequence of the friendship I know to exist between you and my brother,' her letter to the Royal Society's secretary began, 'I venture to trouble you in his absence with the following imperfect account of a comet.' Over time her confidence grew and, at her suggestion, William applied to George III for her to be given 'a small annual bounty'; at £50 a year, he argued, the 'good, industrious' Caroline was a bargain – for a man to do the same work would cost twice as much. As well as comet-hunting, she revised Flamsteed's century-old map of the night sky. Fellow astronomers were full of praise for her work but wider public recognition was slow to come. By the time the Royal Society awarded her its Gold medal, William was long dead and she had moved back to Hanover, where she died at the age of ninety-seven.

A double portrait painted fifty years later shows Caroline tentatively approaching William with a cup of tea; fixated on his telescope, he doesn't acknowledge her. Even she, in her role as humble sidekick ('I was a mere tool which *he* had the trouble of sharpening'), might have protested at this picture of their relationship. Herschel astronomy was a joint enterprise. She and William depended on each other. They were a team.

Henry, William and Alice James

Collaboration? Perhaps not. But there was certainly inter-dependence: what each produced – and for decades Alice was assumed to have produced *nothing* – came about in part because of the existence of the other two. You could say the same about Osbert, Sacheverell and Edith Sitwell. But the Jameses belong to a higher order of achievement.

'In our family group,' Henry James wrote (as one of four older brothers to the one sister), 'girls seemed scarcely to have a chance.' Which was tough on Alice, whom he considered 'the most remarkable member of the family'. Born in 1848, she was six years younger than William and five years younger than Henry. Though under no pressure from their father, who urged them 'just to be something, something unconnected with specific doing, something free and uncommitted', the two oldest brothers went on to make a name for themselves, William as a Harvard professor, philosopher and psychologist, Henry as a novelist. In different circumstances, Alice might have rivalled them, but as her biographer Jean Strouse puts it, 'the intelligence and energy Alice might have used in some productive way went into the intricate work of being sick.'

By the age of fourteen Alice's health was already a concern: her constitution was thought to be so 'delicate' that any excitements would put it at risk. At eighteen she went to New York to be treated for her 'nerves'. The treatment failed to ward off repeated fainting spells, mysterious pains and breakdowns. She was variously diagnosed – by doctors whom her diaries and letter send up – with nervous hyperaesthesia, spinal neurosis, rheumatic gout, hysteria and melancholy. She herself diagnosed 'physical weakness' and an 'excess of nervous susceptibility', and towards the end of her life (she died aged forty-three) was often confined to bed. But there were earlier periods when she coped by keeping busy – while sightseeing on a tour of Europe, for instance, and by caring for her father for a year after her mother died.

Temperamentally she was closest to Henry, who saw a lot of her when she moved to England in her thirties. Emotionally, the closer tie was with William, who having suffered a mental and physical crisis of his own in his twenties identified with and pitied her for her illness. Too much so, Alice said, complaining that his 'sympathy makes me feel like a horrible humbug' when she thought of herself, on the contrary, as 'one of the most *potent* creations of my time'. Near the end of her life, she wrote to William: 'when I am gone, pray don't think of me simply as a creature who might have been something else, had neurotic science been born. Notwithstanding the poverty of my outside experience, I have always had a significance for myself.'

The self-significance comes through in the diary she kept during the last three years of her life. The wit, humour and irony she adopts towards her invalidism are extraordinary, as is the pleasure she took in thinking about death. 'I am working away as hard as I can to get dead as soon as possible,' she wrote in one entry, joking that the 'complication' was Henry's play *The American*, which was about to be staged ('I don't want to immerse him in a deathbed scene on his "first night", too much of an aesthetic incongruity'), besides which, 'there isn't anything to die of'. Soon enough there would be: a cancerous tumour. Rather than lament the fact, she welcomed it: 'To him who waits, all things come! My aspirations may have been eccentric, but I cannot complain now that they have not been brilliantly fulfilled!' At last she'd been given a 'palpable' diagnosis and had her imminent death to focus on, 'the only drawback being that it will probably be in my sleep so that I shall not be one of the audience, dreadful fraud! A creature who has been denied all dramatic episodes might be allowed, I think, to assist at her extinction."* Her absence at a moment when she desperately wanted to be present became a running joke: 'The difficulty about all this dying is, that you can't tell a fellow anything about it after it has happened, so where does the fun come in?' The fun lay in facing the worst and making light of it.

Privately printed for the family after Alice's death by her friend Katharine Loring, the diary remained unpublished until 1934, when it appeared, heavily edited, as part of a book called *Alice James: Her Brothers, Her Journal*, and it didn't emerge in full until 1964, when it was acclaimed as 'one of the neglected masterpieces of American literature'. Neither Henry nor William had wanted it to come out in their lifetime but both thought it remarkable: 'I am proud of it as a new leaf in the

---

*The no less jokey Woody Allen famously takes the opposite view: 'I'm not afraid of dying, I just don't want to be there when it happens.'

family laurel crown,' William said, while Henry thought it 'magnificent', 'heroic in its individuality' and 'a new claim for the family renown'.

She left her mark on their work, too. William's ground-breaking *The Principles of Psychology*, with its famous notion of 'stream of consciousness' and reflections on the link between mind and body, would arguably not have come to fruition without the years he spent reflecting on the physical and mental afflictions from which he and Alice suffered. She recognised herself, both as subject and as sceptical reader, in his essay 'The Hidden Self', which explores split selves and trance-like states. And his 1895 lecture 'Is Life Worth Living?' owed much to family discussion of suicide after Alice, at the age of thirty, seriously contemplated it and was told by her father 'that so far as I was concerned she had my full permission to end her life whenever she pleased.' His consent was counter-intuitive: even when her condition was terminal and morphine available to speed her exit, Alice resisted suicide. William's lecture is equally adamant that, whatever its torments, life is still worth living.

As for Henry, two years after Alice's death he had the idea for a story based on 'a peculiar and interesting affection between a brother and sister . . . with some unspeakable intensity of feeling, of tenderness, of sacred compunction . . . Two lives, two beings, and one experience', twin souls whose problem is 'under-standing each other too well – fatally well.' He saw the story ending with a 'kind of resigned, inevitable, disenchanted, double suicide'. In the event, he never wrote it. But he had already written *The Princess Casamassima*, which features Paul and Rosy Muniment, he an anarchist, she 'a strange, bedizened little invalid', a 'small, odd, sharp, crippled, chattering sister'. There's nothing in Alice's diary or letters to suggest she recognised herself as Rosy, who is snobbish and dislikeable. But to Lionel Trilling and other critics there's no question that the siblings 'stand for' William and Alice.

A friend recently alerted me to a book called *Famous Sisters of Great Men*, which came out in 1906. *Sisters of Famous Men* or *Sisters of Great Men* would be more objectionable titles but the underlying assumption is similar: only men can achieve greatness while a few lucky sisters become famous by association. To be fair, the author, Marianne Kirlew, is a feminist ahead of her time, pitying her famous sisters for their subjugation and self-sacrifice ('I am modern enough to believe it a mistake'). And though the title may have been her choice, she borrowed it from a leading article in the *Manchester Guardian*, unsigned but almost certainly written by a man. A book called *Famous Brothers of Great Women* has yet to see the light of day.

Contemporary examples of brothers and sisters collaborating artistically (or scientifically) are hard to find. Even in the past, such relationships were rare. When they happened, it was usually because the sister remained single, as was the case with four of the five women here. No self-respecting sister today would choose a life of subservience; no half-decent brother would want it for her. But such arrangements have produced a handful of outstanding achievements that wouldn't otherwise exist.

11

'A comparison of my fate with my sister's is very revealing;
her road was far harder than mine . . . It took her a long
time to make a complete break with her childhood.'

Simone de Beauvoir, *All Said and Done*

While I was at university, Gill stayed on at the high school, to
retake a couple of O levels. She spent another year there but
left before taking A levels. Her teachers thought she'd be better
off doing something vocational. She thought so too.

She got a place on a textile and fashion programme at a
college in Leeds, thirty miles from home. The programme must
have lasted two years, because I wrote to her from Canada,
where I went on from Nottingham to do an MA, wishing her
luck with the new courses she was starting halfway through.
Fearing the Canadian winter, and knowing her skills as a seamstress, I asked if she 'could consider making me a lining for my
coat. I'm being soft but if you do see any kind of warm padding,
and had time to do that for me . . .'

She had her twenty-first birthday party that December, eight
weeks early – under pressure from Mum and Dad, she held it
while I was home for Christmas. She wrote to me beforehand,
to sound me out about potential guests, and to report that she

was 'happier at the moment, as everything seems to be going right, especially after this weekend. It changes everything when you find out that someone whom you like likes you – no names mentioned and I don't think I need to.' I'm sure at the time she didn't need to. Now I wish she had. In my memory there was no serious love interest till a few years later. Feeling liked by someone wasn't her only bright spot. After a trip round a leather factory in Beverley ('I don't think I shall buy anything made of suede or leather again – a revolting process'), she'd gone to London, where she enjoyed herself buying material from Liberty. She was now thinking seriously of a career in fashion and asked if I came across any good fashion magazines to bring them home with me.

I was pleased to turn up that letter from her. As far as I can tell, it's the only one she sent during the four years I spent in Nottingham and Canada. Which is probably as many letters as I sent her. The lack of correspondence isn't unusual: how many brothers and sisters of our generation did write to each other? These days we'd have texted or emailed but to go to the trouble of writing a letter *and* leaving the house to stick it in the post (knowing it would take days or weeks to arrive) was more than we could manage. Yes, Dad and his sister Mary exchanged letters during his years in the RAF, and he'd have liked the two of us to do the same. But there wasn't a war on and we knew we'd see each other again before too long. Why be arsed?

Dad thought differently and so did V. S. Naipaul, who while a student at Oxford not only wrote home regularly to his parents in Trinidad but exchanged fond letters with his sister Kamla at her university in India. 'I would like to have you close to me,' he tells her, 'it would give *me* a feeling of deeper security', while she teasingly begs him 'don't go and get yourself hitched to anybody' and to 'have some room in your heart and home for me'. Gill and I didn't write, and our lives were diverging. But neither of us had got hitched. We still had some heart-room for each other.

After a spell in 'horrible' digs, Gill moved back home and commuted to Leeds for the rest of the course. She had her own car, an asset few girls she knew enjoyed. As a child in the era before seat belts, she'd been the front seat passenger when Mum had a collision on a muddy lane; apart from a grossly swollen upper lip, she'd not been injured but was badly shocked. It might easily have damaged her confidence. But she passed her test at eighteen and proved to be a good driver: steady, cautious, disinclined to speed.

The challenge was to exploit her mobility and escape the confinement of living at home. Skipton was only six miles away but she wasn't sporty, had no interest in amateur dramatics and hated the idea of evening classes, which left only the cinema, when a decent film was on, or one of the town's many pubs, the Castle, Red Lion, Cock and Bottle, Craven Heifer, Albion and Black Horse among them. Some had live music, others karaoke or disco. She became a regular. But she wasn't daft. Now and then she might have driven home over the limit, as most of us did, but never when seriously drunk.

I'd a glimpse of her social life one Christmas, in my early twenties, when I went on a pub crawl in Skipton with a couple of old schoolfriends. By 9 p.m., there was a lively crowd in the Albion, with Gill at the centre and lots of kissing under mistletoe. She had hooked up with someone who claimed to be a pop manager and at closing time we all piled off to a party. A beer keg was produced and a joint went round. Skipton's most extrovert gay, 'Popsy' as we knew him, kept exposing himself and was led from the kitchen by his penis. Gill had meanwhile switched her attention to a boy called Julian, who she disappeared with and whose girlfriend eventually noticed they'd gone missing. She threatened to 'kill' Gill and let out a scream when Julian reappeared. (When I saw him the next day he had a cut nose and swollen lip.) Before Gill re-entered the house I intercepted her outside and suggested we leave the party sharpish.

Since my mid-teens Skipton had seemed a dead end. Now I saw it differently: as a hotbed of sex, drugs and violence. I saw Gill differently, too – as gregarious and assertive. My earlier worries about her future seemed misplaced. I didn't put her confidence down to drink.

Mum and Dad were more doubtful. 'They don't approve of me going out,' she confided in a letter she sent me aged twenty-four, 'but as I didn't for nearly two years I am now making up for it. I know they worry, because they are that sort, but I can assure you I am a no-action woman nowadays . . . I don't know why they should be lonely – at least I am living there and they have the pups* to keep them company.'

A no-action woman doesn't sound like a great thing to be, and not what I'd have wanted for her. But she was signalling her trustworthiness – she wasn't taking drugs, drinking too much

---

*The pups were long-haired dachshunds, successors to Nikki, whose death she'd written about in another letter (with a little dig at me at the outset): 'I know that it doesn't really mean anything to you but his death has really upset us all. The most terrible thing is that I dreamed about it happening two months ago so I really blame myself for going on holiday. I know it could have happened at any time but I just wish I had been here. We shouldn't be upset about a dog's death but to me he meant more than anything.'

or having sex with unsuitable men. If I could convey as much to Mum and Dad, that would be helpful.

Gill's feelings of oppression – of being monitored and controlled at a time when she was old enough to be independent – reminded me of my own experiences before leaving home: of Dad trying to catch me out having sex with Pat or Jill; of him criticising the way I scowled, mumbled, mooched about, did nothing to help around the house; of him accusing me of being infantile and 'still wearing nappies' at eighteen. As kids, we craved his attention; as we got older, his inattention. Freedom lay in doing our own thing, which meant doing things on our own, without his involvement. We knew he loved us. But his love allowed no room.

I'd got away, first to Nottingham, then to Canada. Gill hadn't and wondered if she ever would.

12

I was reading Kafka at the time and his story seemed pertinent. Both he and his sister Ottla felt stultified by life at home and resented their father's demands on them. Kafka hated his job in an insurance firm and Ottla was equally frustrated working in the family haberdashery store. In 1917, aged twenty-five, she made a bid for independence, by moving from Prague to a small farm; Kafka joined her there, taking a break from work to recover his health, help her in the garden and fields, and write. At home that Christmas, their father laid into them for 'abandoning' their parents; such 'abnormal' behaviour was a result of them 'having it too easy', he said. To stay on reasonable terms with him, Kafka suggested that they pretend to defer to his views. There were notable acts of joint rebellion nonetheless. When Ottla expressed an interest in going to agricultural school, in Friedland, Kafka supported her: she became the first woman to be admitted there. Later he encouraged her to 'self-confidently step out of line' and marry the man she loved, Josef David, despite his not being Jewish, which was one of 'several objections' to him voiced by their father. 'You know you are doing something extraordinary,' Kafka told her, 'more . . . than if you married ten Jews'.* Neither

---

*Ottla's marriage lasted two decades before ending in divorce in 1942.

of them was suited to marriage, he added, but she could marry for them both, while he stayed single for them both.* He had two other sisters, Valli and Elli, but it's to Ottla that his letters and diaries tenderly refer. He never forgot what he owed her for nursing him when he was ill and for applying to get him leave from his work. 'Ottla was very kind to me', he told his girlfriend Milena.

Was Ottla the model for Gregor Samsa's sister Grete in Kafka's 'Metamorphosis'? Or was it one of his other two sisters, Valli? 'The love between a brother and sister is a repetition of the love between a father and mother,' he wrote in his diary on 15 September 1912, the day Valli's engagement was announced. It's a strange idea and Ronald Hayman, one of Kafka's biographers, speculates that 'he may have entertained sexual fantasies' about Valli; it was between the engagement in September and Valli's wedding in December that he wrote 'Metamorphosis',

---

Despite marrying a Jewish woman, David seems to have subscribed to the anti-semitism of the times; in a 1918 letter to him, Ottla is forced to defend Jews ('perhaps a certain group among them and perhaps the larger group act in a way they should not, but this cannot be said of them all and you surely know that'). For this or other reasons, she may have found David too hard to live with by the end. But it's more likely that she divorced him in order that he and their two daughters (as gentiles) be spared death in a concentration camp. When her daughters came with her to the assembly area from which Jews were transported to Theresienstadt, it was to say goodbye: they weren't made to go with her. After a year in the camp, Ottla volunteered to escort a group of children to what they were told was a safe haven in Denmark or Sweden – in fact, Auschwitz, where she died. Her two sisters died at Chelmno.

*Henry James congratulating his brother William on his engagement: 'I had long wished to see you married; I believe almost as much in matrimony for other people as I believe in it little for myself.'

which does have sexual undertones. More significant, though, is the family row that took place on the evening of 7 October, when Ottla, normally supportive, turned on him. His parents were putting pressure on him to put in more time at his brother-in-law's asbestos factory (at which he was a business partner) and Ottla took their side. The row intensified the suffocating atmosphere at home and his suicidal depression ('I hate them all'). He felt betrayed by Ottla and stood at the window with thoughts of throwing himself out.*

Family tension, a high window, a loving sister who changes sides – all find their way into the story. When Gregor Samsa wakes, transformed into an insect, only Grete shows him any kindness. It's she who tries to find him a doctor; she who notices that he hasn't touched his dish of bread and milk and brings him a range of different foods to eat (vegetables, cheese, raisins and almonds, a buttered bread roll); she who takes charge of tidying his room and clears it of furniture to give him more freedom. 'With his sister alone had he remained intimate, and it was a secret plan of his that she, who loved music, unlike himself, and could play movingly on the violin, should be sent next year to study at the Conservatorium'.

Grete's violin-playing triggers the climactic scene in 'Metamorphosis'. By this point she has lost patience with him, become perfunctory in her tidying of his room, and been forced (now he's not earning) to take a job as a salesgirl, learning French and shorthand in the evenings. The family has also taken in

---

*As his biographer Reiner Stach puts it in *Kafka: The Decisive Years*, 'Kafka panicked. That Ottla, his only confidante, was opposing him in front of their mother was a blow: she represented his last connection to the family. Her turning on him meant his expulsion.' Or again: 'A single angry word from his sister could make Kafka's self-esteem collapse.'

three lodgers; Gregor is careful to keep to his room, in order not to alarm them. But one evening he's roused by the sound of Grete's violin from the kitchen:

Gregor's sister was playing so beautifully. Her face leaned sideways, intently and sadly her eyes followed the notes of the music. Gregor crawled a little farther forward and lowered his head to the ground so that it might be possible for his eyes to meet hers. Was he an animal, when music had such an effect upon him? He felt as if the way were opening before him to the unknown nourishment he craved. He was determined to push forward till he reached his sister, to pull at her skirt and so let her know that she was to come into his room with her violin, for no one here appreciated her playing as he would appreciate it. He would never let her out of his room, at least not as long as he lived; his frightful appearance would become, for the first time, useful to him; he would watch all the doors of his room at once and spit at intruders; but his sister should need no constraint, she would stay with him of her own free will; she should sit beside him on the sofa, bend down her ear to him and he confide that he had had the firm intention of sending her to the Conservatorium . . . After this confession his sister would be so touched that she would burst into tears and Gregor would then raise himself to her shoulder and kiss her on the neck . . .

This fantasy of perfect sibling union is rudely interrupted when Gregor is spotted by the lodgers, who – horrified – promptly give notice. Exasperated, Grete finally abandons and disowns Gregor: 'We must try to get rid of it,' she says, and 'get rid of the idea that this is Gregor . . . If this were Gregor, he would have realized long ago that human beings can't live with such a creature, and he'd have gone away of his own accord. Then we wouldn't have any brother, but we'd be able to go on living and keep his memory in honour.'

In his long essay on the story, Nabokov describes Grete as 'the villain of the piece' and misreads the scene as one in which she 'is completely unmasked; her betrayal is absolute and fatal to Gregor.' Her music, he claims, has such a 'stupefying, numbing, animal-like quality' that the answer to the question 'Was he an animal, when music had such an effect upon him?' is yes: were he human, he'd despise Grete's pitiful scraping of the fiddle; it's only because of his 'beetlehood' that he succumbs to it. But Kafka's question is rhetorical. Gregor's love of Grete's music proves he isn't an animal. And because he's no mere creature (an 'it'), he does as she wishes: crawls back to his room, and 'goes' – dies – of his own free will: as Kafka puts it, 'The decision that he must disappear was one that he held to even more strongly than his sister.' His death leaves the family free to make a new life and they begin by taking a trip to the countryside. The final image is of Grete, who has 'bloomed into a pretty girl with a good figure' and whose parents 'come to the conclusion that it would soon be time to find a good husband for her. And it was like a confirmation of their new dreams and excellent intentions that at the end of their journey their daughter sprang to her feet first and stretched her young body.' It's only with her brother's death, in other words, that Grete comes into her own as a sexual being: thanks to his self-sacrifice, she's free to love other men. The story is as much about her metamorphosis as his.

'Metamorphosis' has been interpreted in many ways: as an allegory of loneliness, existential alienation, capitalist exploitation, the Oedipal struggle between father and son, the claustrophobia of family life. But Kafka's interest in exploring the brother-sister bond is implicit in the overlap of the names (Gregor/Grete). The name Grete also echoes Gretel, in 'Hansel and Gretel', a classic tale of brother-sister harmony. There, both siblings survive by working together; here, the brother dies in order that his sister might live.

I've wandered a long way from Gill. But Kafka is a rare example of a man who writes well about a sister. When I read 'Metamorphosis' in my teens, I identified with Gregor's ugliness and confinement. And when I re-read it in my twenties, I thought of Gill, making the best of things at home like Grete but struggling to get free. She didn't need me to die in order to flourish. But she did look to me for support.

At twenty-five, she had yet to find a job that suited her. When one was offered locally, as a telephonist, she dithered about taking it: 'the money isn't too bad, starting at £1800, but I am still looking around,' she told me in a letter. She had a nice voice, a Yorkshire accent slightly softened by boarding school RP, neither posh nor eeh-bah-gum. The job wasn't what college had trained her for but Mum and Dad thought it worth taking. She nearly caved in and took it. But then an offer came, from Christian Dior, to whom she'd written some months before – a chance to work for them, in London.

I was now based in London, studying for a PhD and sharing a flat with my girlfriend Kathy. We had a spare bed. The offer was there.

13

Gill began in high spirits, commuting to central London from our flat in SE3. When she'd applied to Dior, it was to work as a seamstress. She imagined herself in a room of colourful fabrics, among friendly young women, under the watch of an inspirational designer, an Ossie Clark or Mary Quant or Pierre Cardin, stitching dresses for fashionable clients – pop stars, actors, foreign princesses. But the work was menial, her boss a harridan and the wage a pathetic £7 a week. It was more like work experience, or a token internship, than the first rung of a career ladder. She stuck at it, nonetheless, hoping it might lead to something better.

A harridan boss? That's as much as I know. If I've little sense of the conditions in which Gill worked, it's partly because of her reluctance to talk about them and partly my lamentable incuriosity. I can only imagine it through the lens of Dickens, a century earlier, describing the room where Kate Nickleby worked, 'at the back of the premises, where were [sic] a number of young women employed in sewing, cutting out, making up, altering, and various other processes known only to those who are cunning in the arts of millinery and dress-making. It was a close room with a skylight, and as dull and quiet as a room could be.' As to Gill's boss, I see her as the nasty Miss Knag, who tells Kate that 'she would never do for the business', tries to 'keep her as much as possible in the background', makes the other seamstresses ('the group of little satellites who clustered round their ruling planet') gang up against her, and finally dispenses with her services.

Soon to be married and busy with our work, Kathy and I weren't much fun for Gill to be with in her spare time. And when a girl we knew from university told us a room was going in the flat she shared with two other girls, we encouraged Gill to take it; the flat was nearby; she'd still see us but have more of a social life. Things went well to begin with and when her job at Dior ended abruptly she found another one at Boots. The job was as a shop assistant, a far cry from what she'd come south for. She didn't say why she'd left Dior and tried not to sound demoralised. But I knew she was.

In an old notebook the other day, I came across a poem I wrote when Gill was staying with us called 'The Crime'. Unlike the other poems I was writing at the time, I hadn't typed it up to send out to magazines. It was more like a confessional diary entry than a poem for publication.

> Reading my sister's diary
> (quite unforgivable, I know)
> I find tomorrow, July 4th,
> already filled, lived out
> before its time has come,
> as if the hourglass had
> sanded up both ends,
> the clock grown thirteen hands.

I've no memory of ever reading Gill's diary, let alone of what she might have written in it, but I'm unlikely to have made it up. Was I looking for evidence of why she'd left Dior? Or just snooping?

Rather than ushering in the future, London sent Gill back to her past. She felt as she had at St Anne's – not bullied so much, though there was some of that at work, but homesick.

She missed her bed.

She missed her car.

She missed going to the pub or the pictures with Pat.

She missed the things she thought she never would miss – Dad telling her off, the condensation on her bedroom window, gales, icicles, cows closing in as she walked Heidi (Nikki's successor) through the fields.

She missed gossiping with Christine.

She missed the giant horse chestnut tree on the front lawn.

She missed getting to choose which television programmes to watch.

She missed waking up to silence.

She missed having lie-ins.

She missed sunbathing in a bikini on the lawn.

I knew she was unhappy but the suddenness of her return to Yorkshire took us all by surprise. Fairly or not, for reasons she never explained to us and which were perhaps never explained to her, she was 'let go of' at Boots just as she had been at Dior. Shortly afterwards the girls she'd been sharing a house with got in touch: some of their clothes, LPs and cosmetics had gone missing – perhaps Gill had taken them by mistake when she left? A pair of Kathy's sandals had gone missing too, after a recent party – Gill claimed to have seen someone taking them but now we began to wonder.

These were bound-to-be-found-out petty thefts from family and flatmates, committed as if to hurt and punish herself (rather like the killer in one of Chabrol's films who finds the justice of others too lenient and ends up sentencing himself to death). Perhaps she targeted girls she was jealous of, as if by taking their things she could *become* them. Or the stealing was an expression of despair – a cry for help. Either way it was deeply sad. She had tried to leave home and make a life for herself in London. But the experiment had failed.

When the truth came out about what had happened at the flat, Dad locked her in the cellar for thirty-six hours. Doing it made him feel physically sick, he said later; it was extraordinarily cruel and abusive all the same. (She also claimed that he hit her.) His intention was to make her own up to her bad behaviour then start afresh. But how could he think that confining her to a cellar would help with that? How could he have been so crude – so medieval and barbaric – in his methods? And why did Mum allow it?

His suspicion was that theft – of money, clothes or cosmetics – was why she'd lost the two jobs. Gill denied it; it was only after leaving Dior, unhappy by day in Boots and at night in the Hither Green flat, that she'd done anything wrong. In a shared flat, possessions are easily mixed up. And she'd not been herself when it happened. She'd had a kind of breakdown and couldn't recall the sequence of events.

'She is sensitive,' I wrote in my diary, 'and may have been damaged by the lie about life (the version of it peculiar to my parents) put across to her as a child. When parents insist that their children must behave in such-and-such a way, rather than catering for their individuality, they do fuck them up. Next year she's due to go to secretarial college. Maybe things will get better.

But I sense the agony underneath, always ready to break out in some huge anti-social explosion. What will become of her when our parents die? I fear that, like Auntie Sheila,* she'll be bad and mad. I'm supposedly the sane one, the balanced Libran. But it's as if I'm stealing all the life which should have been hers. I sometimes worry about her committing suicide.'

There's my Irish-twin guilt talking – a bit too piously but (not for the last time) with a genuine worry about where her self-destructiveness might end.

Now there's no one alive to check the truth, I sometimes wonder about the cellar story. Who told me about it? Dad? More likely Mum, from shame, trauma and a need to exonerate Dad for having over-reacted. Was Gill really kept there for thirty-six hours? The figure may have come from Gill or from my own uncertain memory. At any rate, I can't swear that it's correct. The rest is unclear too – how cold, frightened and hungry she was in the cellar, and whether a light stayed on, and if she was given blankets and had meals brought to her. The more I think about it, the less likely it seems she was kept there for long – a few hours at most, perhaps. It's horrible to think about all the same.

The locking-up disturbs me as much as the cellar. There'd be other locked doors in the years ahead: Gill being locked in a bedroom 'for her own protection' or locking herself in so as to drink without being disturbed. This was the prequel.

---

*Mum's closest sister, the sixteenth of the twenty O'Shea children. For many years she worked as a teacher in the Midlands and would come to stay with us every holiday. Unlike Mum, she kept up her Catholicism. Endearingly eccentric to begin with, she became increasingly disturbed and developed a drink problem. She died some years before Mum.

A glimpse of future lockings-up. Though it sounds like the past – an episode from a nineteenth-century Gothic novel. Not tough love but torture.

Kathy, horrified at hearing the story, wondered why Gill – twenty-two or twenty-three at the time – didn't leave home straight afterwards. I'm horrified, too, in retrospect, though I can't remember speaking out at the time. I'm sure there were tears – Dad's mostly. And apologies all round, for the bad that had been done and the worse that followed as punishment. Gill knew that Dad loved her, so they forgave each other and put it behind them. Tried to anyway. Can such abuse ever be expunged?

In the event, Gill didn't go to secretarial college. Or if she did, she quickly packed it in. College meant school and after St Anne's, Skipton Girls' High and the textile course in Leeds, she'd had enough of education. She was at a loose end, living at home, bored, lonely and, after the London debacle, in disgrace. There were vague thoughts (mostly Mum and Dad's thoughts) of looking for seamstress work somewhere nearer home. Dressmaking was still a passion of hers. She'd have liked to set up her own business. But she'd had the chance to learn her trade at Dior and blown it. To put it a kinder way – and Mum and Dad, repenting their severity, were eventually more willing to believe her version of events – there never really *had* been a chance at Dior. She'd been taken in, exploited and, 'not the right kind of girl', summarily dismissed.

She settled for clerical work instead – short-term posts, mostly, including one at the Smith & Nephew factory and another at Skipton Register Office (where she'd later marry). She may have had other jobs but there were none she took to or made her own. She had no shorthand and her typing was slow. Unable to focus (for reasons that became clear only later), she struggled to complete the work assigned to her. If she wasn't sacked within a month or two, she would leave of her own accord.

14

Not long after the Dior disaster, Kathy and I got married. Did Gill feel jealous or resentful? She never said as much but sisters sometimes do. Brothers, too, have been known to kick up, whether from pecuniary motives (in pre-twentieth-century novels there's often a brother who pushes his unwilling sister into a marriage that will benefit him) or from a fear of being sidelined and dislodged. The intended spouse might be a paragon but that's no reason not to hate them: an outsider has muscled in to steal away the loved one. The closer the tie has been, the greater the resentment and distress. Whatever Gill felt about me getting married, I count myself lucky that she didn't react as some sisters have. A number come to mind, several of them alluded to already: perhaps it's no coincidence that where brother and sister have been close and collaborative, marriage is an explosive issue.

The Wordsworths

Dorothy's reaction to William's marriage to Mary in October 1802 was – to put it mildly – overwrought. She wore his wedding ring the night before and when she handed it back to him next morning 'he slipped it again onto my finger and blessed me fervently"* before leaving for church. She didn't attend the ceremony but when she saw two men 'coming to tell us it was over, I could stand it no longer and threw myself on the bed where I lay in stillness, neither hearing nor seeing'. What was 'over' wasn't just the ceremony but the exclusive relationship she shared with William; it's no coincidence that the journal she'd kept – a commemoration of their life together over the previous four years – was abandoned a few weeks later. More immediately, the news that William was returning from church 'forced me from the bed where I lay and I moved I knew not how straight forward, faster than my strength could carry me till I met my beloved William and fell upon his bosom.' The consolation for Dorothy was being allowed to join William and Mary on their honeymoon. More consoling still, the three-day tour of Yorkshire took them to places she and William knew and 'owned' from earlier visits. Most consoling of all, perhaps, was the moment in the coach when 'Wm fell asleep, lying upon my breast and I upon Mary', a configuration in which Dorothy reclaimed her sense of priority – she'd not quite lost him after all.

The Herschels

At fifty, William married a rich widow, Mary Pitt, who insisted on taking charge both of her own home and his – the one his sister Caroline had shared with him and managed for the previous sixteen years. Under the new arrangement, Caroline lived in an apartment over the workshop where she and William

---

*The phrase comes in a sentence that has been scored out in the Journal, either by Dorothy or another party, and may, in the view of recent scholars, read slightly differently: 'he slipped it again onto my finger as I blessed the ring softly.' Either way, a highly charged experience, part erotic, part spiritual, is being described.

carried out their astronomy; instead of being part of the family, she was pushed aside. Her feelings about this can be judged by the missing pages in her diaries; torn out to conceal her anger from posterity, they end with the day of her brother's wedding and don't resume for another nine years. Her feelings weren't easily hidden, though. 'To resign the supreme place by her brother's side,' one of her relatives later wrote, caused her 'bitter suffering'. Mary didn't interfere with William and Caroline's work as astronomers. But only when she gave birth to a son, on whom Caroline doted and to whom she remained close for the rest of her life, did the relationship between the women improve.

The Renans

In her early twenties Henriette Renan turned down a marriage proposal when her suitor told her 'he did not mean to marry them [her mother and brother] also': loyalty to her family, and to Ernest in particular, came first. When Ernest became engaged at the age of thirty her distress was so extreme that he told his fiancée, Cornelie, he could not see her again 'until my sister's heart ceased to bleed at the thought of our meetings'. When Henriette heard what he'd done, she went to see Cornelie's father to apologise and the wedding went ahead after all. As it turned out, the marriage didn't mean her ceding her place by his side. When the three of them went on an archaeological trip to Syria and Palestine, an ailing Cornelie returned after two months, allowing Henriette to have Ernest all to herself. The pleasure was short-lived; soon afterwards she fell ill. Before the end, in a premonition of death, she told him. 'I have been unjust, exclusive, but I have loved you as people do not love nowadays – as one has no right to love perhaps.'

The Mendelssohns

In this case it's not the brother's marriage upsetting the sister, but the sister fretting that her marriage will upset the brother. 'Dear lamb,' Fanny calls Felix in her letters, her tone gradually changing over the years from the maternal through the familial ('You are our alpha and omega and everything in between') to that of a romantic lover: 'I never stop thinking about you', 'You are a kind of angel – for God's sake, don't change'. In the months before her wedding to Paul Hensel her passion becomes intense, as if she has transferred to Felix what she should be feeling for Paul: 'I stand in front of your picture, and kiss it, and immerse myself so completely in your presence . . . I'm extremely happy and love you very much. Very much.' Hensel's main qualification as a husband, it seems, is his admiration for Felix: 'what I've always valued about him is that he possesses no trace of envy towards you – only love.' But she continues to worry, trying desperately to persuade herself that marriage will not dilute their intimacy: 'Hensel is a good man, Felix, and I am content in the widest sense of the word, happier than I ever imagined possible. For I dreamed and feared that such a relationship would tear me away from you, or rather alienate us, but it is, *if possible*, just the opposite. I've gained more awareness than before, and therefore am closer to you.' Having informed him about the wedding preparations ('I think my outfit will please you'), she writes again on the morning of the ceremony:

> I am very composed, dear Felix, and your picture is next to me, but as I write your name again and almost see you in person before my very eyes, I cry, as you do deep inside, but I cry. Actually I've always known that I could never experience anything that would remove you from my

memory for even one-tenth of a moment. Nevertheless I'm glad to have experienced it, and will be able to repeat the same thing to you tomorrow and in every moment of my life. And I don't believe I am doing Hensel an injustice through it. Your love has provided me with a great inner worth, and I will never stop holding myself in high esteem as long as you love me.

The thought of seeing Felix again – 'only six more weeks' – is as exciting to her as the wedding itself. Ten months on, now the mother of a son, she tells him 'I am, was and will remain yours as long as we live.'

The Macaulays

A man's distress this time. Thomas Macaulay said that his sisters' marriages were a 'living death' to him, after which he was left 'with nothing else to love'. Ten and twelve years his juniors, Hannah and Margaret were his favourite audience when writing or talking. For three years, in his early thirties, he bombarded them with amorous letters. 'I pine for your society, for your voice, for your caresses,' he wrote to Hannah, 'there is nothing on earth that I love as I love you.' Nothing or no one except Margaret, maybe, to whom he wrote with equal ardour: 'no change of situation or lapse of time can alter a love like that to which I bear to you.' Love for his sisters 'has prevented me from forming any serious attachment,' he confessed, and he hoped their love for him would have the same outcome. But first Margaret married, then, despite all his pleas, reproaches and self-pity ('I am alone in the world. I have lost everything'), Hannah followed suit. On her wedding night, friends urged the newlyweds to return from their honeymoon as soon as they could, 'as they were frightened about him'. He survived but 'spent many months in great unhappiness' and, single till the end of his life, continued to mourn that he 'lost M & H at once'. Margaret's early death compounded his grief but in his mind he'd lost her already. If only he had loved his 'darling sisters' less deeply: 'The affection of brothers for sisters, blameless and amiable as it is beyond almost any human affection, is yet so liable to be interrupted that no man ought to suffer it to become necessary to him.'

The Jameses

From childhood into his thirties, William James loved to tease his sister Alice, mock-courting her as his 'lovely babe', 'beloved sisterkin', 'sweetlington', 'beautlet', 'dear incomparable', 'little beauty', 'most kissworthy', 'sweet lovely delicious grey-eyed Alice'. When she was eleven he composed a song, performed in the presence of the family, which cast him as a courtly lover and her as a cruel, rejecting mistress: 'You told me I must never dare/To hope for love from you./Your childlike form, your golden hair/I never more may see,/But goaded on by dire despair/I'll drown within the sea'. It was a tone William kept up for many years, as if they were pledged to each other in sickness and health, mostly sickness. In his mid-twenties, writing to her from Dresden, he fantasised about being nursed by her: 'A fortnight ago I caught the "influenza" in Teplitz and was sick for a week, 36 hours with raging fever and me cryin' all the time to have you sitting by me stroking my brow, and asking me if there was nothing, *nothing* you could do to alleviate my sufferings . . . Whole dialogues did I frame of how I wd. work on your feelings if you were there and longed to cleave the Ocean once more to press you in my arms.' As their mother Mary saw it, William's flirting was a tonic to Alice: 'He is very sweet upon her, in his own original way, and I think she enjoys very much his charming badinage.' In his troubadour attentiveness, he stood in for the suitors she'd never had – and never would have. The sexual undertone in the fraternal affection is hard to miss: 'Thou seemest to me so beautiful from here, so intelligent, so affectionate, so in all respects *the thing* that a brother should most desire that I don't see how when I get home I can do any thing else than sit with my arm round thy waist.'

The spell was broken when he got himself a girlfriend. To compound the offence, he chose a woman called Alice. (Henry, writing from England, wondered how the family would avoid confusing the two of them: 'What *do* you call each other, for distinction's sake?') The courtship was drawn out over two years, in part because of William's hypochondria, but eventually, in May 1878, the engagement was announced. Seeing it coming, Alice took to her bed. She can't have warmed to William's fiancée and evidence suggests the feeling was mutual: if nothing else, Alice's breakdown – the 'feeling of inability to meet life' – disrupted the engagement and wedding preparations.

The marriage went ahead in July. Alice didn't attend. Henry hoped that after this 'abnegation' she might be able to enjoy the married couple's 'conjugal and fraternal society'. But only when she went to England, at a safe transatlantic remove, did relations with her sister-in-law recover. In the short term William's marriage – or desertion – caused a breakdown worse than any she'd experienced before. She was thirty that year and, having seen him marry and friends of hers marry but with no prospects of marrying herself, she was forced to accept that she might spend the rest of her life alone. In a late diary entry she referred back to 'that hideous summer of '78 when I went down to the deep sea, its dark waters closed over me, and I knew neither hope nor peace'.

And then there was Friedrich Nietzsche and his sister Elizabeth, who (so one biographer reports) 'were so close to each other that each had an inhibiting effect on the other's chances of finding a marriage partner'. She was so jealous of his relationship with Lou Andreas-Salomé that she effectively destroyed it, for which he never forgave her.[*]

What a catalogue of pain! It's a relief to think that Gill and I didn't suffer in that way. We weren't, as Sylvia Townsend Warner puts it in her story 'A Love Match', 'the kind of brother and sister of whom one says "It will be rather hard for her when he marries".' Gill might not have been especially warm towards Kathy, whom she regarded suspiciously as an exotic from Down South. But now that we'd been together for several years she accepted her. And there's nothing in my memory, or in the wedding photos, to suggest even a sliver of distress.

The only effect was to make her consider her own situation. She was barely any younger than me – should she be thinking of marriage too?

---

[*] For a compelling account of a sister trying to kibosh a *sister's* wedding, see Dorothy Baker's 1962 novel *Cassandra at the Wedding*, in which the eponymous heroine tries to dissuade her twin, Judith, from marrying. When her efforts fail, she takes an overdose. It's left to Judith's husband, a doctor, to save her.

15

She didn't have a steady boyfriend. Sometimes she went out with Pat. But whenever Pat had a new boyfriend she'd be stuck. For a girl to go to a pub on her own was awkward. Some men got the idea you were a slut.

She began to worry that she'd end up living with Mum and Dad till they died. When they behaved as if it worried them too ('Not going out then?' 'Have you thought about joining a club?' 'That engineer down at Armorides seems a nice lad'), it made her worry all the more. She was still in her twenties – hardly over the hill. But most girls she'd known at school were married with kids by then. She felt a little under pressure. And after Mum and Dad retired,* with more time on their hands to fret about her future, the pressure increased.

They retired a week after Mum's sixtieth birthday and went to France for a month, leaving Gill behind with Pat. She suggested

---

* Even in retirement, they kept up with their patients. Every Christmas, as Dad's diary recorded, they made a point of visiting the elderly ones at home. Between 5 and 20 December 1984, for instance, they visited 208 former patients, seventy-three of them aged over eighty. In 1986 the total was 231 and the following year 266. They'd been retired ten years by then.

I come up in their absence but I was busy with work and had booked a week in Sicily ('if you have any money to spare,' she wrote, 'and if they have any nice costume dolls, would you get me one'). Did she and Pat throw a party or two? Was that how she met a boy called Nick? The relationship looked promising but then she wrote to tell me 'I have been ditched in a very heartless way. Still maybe it's for the best. I shall wait and hope he comes back to me. I have had offers of dates but at the moment I don't want them.'

She loved to sunbathe. The Yorkshire Dales weren't the best place for it but she'd lie out at every opportunity; if the wind was blowing, she could always wrap herself in a rug and feel the warmth on her face. She got the habit from Dad who'd picked it up as a young man in the 1930s – a benign anglicised version of the Nazi Youth veneration of the Great Outdoors. 'Fresh air and exercise' was his motto; the latter meant moving your sunbed now and then. When we were kids, he bought a sunlamp and set it up in the back bedroom. We'd sit there, in sunblock and black goggles, while our faces and shoulders burned. The sunlamp was meant to be good for your health, raising your serotonin levels and warding off what later became known as Seasonal Affective Disorder. But all Dad wanted was to get brown. Gill too. Everyone looked better with a tan.

Not ready to start dating again, Gill lay out a lot that summer. She enjoyed shutting out the world and feeling warmth flood through her body. I used to tease her about it. And when I read D. H. Lawrence's story 'Sun', in which the female protagonist imagines the sun's intensity as 'focused on her alone', I thought of Gill: 'She could feel the sun penetrating even into her bones . . . The dark tensions of her emotion began to give way, the cold dark clots of the thoughts began to dissolve . . . she lay half stunned with wonder at the thing that was happening to her. Her weary, chilled heart was melting . . ."

By the following March, she was working as a barmaid and dating again. 'I think I've met my man,' she wrote to me, 'even though complications do exist. I've only known him a month but I feel like I've known him for ages mainly because there are no secrets between us. He's in the navy and goes back in April to Portsmouth to his ship for another year before he comes out. The other complications are that he's married and is waiting for a divorce if she'll give him one and has a little boy of two. But that doesn't bother me, so we will have to wait & see what happens.'

It sounded deeply unpromising and by the time she wrote again in November, the relationship was over. I don't have many of her letters – there weren't that many and they tended to be short. But this one was long, as if she needed to unburden

---

* 'Sun' was written round the time Lawrence was working on *Lady Chatterley's Lover* and there are clear similarities between the two. It's a story about a woman finding sensual fulfilment and ends with her fantasising about having children with an animalistic local peasant rather than with her pallid, ineffectual husband. The erotic self-transcendence or 'actirasty' that she experiences through sunbathing is reminiscent of what Connie Chatterley feels after being fucked by Mellors: 'Something deep inside her unfolded and relaxed. By some mysterious power inside her, deeper than her known consciousness and will, she was put into connection . . . She herself, her conscious self, was secondary, a secondary person, almost an onlooker.' Some of Lawrence's prose from this period, the 1920s, now makes me cringe but in Canada I wrote an MA thesis on 'the female quest' in his fiction: at the time Gill was getting into sunbathing, I was getting into him.

herself as she couldn't when we spoke on the phone. 'I'm going to write this year off as not having existed', it began. First there'd been 'this older bloke, who was a good laugh until I found out he was married & a wife batterer. Then I met Pete – that silly sod – whom I unfortunately got myself involved with and thought I thought something about. Then I smashed my car, once not too badly, & then good & proper, & the outcome of that was that the only other person who was hurt is now trying to get compensation to the amount of £300, even though my insurance company say they won't pay, so if anything comes of that the whole enquiry will have to be re-opened & it will probably end by me going to court . . .'

Only halfway through the letter did she come to the point:

When I started work at the Anchor I wasn't interested at all in men, but after a couple of nights I got asked out by quite a few blokes, especially Wynn, who kept pestering me until I eventually relented & went out with him & found out that he wasn't as bad as the rumours made him out to be . . . and it's just snowballed from then until he's fallen for me & I'm still not sure.

Anyway about a month ago he and his wife started talking about divorce again. Unfortunately when she went to see her solicitor he told her that to avoid any risk of her losing their two kids the best thing was for Wynn to admit adultery. No names had to be mentioned BUT his wife's solicitor pressurized Wynn into giving a name & mine was uppermost in his mind. So, I have been named as co-respondent, and you can imagine how that went down with Mum & Dad. I won't have to go to court, but they think I've been labelled. They also think him not good enough for me, because he is a labourer & not a professional person, the sort Dad would talk to in a pub but would never expect me to get involved with, so I have been getting myself into a bit of a state trying to keep things right on both sides and only upsetting myself. I hope in time if I do decide to stay with Wynn that Mum & Dad will accept him. I might change my mind about him but I know he won't change his mind about me.

Another thing they are worrying about is how I am going to cope when they are not here. They don't think I could manage on my own but I'm sure I could. One minute they're trying to marry me off to the 'right' person & the next minute they're saying I've got all the time in the world to meet someone. You can imagine how confused I've managed to become with all of it.

So there you are, my bad 1978 is nearly over, but if you want to give me any advice about it at all don't hesitate to do so as I know I shall accept & think about what you may say. Anyway I'll leave that decision to you . . .

Did I advise Gill? Not that I can remember. I listened to her, I hope, and sympathised with her. But how could I give advice without knowing Wynn? Even if I had known him, it wasn't my place to tell her what to do.

Did Gill seriously *expect* me to advise her? Maybe. Dad would have encouraged the idea. He'd been free with advice to his sister Mary when her husband Michael, an RAF pilot, went missing over France in 1943 – suggesting names for the girl she gave birth to a month afterwards (suggestions which Mary ignored, choosing Michaela in memory of Michael), prescribing rest and relaxation, and urging her to stay with their parents for a while rather than living on her own. Later, when Michael's death was confirmed, he helped set her up with his best friend Ron, whom she married.*

Historically, in middle-class society at least, brothers were supposed to behave this way – to restrain their sisters' impulses, protect their 'reputation' and control their choice of partners. Protecting also meant policing and, if need be, avenging. As Carolyne Larrington puts it in her book *Brothers and Sisters in Medieval European Literature*, 'One consequence of the power asymmetry between brothers and sisters is that brothers are expected to take responsibility for their sisters' conduct. Thus they are depicted compelling their sisters to conform to social norms or defending their honour – usually defined in sexual terms.' The idea was still alive in the nineteenth century: in *The Mill on the Floss* Tom Tulliver tells his sister Maggie that 'a brother who goes out into the world and mixes with men necessarily knows better what is right and respectable for his sister than she knows herself.'† Tom forbids Maggie from seeing one suitor (Philip) and banishes her from home because of her behaviour with a second (Stephen). Such fratriarchal despotism is still evident in many cultures today, where the murder of 'immoral' sisters (unmarried sisters who've lost their virginity

---

* She died of cancer in March 1983 aged sixty-three (or officially – since she was born on 29 February – aged fifteen). Dad's diary is laconic: her funeral takes its place between 'got seed potatoes' and 'put clothes rack up in utility room'. But her death affected him deeply. To lose your younger sister is a terrible thing.

† Charlotte Brontë took the opposite view: 'Girls are protected as if they were something very frail and silly indeed while boys are turned loose on the world as if they – of all beings in existence – were the wisest and the least liable to be led astray.' From having Branwell as a brother, she well knew how gullible and wayward boys – and men – could be.

or married ones who've left their husbands) is dignified as honour killing.

I'd no murderous impulses towards Wynn and didn't share Mum and Dad's snobbish reservations about him. More to the point, it didn't feel right to intervene.

If I'd read it at the time, L. P. Hartley's 1970 novel *My Sisters' Keeper*, a cautionary tale about fraternal interference, would have confirmed those instincts. It tells the story of Basil, a repressed homosexual who has three sisters and who suffers from what his friend Dr Powell calls 'sisteritis, an age-old complaint that mustn't be confused with cystitis'. Sisteritis means an excessive concern for your sister's (or sisters') interests, at the expense of your own. Less altruistically, it means meddling in their affairs, which in Basil's case takes the form of finding them husbands.

With his older sister, Gwendolen, his error isn't poor judgment but cowardice. When she becomes engaged to a former schoolfriend of his, Terry, who has a reputation for pursuing boys, Basil steels himself to warn her off but loses his nerve. The marriage turns out better than expected till Terry is caught cottaging with a boy.

Evelyn, Basil's second sister, is a bluestocking archaeology enthusiast who follows him to 'Oxenbridge' university. Knowing how fond she is of fast driving, he helps his friend Ralph to buy a sports car, in the hope she'll be impressed and fall in love with him. The strategy works but disaster follows, when she's seriously hurt in an accident while driving the car. Against the odds, both she and the relationship survive.

There's no such luck with Basil's third sister, the beautiful Amabel, from whose many suitors he recommends the mysterious Alan. They quickly marry, by which time she is already pregnant. Soon afterwards Alan disappears on a work mission; Amabel tells

Basil that she wants an abortion and will never take Alan back. He persuades her to have the baby but she dies in childbirth.

Dr Powell is consoling. 'If every man felt responsible for his sister's conjugal adventures, there would be no end of it,' he tells Basil, and quotes from *King Lear*: 'We are not the first/ Who, with best meaning, have incurred the worst.' The novel ends with Basil's recognition that 'Too much concern with how my sisters should arrange their lives' has been his failing.

L. P. Hartley was no feminist but the message is clear; sisters must make their own way in life; brothers should butt out.

Gill and Wynn were regulars at the same pub even before she got a bar job there. He was separated from his wife; their two small boys lived with her but he saw them at weekends. He had a steady job, as a technician with the Yorkshire Water Board. When Gill described him as a 'labourer' she was using Dad's terminology. But far from being a swarthy farmhand or hired man, he had taken a college course to qualify for the job and by the time he retired, on a good pension, would become area manager. He was older than Gill but (she decided) not too much so. They thought of themselves as loners. Together they felt less like loners. Change a consonant and they could be lovers.

It was no whirlwind romance. Four years passed before they married. The delay wasn't down to her doubts or Mum and Dad's objections but the time it took for his divorce to come through. By then, any qualms about his suitability or devotion to Gill had been dispelled. At the time Dad was building a house, at the back of our old one, and enlisted Wynn in the work. Despite being full-time at the Water Board he spent every weekend, holiday and most evenings onsite. It took three years: first the exterior work, with Wynn driving a JCB, then the wiring, plumbing and decorating. Dad's diaries list the hours his various workmen put in, so he knew how much to pay them. Wynn's payment was in beer, swigged in a bottle at the house or a tankard at the pub. He was family now.

Jacking in her bar work, Gill got a job at the local education office. It must have been part-time because the diaries record her spending long days on the new house, sanding, painting, wallpapering, making curtains. Along with Dad's entries ('Fallow deer in garden, 3-5.30'), there are some in her handwriting. Happy and in love, she no longer resented being at home. It was a new home and she enjoyed being in on the start of something: the smell of fresh paint, planed pine, woodstain, felt underlay.

They announced their engagement two weeks after the work was finished and in June she went to Manchester to buy her wedding dress (seeing a ballet the same evening for good measure). The following week she and Wynn exchanged contracts on Orchard Cottage, a pretty two-bedroom house down the village that belonged to Mrs Leach, whose daughter Janice was a childhood friend of ours. They began renovating and decorating it even before the sale went through, then moved in at the start of August and married later that month.

Her dress showed no bulge. They didn't know she was four weeks pregnant.

The ceremony was at the register office in Skipton, with a reception at the Cross Keys afterwards. It was a modest reception but big enough to accommodate aunts, uncles, cousins and godparents. Not Beaty and Josie, though. Were they invited? Probably not. For an occasion like this, despite the holidays they'd spent with us and their assimilation into the family, they *weren't* family. Did their absence stem from a worry that Josie's resemblance to Dad would be recognised? Or was some snobbery involved, Beaty and Sam being a couple who ran the local pub, not the middle-class professionals with whom Mum and Dad mostly socialised? Dad was no snob but he might have feared the reaction of his sister Mary, who'd a shrewd idea of Josie's paternity. At any rate, though she'd be there for Mum and Dad's funerals some years later, Josie wasn't present at the wedding. She was in her early twenties by then, an attractive young woman with a laugh just like Beaty's. She'd have brought some fun to the occasion. They both would. But embarrassment too. Shame even. It was safer for them not to come.

Afterwards I jotted some notes down about the day, which I later drafted as a poem, perhaps intending to give it to Gill and Wynn as a souvenir but failing to finish it.

There's migraine thunder like a fat goddess
Rolling over in bed. Rain all morning
Raises smoke above the drive's new tarmac
And the lawn-bedded flagstones are awash.

So much to do, so little time to do it.
We're back and forth, manic with the worry
About place-cards, telegrams, last-minute salads
And carnations for every lapel.

I stow the cake with its Roman columns
On the back seat of the car. I grate onions
And carrots for coleslaw. I unload goblets
From the bee-cells of a cardboard box.

Then I put on the double-breasted cream suit,
Last worn at my own wedding,
And try to aerosol the stain from my tie,
Leaving a haze on the silk like steam.

Two Sisters

In the cave of her bedroom, my sister
Fiddles with the catch of her necklace,
Her earrings dangling like icicles,
Her wedding dress the colour of frost.

We're late, we're certain to be late,
And the car's low on petrol, but we make it,
To a building that's also the Jobcentre,
With a pair of women who officiate.

A baby screams during the marriage vows
And there's a problem with the rings,
The groom's wedding finger is too swollen –
Gill slips it on his pinkie instead.

We stand on the steps with Wynn's sons
From his first marriage, smiling for the lens.
In a house across the street, there's a woman
Behind net curtains, a mirroring of Gill in her veil.

Wynn shakes my hand as if gripping a spade.
I delete the joke about his first marriage being 'practice',
Making do with how he works for the Water Board
Though water's not his favourite drink.

Back at the house, my cousin takes six children
For a walk and they head off across the fields
Hand in hand, like skydivers or angels
Or a blessing for the happy couple . . .

16

'Happy couple' may be a cliché but it was true. They enjoyed themselves at Orchard Cottage, taking turns to cook, toing and froing to the pub, throwing a housewarming (and pregnancy) party just before Christmas. Louise was born the following April, on the same day as our daughter Aphra. 'Two grand-daughters born within eight hours, 230 miles apart,' Dad's diary recorded. 'Gill & Louise settling well' he reported three weeks later. He'd always known Gill would 'make a good little mother'.

There was one downside. Whereas Wynn saw no reason to curtail his pub-going, Gill, with a small baby, was confined to home. On nights when he didn't go out, they drank together at home. On nights when he did go out, she drank alone: a glass of wine or two made her feel better and distracted her from worrying what he might be up to – he'd met her in a pub, why not another woman? One Sunday she lost it and pushed the pram along the main road to the nearest pub (no small distance) in search of him; next day Dad 'saw Wynn at work to apologise for Gill's stupidity'. On another evening, when Louise was five months, she and Wynn took her to the pub with them, which Mum found unacceptable: 'Kim had row with Gillian re babies in pubs at 10pm,' Dad's diary noted.

Gill promised to give up her drinking. Half the problem was

her small stature: whereas Wynn could drink six pints and still be sober, she'd get tipsy from a couple of glasses. But she'd only ever done it when Louise was asleep for the night, she said, not during the day. It wasn't like she was addicted.

In June 1985, a friend asked Gill and Wynn to join them in Spain for a week's holiday. It was a big moment for Wynn, who'd never been out of the country before, indeed rarely out of the area where he grew up; he'd seen no need and harboured a suspicion of Abroad. But Gill was keen to have a break: however helpful her parents, spending all day at home with a one-year-old was hard. They flew together from Manchester – the friend, his wife, Wynn, Gill and Louise – and celebrated their arrival, on the first evening, by going out to a restaurant. Round midnight they set off back to the villa they were renting. The friend was driving. As they climbed a short hill, a lorry carrying fruit appeared at speed around the corner. Gill was sitting in the back, with Louise in her arms but no seat belt. Though the crash wasn't head-on, the impact threw Louise through the windscreen. She ended up by the side of the road, alive but with a depressed skull fracture: some of the bone in the middle of her forehead was pushing back against her brain. Quickly on the scene, an ambulance took her to the local hospital, where the broken skull fragment (1¾ inches by 1¼) was removed, relieving the pressure on her cortex. Gill also needed medical treatment, for scalp lacerations and whiplash; she suffered from neck pain and migraines for a long time afterwards. The other passengers were uninjured and returned to the villa. Louise was kept in hospital, with Gill at her bedside.

Back in Yorkshire, Mum and Dad got to hear about the accident second-hand and contacted the British Consulate. Gill phoned them two hours later; Louise had been in intensive care for five days by then but Gill 'hadn't wanted to worry' them. Mum flew out to help; they all returned six days later. Back home a frantic round of x-rays and consultations began. There was no evidence of brain injury though the scarring carried a risk of dizzy spells and epilepsy in future. More to the point, there was a hole, the size of a large coin, in Louise's forehead, with only skin and tissue covering it. Dad thought some kind of plate should be fitted to her cranium, to prevent the risk of a sharp object penetrating the brain. The consultant, who'd not come across a case like this before and questioned whether the Spanish hospital had done the right thing (might the piece of bone have been saved and regrafted?), suggested twice-yearly monitoring, with surgery an option but 'wait and see' the best policy. There was a thought that the soft tissue at the front of the skull might harden and the risk go away of its own accord. Meanwhile Louise was measured for a protective helmet and, later, a lightweight plastic headshield, to be worn when she played outside.

The arguments about her skull fracture dragged on for years. So did the insurance claim for her injury. Had the fruit lorry been across the white line as it came round the bend? Or had the Brits, on their first night in continental Europe, been driving on the wrong side of the road? Eventually, in her teens, Louise was awarded compensation. (The money was put in an account and later used to buy a small house in Barnoldswick, which her half-brother lived in and renovated.)

If the accident had affected her, she showed no signs. But the anxiety took its toll on Gill, who'd been the one holding her and was tormented by the memory: if only the car had been fitted with a child seat, or the fruit lorry hadn't appeared at that moment, or they'd not gone out at that night, or they'd never gone on holiday in the first place.

*

She became a homebody after that. Being away was associated with unhappiness.

1. St Anne's: bullying.
2. Leeds: horrible digs.
3. London: homesickness.
4. Spain: the car accident.

However intrusive Mum and Dad were, she felt safe in the village where she'd grown up. No more leaving Thornton-in-Craven.

Apart from the last four years, it would be home for the rest of her life.

Reliving the trauma of Spain, she drank to subdue it – not just the odd glass now but bottles or wine boxes, and not just at night, with Louise asleep, but during the day. Sometimes Wynn would come home from work and find her crashed out on the sofa, with Louise playing at her feet. 'PISSED', a marginal entry from Dad's diary that October reports. After another episode a month later ('Gillian v fresh – Upset Mum & I'), he spent several hours composing a long letter to Gill, which Mum delivered the next day. 'No doubt I will be wrong', he reflected, anticipating denials and protests.

The letter gave Gill pause. And when she became pregnant again the following spring (with a boy this time), the drinking stopped. But the things that lay behind it (post-traumatic stress, migraines, neck pain, depression, guilt, jealousy) hadn't gone away.

There was a further worry: her eyesight, never the best, was getting worse. The first sign was her difficulty seeing in low light. Her eyes were checked several times, with inconclusive results; 'a waste of time' was Dad's verdict on one of the trips they made to Bradford Royal for a visual field test. Then the

GP referred her to a Professor Bird, who diagnosed nyctalopia, night blindness, and attributed it to retinitis pigmentosa, a disorder in which the retina loses its ability to respond to the light. In her case the condition was bilateral, he told her, and – being progressive – might eventually affect her daytime vision as well; no known treatment existed. If that wasn't bad enough, he discovered a second condition, bilateral macular degeneration, a breakdown of cells in the retina, which explained her peripheral vision. The two were 'an extremely rare combination', he said. Sod's Law.

Mum and Dad blamed themselves: if only they'd made Gill have regular eye checks when young ('so typical of doctors to neglect the health of their children'). Though she hadn't complained of problems with her vision, that might be because she'd never known anything else. And if the problem did date back to childhood, it would part-explain her struggles at school. Whatever the case, she was terrified of the prospect of going blind one day, all the more so now she was a mother. 'Not to be able to see my own kids': what could be worse?

Josie had her health issues too. I'd mostly lost touch with her since university and only heard about her second-hand, through Mum and Dad, who downplayed the problems she'd had as a teenager – first anorexia, then bulimia, then a spell in a clinic in York. Whenever I saw her, she seemed cheery and relaxed – the same smile was there, the one she'd had as a small child; the same energy and enthusiasm. Dad knew different but didn't confide in me, only to his diary: 'Called on Josie. Josie emotional – suggest Dr', goes one entry for 1983, when she was twenty-four. Or there's this from the following year: 'Josie came over. Had had row with Beaty – stayed night and caught bus at 1.30pm'. A week later he and Mum took the pair of them off to Abersoch. A truth and reconciliation exercise? Reconciliation anyway: the truth about Josie's paternity wasn't a matter for discussion.

When Josie was diagnosed with diabetes, the worries over her health increased. But she quickly got used to injecting herself. And by the time Wynn and Gill were having children, she'd turned a corner: no longer hyper and anxious, she'd met the man who would become her husband. Beaty and Sam both liked him, not least for helping to stabilise Josie. The relationship flourished while Beaty and Sam's continued to be rocky: 'an impossible situation', Beaty called it.

I saw for myself how Josie had blossomed when we all went to Cartmel races one day. Photos around the time tell the same story. There she is, blonde-haired in a long white dress standing next to her mother in a flower garden; bright-eyed in brown slacks and a white jumper, with her husband's arm around her; pale-faced in a yellow frock holding her first baby. The shape of her face, the expression, the eyes: they're Dad's. And she's smiling. Whatever her troubles, she has come through.

When Mum and Dad's partner in the GP practice, the wonderfully named Dr Love (successor to the less wonderfully named Dr Dick), put up his house for sale, they thought it would be perfect for Gill. Built in the field they'd sold to him twenty years earlier, Arley House was roomier than Orchard Cottage. It was also closer, the nearest house to theirs in fact, just fifty yards away: she'd no longer have to cross the busy main road to visit them, and Louise, now walking, could safely come round to see them by herself. Just as he'd moved his mother in next door, after she'd been widowed, so Dad did the same with his daughter. And for the same reason: to keep the family close and give children easy access to their grandparents.

The house cost £80,000, more than was easily affordable, but with a £20,000 mortgage, £20,000 from Gill's investments, and Mum and Dad paying the rest, the money was raised. Dad wrote us a letter explaining how, in the event of his death, Gill and I would jointly inherit his quarter share and she would buy me out – ditto when Mum died. For all its careful reasoning, the letter read awkwardly in places, as if he was conscious that Gill might be troubled by the idea of her parents having a share in the house and of me part-inheriting it. It wasn't that Gill and Wynn only half owned the house, he insisted. But I guessed, from his defensiveness, that Gill must have suggested as much, in an anxious or accusing voice. Three years later, in another letter to me, he was still explaining his logic: that he had always treated his children equally and that any future share I might have in her house existed only 'transiently, on paper'.

Maybe it was my financial naivety but I found the logic hard to follow. Why not simply *give* Gill and Wynn the £40,000? There were inheritance tax implications, should he die within seven years (which he did). But a gift or never-to-be-repaid loan would have been the simplest solution – and would have stopped Gill feeling that the house wasn't truly hers. She suspected Dad was hedging his bets, either because he still distrusted Wynn (as a working-class man, on a modest wage and with alimony to pay, might he have hitched himself to a wealthier young woman out of expedience rather than love?) or from a worry about Gill's drinking. Wasn't Dad keeping his hand in as a protective measure, in the event of disaster or divorce? She believed so – and resented the right it gave him to monitor and control her.

Despite the earlier drinking lapses, she was a good mum, as Dad was the first to acknowledge. A full-time one, too: she'd not had a job since marrying. She spent hours helping Louise and Liam to read and do sums. There were lessons in table manners too: elbows off the table and use a knife and fork, please – no fingers. Later, when they started at the village school (the one Gill and I had gone to, with a bigger intake but otherwise little changed), she spent the day cooking and baking for them, even when her failing vision made it difficult. In the evenings she'd watch *Coronation Street* and police dramas, or a classic Disney on videotape. *Dirty Dancing* and (later) *The Full Monty* were favourites too – for the songs. Her musical tastes were eclectic and Liam shared her enthusiasm. Later, in his teens, adept on both guitar and drums, he formed a band, and they'd rehearse in the playroom next to the garage. Rather than complain about the noise, Gill listened.

In the summer of 1990, the year before Dad died, I borrowed his camper van for a week, for a holiday with Kathy and our kids (three of them by now) in Pembrokeshire. We met to swap vehicles in North Wales, where I'd just spent a week on Bardsey Island. He brought Gill and her kids with him, making ten of us in all, the kind of gathering Dad loved, 'one big happy family'. But during the meal, there were tensions between Gill and Mum. When Gill stomped off, I caught up with her outside. 'They're always bloody interfering,' she said, and complained of being spied on. I had a word with Dad before parting ways. 'You need to back off,' I told him.

Home from holiday, I found a six-page letter waiting. He was sorry the lunch had been ruined, he said, but I hadn't understood the context. In many ways, having Gill and her family next door was a perfect arrangement. They did shopping for her (or she for them), Mum babysat on Saturday nights, he and Wynn went for a pint every week, etc. But in the past few months there'd been increasing tensions and Gill had become very depressed: 'She talks of Wynn leaving her and "who'll want a half-blind woman with kids if he does?".' The letter went on both to blame Wynn for being 'too much the Victorian husband' and to praise him for looking after Gill. The problem was hers to solve, he concluded. All the same, he said, in his last sentence: 'I must remind you that when I am gone it will be your job as Trustee to manage the financial affairs and see to the welfare of your sister and her children as long as you live.'

Ah, right. No pressure then.

> 'Ah, but [sisters] must turn out and fend for themselves,'
> said Mr Tulliver . . . 'They mustn't look to hanging on
> their brothers.'
> 'No, but I hope their brothers 'ull love the poor things,
> and remember they came o' one father and mother.'
> (George Eliot, *The Mill on the Floss*)

In November that year, Dad sent me a letter with photocopies of two handwritten profiles, or character assessments, one of Wynn, the other of Gill. They'd been written for himself, primarily, to clarify his thinking. Both ran to several pages; it must have taken him hours to put them together. I imagined him coming back from the pub, pouring himself a whisky, and sitting at his desk into the small hours, just as he used to in the old house, at the billiard table, when sorting out his stocks and shares. The effort involved was a mark of his worry about Gill – and of a fear, though his cancer hadn't yet been diagnosed, that he might not be around for much longer. It was also characteristically controlling. He'd posted the profiles to me as preparation for the moment when he'd be handing on the baton – when patriarchy gave way to fratriarchy.

Gill, he said, felt criticised by Wynn even for stuff she couldn't help – over-cooking the veg or leaving pans dirty when she washed up because her vision was poor. Of course his patience had been tried of late. And despite having once said that marriage wouldn't alter his lifestyle, he had recently modified his habits, staying home most evenings. Hard-working and good about the garden, he had many redeeming features. The main problem was the legacy of his difficult childhood (a Jehovah's Witness mother, a father who drove HGVs and was often away), which made him suspicious of close family ties. He was at any rate suspicious of too close a tie with the Morrisons: 'He refuses to join our family and has tried to distance our daughter from us. By regarding our two houses as isolated units, each with its own family inside, he's driving a wedge between Gillian and ourselves.'

As for Gill, she seemed very low. Along with a fear that Wynn no longer loved her, there were several factors behind her depression, among them an inferiority complex, eyesight problems and the trauma of the car accident. Deep down, he said, she was 'a sensitive, loving girl and a wonderful mother and wife'. But her paranoia and persecution complex had become extreme. His profile cited things he'd heard her say in recent months:

'You're trying to take my children away.'

'Blake has always been your favourite.'

'You sent me to boarding school to get rid of me.'

'You live too near – you're always spying.'

'I thought I'd be independent when I got married but I'm not.'

'If Dad dies of a heart attack, it'll be my fault.'

'Wynn wants to go back to his first wife. If not, he'll leave me for someone else – who wants a woman going blind?'

Worst of all was what she'd said to Mum, grabbing her wrist

(which was broken and in plaster at the time): 'I don't care if it hurts. I hate you. Get out of my house.'

He and Wynn had discussed the problem many times, he said, and between them they'd tried everything – 'blasting, cajoling, sympathizing, the lot'. But in the end, it came down to one thing: booze. No getting round it. Her drinking was out of control.

17

'Madness & booze, madness & booze,
Which'll can tell who preceded whose?'

John Berryman, 'Dream Song 225'

I saw for myself the state Gill was in a few weeks after that letter from Dad – at New Year, on the day I found her hiding out in our parents' garage, drunk, bitter and despairing. It's tempting to let that episode stand for all the others. I don't want to rob her of her dignity. But when she was pissed she had no dignity. And I'm on a mission here – not just to be honest about her addiction and its impact on the people close to her, but to demythologise the romance of heavy drinking.

Literature – American literature especially – is rich in examples of alcoholic excess, mostly glamorised. Hemingway, Faulkner, Hart Crane, Tennessee Williams, Dorothy Parker ('I'd rather have a bottle in front of me than a frontal lobotomy'), Ring Lardner, Raymond Chandler, O. Henry, Jack London, Delmore Schwartz, Scott Fitzgerald, ('Too much champagne is just right'), John Berryman, Jack Kerouac, Charles Bukowski, Anne Sexton, Patricia Highsmith – the list is long even without those, like Hunter S. Thompson, more renowned for their experiments with other substances ('I hate to advocate drugs, alcohol, violence or insanity to anyone, but they've always worked for me'). There are embarrassing episodes, but little to suggest the fallout from constant heavy drinking: illness, injury, insomnia, squalor, violence, misery for oneself and others. A bohemian chic is still associated with boozy writers, with websites that give you the recipes for their trademark drinks: Faulkner's mint julep, Hemingway's mojito, Chandler's gimlet, Kerouac's margarita, Scott Fitzgerald's gin rickey. And it's not just the Americans. All literature abounds with paeans to the hard stuff. Sometimes it's a matter of national pride, with ale, stout, vodka, absinthe, Chianti or, for Robert Burns, the peaty goodness of Scotch whisky being celebrated for their miraculous powers ('O whisky, soul o' plays an' pranks,/Accept a bardie's gratefu' thanks'). The spirit is one of *carpe diem* – drink now because who knows what tomorrow will bring. As Byron puts it:

> And for the future – (but I write this reeling,
> Having got drunk exceedingly today,
> So that I seem to stand upon the ceiling)
> I say – the future is a serious matter –
> And so – for God's sake – hock and soda water!

The positive spin put on alcohol both in the Bible (with the marriage feast at Cana – 'the only worthwhile miracle in the New Testament' as Christopher Hitchens called it) and in classical legend (with Dionysus the god of ecstasy and wine) is something that John Cheever puzzled over. Why is drunkenness not among the deadly sins, he wondered? Why in early religious myths and legends is alcohol presented as one of the gifts of the gods? In rehab – briefly brought to his senses – he wrote: 'The belief that to be drunk is to be blessed is very deep. To die of drink is sometimes thought a graceful and natural death – over-looking wet-brains, convulsions, delirium tremens, hallucinations, hideous automobile accidents and botched suicides . . . To drink oneself to death was not in any way alarming, I thought, until I found that I was drinking myself to death.'

More typically, Cheever justified his reliance on alcohol as integral to his writing: 'The writer cultivates, extends, raises and inflames his imagination.' Alcoholics are never short of justifi-cations for their addiction. Someone or something else is always to blame. 'Wine was almost a necessity for me to be able to stand her [Zelda's] long monologues about ballet' (Scott Fitzgerald). 'Modern life . . . is often a mechanical oppression and liquor is the only mechanical relief' (Hemingway). 'I began to drink heavily after I'd realised that the things I'd most wanted in life for myself and my writing, and my wife and children, were simply not going to happen' (Raymond Carver). Best of all is John Berryman: 'Why drink so, two days running?/two months, O seasons, years, two decades running?/I answer (smiles, my question on the cuff)/Man, I been thirsty.'*

Why do writers drink? Why does anyone drink? Don Birnam, the hero of the definitive novel about alcoholism, Charles Jackson's *The Lost Weekend*, thinks it a futile question:

------

*Olivia Laing's study of six American writers who drank to excess, *The Trip to Echo Spring*, is a fine examination of the self-delusions involved and of the tragedies that can ensue – it's a book enriched by personal experience, tough-minded and refreshingly unglamorising. Leslie Jamison's *The Recovering* covers some of the same ground and is more overtly auto-biographical. It's also sceptical about finding answers for addiction: 'My drinking had something to do with my family, and something to do with my brain, and something to do with the values I was raised to worship . . . All these tales of *why* are true and also insufficient.'

Why? You were a drunk; that's all there was to it. You drank; period. And once you took a drink, once you got under way, what difference did it make. Why? There were so many dozen reasons that didn't count at all; none that did . . . To hell with the causes . . . They counted for nothing in the face of the one fact: you drank and it was killing you. Why? Because alcohol was something you couldn't handle, it had you licked. Why? Because you had reached a point where one drink was too many and a hundred not enough.

It's a great riff and a seductive premise: once addicted, you're addicted, end of story. But there are reasons for becoming addicted: illness, boredom, loneliness, trauma, hedonism, lack of self-confidence; drink as stress relief or a short-cut to euphoria; drink as a way to bury the past, obliterate the present and escape the future. Genes are also crucial, with certain chromosomes, so science suggests, creating a predisposition. In the past, men and women on both sides of our family, the Morrisons and the O'Sheas, lost their way because of alcohol. And then there's nurture: that's the part I'm trying to understand.

Pubs were an integral part of our childhood, all the more so once Dad's affair with Beaty began and Sunday lunchtimes at the pub became an excuse for him to see her. By twelve or so, Gill and I graduated from orangeade to shandy – getting a taste for alcohol at that age would destroy its mystique and stop us going mad for it later, Dad reasoned. (When he took me to see his father's corpse in an open coffin, when I was eight, it was with a similar therapeutic motive: to get me used to death at an early age, so I wouldn't be tormented by it later.) As he saw it, his own consumption was moderate – two or three pints at the pub on a weekday evening, with maybe a whisky or two when he got home. Mum was more abstemious but the crowd they mixed with were all good drinkers: Charles and Selene, Gordon and Edna, Stephen and Val. There was no taboo about getting squiffy. Dad's word for that was 'fresh', as in 'I could tell Uncle Gordon was fresh last night'. To 'get fresh' suggests rejuvenation – a good thing not a bad one. Smoking was also deemed harmless. But two of the daughters in Mum and Dad's small circle became alcoholic and another died of lung cancer.

I'm not sure that irony is the right word for it but I'm struck how we abbreviated Gillian's name to Gill – the word, in old imperial measures, for a quarter-pint. Gill was small (not pint-sized but quarter-pint-sized) which made her more susceptible to the effects of alcohol. Had she stuck to quarter-pints of beer (you can't get them in a pub, but you can buy 25cl cans and bottles at the supermarket), she might not have developed a drink problem. But she didn't do things in halves, let alone quarters. It was the full 5-litre wine box, nothing less.

Did Mum and Dad blame themselves for her drinking? They never said as much. But the thought must have occurred. When a child goes off the rails, parents can't help but feel responsible. Siblings can feel guilty, too. My guilt is exacerbated through a sense of kinship. I drink more than I should.

I've never subscribed to the sentiments of Larkin's 'This Be the Verse'. Yes, they fuck you up, your mum and dad, and they were fucked up in their turn, but most of what happens in life is your own responsibility. Still, in my head I keep rewriting the last stanza:

Man hands on alcohol to man.
It passes down through blood and bone.
Stick to water if you can
And don't keep booze at home.

The March after her New Year meltdown, Gill went into rehab for a month. She'd been under pressure from Mum and Dad to 'straighten herself out', and even Wynn, who had no faith in therapy, thought it worth a go. Dad vowed to change the family lifestyle when she came out: less pub-going and more excursions up the Dales, perhaps a little golf too. I phoned Gill at the rehab place, Gisburne Park. She missed the kids terribly, she said ('I don't suppose I'd be a normal mother if I didn't'), but Wynn had been good about bringing them to see her. At the end of the call I encouraged her to write and describe what Gisburne Park was like. I didn't expect her to – that would mean owning up to why she was there – but she did. After saying how pleasant the setting was (hills, woods and a river running by) she itemised her daily routine, from a gym workout on an exercise bike or rowing machine to hydrotherapy. More to the point was the late-morning group session 'which is really a lesson in learning to talk about yourself – which for someone like me was very hard to do at first'. There were further meetings during the day, with a chance to watch videotapes or hear former patients talk about their recovery. 'I suppose if I go home better than I came in things should improve for everyone,' she said. She was glad I'd phoned: 'It makes me realize people do care even when I think they don't or when I think they're interfering – I suppose they're only trying to help.'

Reading the letter again now, I'm struck by the repetition of the phrase 'I suppose'. It's as if she's trying to persuade herself that she can get better but doesn't quite believe it.

Perhaps in the short term she did improve. But then Dad was diagnosed with cancer. He died three months later. She took it hard – and took to hard drinking again.

For a time Wynn tried watering down the wine, rather than confiscating it. Then he removed all alcohol from the house and locked it in his car boot. He also filmed Gill with a camcorder, hoping the playback, when she sobered up, would shame her into abstinence. The blank cheques she wrote to taxi drivers were especially worrying. Despite the worry, though, he had a secret admiration for her sneakiness. She'd always had it, even in the early days, pre-children. If they were at the pub, and he went to the gents, she'd buy herself an extra drink. Or if he bought them each a rum and Coke, then went to play pool, he would find, on his return, that she had drunk both. Often his mates would be there, and he'd feel ashamed because of the state she was in. Eventually he stopped taking her with him. Not that it stopped the drinking. She did it at home instead.*

She was resourceful there as well. She'd be in the kitchen chatting to him or the kids, then if they went to watch telly and left her alone for a minute, woomph, like magic, she'd be gone, in a taxi which somehow, despite their watchful presence, she had managed to phone for and had arranged to be waiting at the end of the drive. (All this in the days before mobiles and texts, and despite having eyes too poor to read a watch face.)

---

*Stephen Blackpool on his alcoholic wife in Dickens's *Hard Times*: 'I were very patient wi' her. I tried to wean her fra't ower and ower agen. I tried this, I tried that, I tried t'other. I ha' gone home, many's the time, and found all vanished as I had in the world, and her without a sense left to bless herself lying on bare ground. I ha' dun't not once, not twice – twenty time! . . . I ha' bore that much, that I were owd when I were young.'

Then after an absence of several hours, she'd be back, ideally with the next day's drinking secreted about the garden before she entered the house.

If she had been male, heavy drinking would have been less transgressive. Men, 'roaring drunk', had a licence to misbehave which even single women in their twenties were denied. And if a woman was older, married and a mother she would be stigmatised. As Leslie Jamison puts it, 'Male drunks are thrilling. Female drunks are bad moms." Whenever Gill succumbed after a spell of abstinence and took a first drink – furtively, in private – she would tell herself 'Just the one: I'm not a bad mother and this won't be a binge.' But then the drink took over. The bully booze.

She drank to excess from distress. It wasn't just losing Dad but, in the years that followed, losing the mother she knew. Though free of dementia, Mum had spells of confusion, through not eating or urinary tract infections or the pills she took. Occasionally she'd wander down the drive and into the road, as if looking for someone or something – just as Gill did too, when drunk, though never (as far as I know) at the same time. The two errant women of Thornton.

Mum's decline was hastened by the strain of seeing Gill drink too much. Equally, Gill's drinking escalated from the strain of seeing Mum decline. Gill herself said as much, though competing culprits were Wynn (a rotten husband), me (a neglectful and

---

*Or as Marguerite Duras puts it more dramatically: 'when a woman drinks it's as if an animal were drinking or a child. Alcoholism is a scandal in a woman and a female alcoholic is a rare, serious matter. It's a slur on the divine in our nature.'

indulged brother) and Dad (a tyrant who went and died on her). And of course her eyesight was deteriorating. She was lonely, unhappy and had two kids to bring up. Who'd not get drunk given all that?

We pitied her and we blamed her, both at the same time.

When she sobered up, I'd start to believe that she could get free of drink for good. But then she'd lapse again. And I'd remind myself of the statistics: one book I read claimed that only one in seven alcoholics beat their addiction, and even the more upbeat studies (it's important to give recovering alcoholics hope) put the figure of those who *stay sober for a year after being at rehab* at less than 20 per cent.

People talk of drinkers 'drowning their sorrows'. But Gill's sorrows didn't drown. They rose to the surface, blackly buoyant, while the good things went under.

The best things were Liam and Louise, whom she loved but, when she was drunk, failed to look after. There's a painting by the seventeenth-century Dutch painter Jan Steen, *The Effects of Intemperance*, which shows a mother slumped in alcoholic stupor (her dress dangerously close to a brazier) while her children run amok; Hogarth's *Gin Lane* tells a similar story. Nothing terrible happened to Liam and Louise; they were used to their mum being insensible and they coped amazingly well. Still, Gill's problems weren't easily hidden. It was lucky no one in the village snitched. She reaped the benefit of being the doctors' daughter or (as she'd become) the doctor's daughter.

There were good times as well, especially when the kids were small. Birthday parties with a bouncy castle, for example, when late in the day, with drink inside them, the dads would have a go, competing to be the one to jump highest, small change falling from their pockets as they did, which the kids would snaffle. And there were barbecues on summer weekends, when Louise and Liam would stay up late and not care, or pretend not to notice, if their mum overdid things, the only drawback being the state she'd be in on Monday morning and the probability that she would continue where she had left off.

Later, as teenagers, they were more embarrassed by her antics. Their friends would sleep over and wake to find Gill drinking the dregs in their glasses from the night before. Or mates who did shifts at the Co-op would phone to tell Liam that his mum had passed out on the pavement outside.

They knew she loved them. But that drink turned her into a stranger. You should keep a diary, Wynn told Louise. You could call it *My Two Mothers*.

Sometimes Wynn – and later Louise and Liam – would share a joke with me about Gill's drinking. It was a way not to cry about it. And funny things did happen.

Once – after Wynn, at the end of his tether, had locked her in an upstairs bedroom to stop her getting at drink – she climbed out of the window and across the roof. Louise was having a piano lesson and looked out to see Gill's hand dangling from the gutter above the window where she and her tutor were sitting.

Another time, crawling about the garden in search of bottles she'd hidden, she got stuck in some bushes and called for help. Wynn was trying to extricate her when a van pulled up in the drive. It was the fish man on his weekly round. Wynn had to stand there, buying cod, hoping Gill wouldn't call out for help again.

Then there were the bottles of elderflower wine that went missing, the ones Wynn had home-brewed and which he assumed had been nicked by his teenage son Mark, who was staying with them at the time and to whom Wynn gave a serious bollocking, before he realised the culprit was Gill. Or the bottle of port Wynn bought for Louise's boyfriend, many years later, and put under the Christmas tree, suitably wrapped, which had disappeared by Christmas morning.

Or there was the time one of Gill's friends phoned me, saying Gill was in a bad way and wanted to go into rehab – could I help? It didn't sound like Gill, who hated rehab, but I called Gisburne Park, where she'd been before, and they said they'd be willing to take her if someone could bring her in. We couldn't get hold of Wynn so the friend drove her there that evening. I called Wynn next morning to put him in the picture.

I expect you've been worrying where Gill's got to, I said.

Why would I? he said. She's here, flat out on the lawn.

She'd sneaked out during the night, walked the half-mile-long drive to the road, and flagged down a passing vehicle to drive her home – despite having no money on her and being unable to see.

Funny? Maybe not. But funnier than my diaries. In Mum and Dad's last years, I shuttled back and forth to Yorkshire a lot. And on the train home to London I'd record what I had heard and seen.

I keep diaries only when I'm upset or miserable. To include them all would paint a false picture of Gill, who had periods of sobriety; to include none would be a denial of the havoc she caused when she did drink. What follows is a selection from the mid-90s, either side of Mum's death.

18

3 January 1995

The usual mixture of Christmas torpor and mayhem. The mayhem came from my sister, who was building up for a bender when I arrived with Kathy and the kids on Boxing Day, then went on it, spectacularly, while we took Mum to the Lakes for three days. 'Abandoned' (her word) on New Year's Eve, she ordered several wine boxes to be delivered by minicab then turned up at the pub where Wynn had gone and in his words 'disgraced herself'. I feel the pull of conflicting sympathies. Towards him, constantly humiliated; against him, for not doing more to help Gill. Towards her, who needs to be held, loved, understood; against her, for being selfish, passive-aggressive, manipulative. On New Year's Night, after walking her home (it took a lot of persuasion), I came back and tried to double-lock the door, knowing she had keys and fearing she would walk up the stairs and knife me. It was an absurd fantasy, perhaps triggered by my reading about Mary Lamb, who stabbed her mother to death. Gill has never been violent towards me – but I lay there in the dark, waiting for the creak on the stairs, the gleam of her knife in the dark.

24 July 1995

According to Mum, Gill's drinking has reached epic proportions. The occasional three-day bender has turned into regular three-week binges. Even when she seems sober she's not, topping herself up surreptitiously during the day. It's gone way past embarrassment. The other week the police arrested her round the back of the local supermarket, in Barnoldswick, as she tried to open a wine box (one of several) while in a state of undress. The police rang Wynn, asking him to take her home since there was nothing they could charge her with – she wasn't a public nuisance, wasn't using threatening behaviour, wasn't a danger to herself or others, just drunk. He wanted them to lock her up for the night, as a shock to the system, but they wouldn't oblige. Back home she's been opening Dad's ancient, giant flasks of home-made wine, which he stored under the eaves – they're the kind you see on bars with coins inside for charity, and he thought them ideal for brewing. On visits to Mum, she slips upstairs for a glug.

In her own house, she hides wine boxes in the children's bedroom (among toys) or in the airing cupboard (among linen sheets) or in the garden: everyone's used to this, including the children, who feel protective of their mum when she's drunk because of the love she gives them when she's sober – and perhaps also because they fear being removed from her care, erratic though it is.

September 1995

The GP, Dr Miller, says that Mum would 'benefit from a spell in hospital because she lacks TLC' – a reproach aimed at Gill, I infer, which he confirms by adding 'Your mother's literally worrying herself sick'.

When I go up to see her in Airedale hospital on the 19th, Gill arrives too. I'd tried to call her the previous night to put her off (no point in both of us visiting at the same time) but didn't get through. She's embarrassed and offers to leave. No need, I say, while she fusses round Mum's underwear, then tries to find a brush for Mum's hair but can't locate it.

Stupidly perhaps, I try to have things out with her in front of Mum.

B   I think we should have a talk.

G   I'd better go now. [tries to leave]

B   There's no need. It doesn't have to be private. Anyway, it *is* private. There's only the three of us.

G   No, I'll let you two talk. I'd better catch that bus.

M   Stay, love.

G   I'll stay but I'm not going to talk about it – not to family.

B   All right, you don't need to talk to us, an outsider makes more sense. But at least admit there's a problem.

Mum changes the subject. Gill remains tearful. I feel a terrible impulse to goad – that she's making her mother ill, that Liam's dislike of school is caused by her picking him up when drunk and the shame that causes him*, that Mum needs someone *reliable* to look after her.

---

*I thought of Liam twenty-five years after writing this, while reading Douglas Stuart's Booker Prize-winning *Shuggie Bain*, a novel that's wonderfully insightful about the impact of a mother's alcoholism on her children – which in Shuggie's case includes having stomach cramps every day when school is about to finish: 'It was the burning bile of anticipation, the rising fear of what might lie at home. Agnes had gotten sober many times before, but the cramps had never really, completely gone away. To Shuggie, the stretches of sobriety were fleeting and unpredictable and not to be fully

Eventually Gill leaves. We try to dissuade her but not very hard. She goes off tearful at having made the noble sacrifice of 'leaving you two to talk together'. She'll have to get herself to the bus stop and start for home, which will take an hour, maybe two. Pissed or not, she sees much more of Mum than I do yet there I was getting angry with her.

Heartbreaking, awful. An hour later, writing this, my body is hurting still.

February 1997

Another GP in the practice takes a different view from Dr Miller. She listened as I described Gill's recent drinking and after stalling for a while, from worry about breaching confidentiality, she said she took Gill's side, and that what she needed was a good solicitor. Evidently Gill had been complaining about Wynn. She said she thought that if Gill were left to sort her life out *on her own*, she would do so – ie stop the drinking and get herself together. She says it's tempting for her to tell Gill 'This is what you should do, this is what's best', but that this would disempower Gill, and that lack of power is her basic problem. I wince as she says it, not so much because she's wrong but because I resent the analysis coming from her. More accurately, what I resent is feeling that she has bought Gill's line that it's all Wynn's fault.

Back at her house, Gill sits on the sofa, monosyllabic or unintelligible when she attempts to speak, mostly just nodding, unable to keep her head raised for more than a moment, her eyes glazed, in and out of sleep – noddy noddy noddy.

---

enjoyed. As with any good weather, there was always more rain on the other side.' For all the suffering she puts him through, Shuggie remains loyal and loving to his mother – as did (does) Liam.

11 March 1997

Gill calls, in tears, to say Mum is going downhill mentally as well as physically. She's often confused and this morning stood naked at the window, waving at Mr Kelly, the gardener. She thinks we should have power of attorney and that a solicitor is coming to arrange it. I worry about this, having come to distrust Gill: is it some scheme to get hold of Mum's money, to fund her binges? I hate myself for thinking this but there, I have thought it.

In the background I can hear Wynn demanding to know where the bottles are that she has hidden about the house. I know she's drunk but reassure her that she's done her best by Mum. This makes her cry even more.

When I'm there next day, Dr Miller says that the pneumonia is aspergillus, a fungal infection slowly filling Mum's lungs – like foam, like milk boiling over, like the snow falling all over Ireland in Joyce's story 'The Dead'. Later I lie in the back bedroom, which has brown wallpaper with white floral sprays that I've never noticed before, and as I stare at it I feel as if I'm entombed, or enwombed, watching my mother's lungs fill up with whiteness. Decades on, I'm back inside her body again.

14 April 1997

I visit Mum in her nursing home, Cromwell's. Last time I came up Gill laid on a generous lunch for me: three sausages, a hard-boiled egg, bread, two kinds of cheese, a pot of tea, biscuits, chocolate and an apple. It was a real effort. And a reminder how sweet and caring she is when sober. She also told me that I might not see her over Easter 'because I'm going into hospital to sort my drinking out'. It seemed like such a breakthrough, after years of denial, that I gushed in encouragement. In the end she didn't go of course. And Mum says she hasn't seen her lately because 'she's back on the drink'.

It's terrible for the kids and for Wynn, who has to check in at work at 7.30 then come back by 8.10 to get Liam off to school – then either pick him up at 3.30 or ask a neighbour to do it. He and Louise share the cooking; at weekends they eat at The Anchor. He finds it almost impossible to do his job and look after her; it's lucky the Water Board is so understanding. The looking-after mostly consists of keeping Gill off the booze but it's still too much.

I made no attempt to see her today, and now, on the Intercity south again, I feel huge guilt about that. Why am I so cold that I didn't feel the need? Why am I so cold that I prefer to spend my time writing about not seeing her rather than seeing her? Then again, why am I writing about her when there are so many other things I could write about? Why is it – why is she – the only subject? Sometimes I feel she is inherently unlovable or me inherently unloving. At other times that one needn't care about siblings (as opposed to friends), because – the old line – 'one doesn't choose them'. But here I am writing this. And hurting.

April/May 1997

Each time she sobers up she assumes a mask of penitence, a shroud of silent remorse, as though the problem is behind her and we mustn't bring it up. As a result, there's no resistance next time she feels the urge. Perhaps there would be none anyway, but being made to think about her drinking, however cruel a process when she's 'all right again', seems like the only hope of a cure.

She would get a lot of sympathy – probably does – by speaking to people outside the family. But as someone who's inside the family, I can't offer much. Even if I try, it doesn't count, because of ancient, unhealed scars. I'm on the wrong side, even when I'm on her side.

19 May 1997

Since Mum went into Cromwell's, across the road, Gill spends more and more time in Mum's house. First it was just the odd night; now it's days at a time. Mostly she sleeps, with brief waking gaps before she bombs herself back to oblivion. The house has become a womb to her.

Wynn says the place smells of wine now and that various ornaments have been smashed. He feels she's abusing the unmeant hospitality – Mum's dimly aware that Gill goes there but has no idea how often. Oddly, Gill says that she doesn't want to move in there when Mum dies, that the place has too many bad memories. Perhaps she's trying to make it a less attractive prospect by wrecking the furniture and décor.

Late May 1997

Gill's problem isn't lack of self-knowledge. It's that she knows herself only as a bad person and can't stand the glare of that knowledge. The good in her (and she has many good qualities) is filtered out.

Wynn reports a recent conversation:

He: What are you trying to do, drink yourself to death?
She: Yes.

Early June 1997

Another day visit to Yorkshire. I'd have liked to tell Gill I was coming but when she's over at Mum's (using it as a battered – or plastered – wife's refuge), she doesn't answer the phone.

Mum suggests a walk, with me pushing her wheelchair. She has been given worrying reports of Gill (one neighbour found her crawling on her knees by the church) and wants to see her. We ring the bell at both houses, without success, circling Mum's to see if we can spot Gill inside, relieved not to find her collapsed on the living-room floor. On the second circuit I spot her sitting on the edge of Mum's bed, on the phone. We dither about what to do. I don't want a nasty scene. We make another circuit, giving Gill the chance to come outside if she has seen us. By the greenhouse we find a brown mohair cardigan of Mum's lying in the flowerbed – presumably worn then discarded as Gill sat outside one night. It's not her fault she has failed to spot it; her eyes are bad. But I feel for Mum. Not that she cares about the cardigan. But what she infers about it being left outside upsets her.

29 June 1997

I'm up seeing Mum again and this time Gill makes a special point of coming over. She's noisy and manic in a way I'm unused to – is it that she's had a nip or two before my arrival and is feeling just right, tip-top? Or has the GP put her on an anti-depressant? She seems lively and positive, anyway, if also erratic. She hates Mum being like this, she says, as we leave. I should be hardened to it by now, she adds. Problem is, I'm sensitive.

It's true. She is.

Late July 1997

In the days after Mum's death, Gill and I are gentle with each other. But once the funeral is over, she starts drinking again and circles back to the same ancient grievances – that Dad hit her, that Wynn does too, that I've shouted at her, that only Mum understood her; that she's useless, a burden, a shit, a Nothing; that she's a bad daughter, bad mother, bad sister, bad wife; that we want her taken off to a loony bin. Round and round she goes, beating us up, beating herself up. Tomorrow she'll probably remember none of this, only that Wynn and I were 'horrible' to her.

[In the middle of writing this – or rather copying it from my diary many years later – Gill phones. However guilty I felt at setting down the words in the first place, now I feel doubly guilty: here I am, recalling events that show her in an unflattering light, as if writing a hostile obituary, and there she is, on the line from Yorkshire, bright, friendly, asking me what I'd like for Christmas. There are years when she's not in a fit state to ask, or not in a fit state to deliver on her promise, but this time looks better. Not that I care about the presents – I usually ask for a CD, knowing she'll get Louise to order it online – but if it's a year when the subject isn't raised I know she's in a bad state.

When she's in a good state like this, it's hard to believe she'll relapse, and that's what's so cruel about it: your heart lifts, you start investing in hope, this time she has turned a corner you think, which makes the inevitable let-down harder to take, and slowly you become more cynical, colder and warier, so that next time she calls in a good state you're less receptive – an ugly outcome for you as well as her.]

Two Sisters

New Year's Day 1998

We're up north again, after a drama on Christmas Eve, when Gill rang me round midnight to complain that she'd smashed up Mum's house after being 'chucked out' by Wynn (she'd attacked the kids, he later told me, and left bruises on their necks, for depriving her of drink). She called me pleading for help and was crying so hard that her voice was lost between sobs, like a tiny boat in an Atlantic storm. I did ring Wynn, and he promised to let her back in the morning, since he was too angry to do it then, and the rain too horizontal. After being allowed in on Christmas Day, she stayed sober for the rest of the week, till last night.

When I go over to Mum's house, I find that the front door has been damaged (the wood splintered) but that it still locks – hardly the catastrophe Gill made it out to be. The bloodstain up the wall is more upsetting. She fell onto the radiator one night and blood spurted from her head – luckily Wynn had an intuition there might be a problem and went round, to find her lying in a puddle of blood. Thinking at first that she had tried to kill herself, he rang for an ambulance. They stitched her up and later that morning he collected her from hospital. [*] She resumed drinking at once.

Her latest trick is to leave credit cards in various pre-arranged spots about the garden for the taxi drivers who secretly deliver her booze. I found one on top of the wall at the end of the

---

[*] On another occasion, finding Gill crashed out on an outdoor swing seat with her leg badly cut open and bleeding heavily, he fetched a little first aid kit, which contained a needle and thread, and rather than take her to hospital stitched her up himself – then took the stitches out a few days later when the wound had healed. Few husbands would have been so resourceful.

path to her house today, and handed it to her casually, playing along – 'Here, Gill, I found this', 'Thanks, however did it get there?' – each of us a feeble actor.

It sometimes seems remarkable that she's still alive. She has the DTs after a bout like this last one. And has her eyesight problems. But is otherwise relatively healthy. At this rate she'll outlive us all.

Reading my diary entries now, I feel bad – a prig, a prat, a prick. They're short on empathy and fraternal warmth. I couldn't get past the anger I felt on Mum and Dad's behalf. In their retirement they might have travelled, taken up new hobbies, rested – instead of which worry about Gill consumed them. It's natural for parents to worry and the worries don't stop when your kids grow up (they don't even stop when you become grandparents, at which point there's a new generation to worry about). But Mum and Dad had more worries than most. I took their side, seeing Gill's addiction as a failure of will, not an illness. Their suffering made me cold towards her. Wynn, Louise and Liam were suffering too. That made me colder still. It's what happens with addicts. They kill your compassion.* For a time Gill's drinking killed mine.

Did I handle things any better than the other men in her life, Dad and Wynn? Hard to say. When their patience ran out,

---

* 'It is hard to love an addict. Not only practically difficult, in the picking up after them and the handling of those aspects of life they're not able for themselves, but metaphysically hard. It feels like bashing yourself against a wall, not just your head, but your whole self. It makes your heart hard. Caught between endless ultimatums (stop drinking) and radical acceptance (I love you no matter what) the person who loves the addict exhausts and renews their love on a daily basis.' (Emilie Pine, *Notes to Self*)

they could be draconian. Both resorted to locking Gill up, whether as punishment or to keep her from getting more booze. I couldn't have done that. Then again, she wasn't in my life every day. And from time to time I did lock her out of my heart.

Now I think I should have done more. Phoned her more often. Reassured her I loved her. Joined Al-Anon, the charity for friends and family of alcoholics, in search of advice. But we stayed in touch. There was no falling-out. I wasn't *that* cold. We were Irish twins. I never hated her.

19

'Brothers and sisters, when they are not friends, are generally the sharpest enemies to each other.'

Samuel Richardson, *Clarissa*

Some brothers do hate their sisters. It's allowed. At any rate it happens. I've read the books – the novels and biographies. Same-sex sibling hatred is more common – Cain and Abel, the Gallagher brothers, Olivia de Havilland and Joan Fontaine. But George Eliot's brother hated her. And then there's Philip Larkin, whose sister Kitty was ten years his senior.

A boy with a much older sister might be expected to look up to her and even romanticise her a little. But Larkin took his cue from his father Sydney, who thought Kitty 'little better than a mental defective' and when Coventry was blitzed in 1940 sent a telegram of reassurance to his son but not to her. In kinder moments Larkin saw Kitty as a fellow victim of their parents' unhappy marriage. At worst he effaced her, describing himself as 'for practical purposes an only child', with Kitty an irritating reminder that his only-ness was an illusion.

In letters written when he was a student at Oxford he treated her on almost equal terms, recounting his difficulties getting access to a copy of *Lady Chatterley's Lover* at the Bodleian, sharing his thoughts about Jungian philosophy, and signing off, in one case, 'with very much love'. He even used her to test out his experiments in poetic prose. His letters to her weren't especially intimate and he mocked her poor spelling, as if to remind her how much better educated he was. But a brotherly affection came through. In a letter to a friend, he quoted something Kitty said when their father died – 'We're nobody now: he did it all' – as if she'd articulated his own feelings.

Afterwards, though, as their widowed mother Eva became more demanding, he was vehement about Kitty. 'My bitch-sister . . . an absolute mean-spirited self-centred little swine of Hell' is how he described her to his girlfriend Monica Jones. They rowed over their respective duties towards Eva, each blaming the other for neglecting her, and his anger boiled over when Kitty asked him to look after Eva while she and her husband Walter went on holiday: 'I've just had that pair of swine from Loughborough on the telephone, & it has left me in a rage . . . they have no feelings at all. I was flabbergasted by their *sheer hoglike gracelessness* . . . The sons of sods.' Whereas his drawings of Eva depicted her as lovably seal-like, and those of Monica as a cute little rabbit, the recurrent verbal image for Kitty was of a hog or swine.

He must have had some respect for her or he wouldn't have instructed his executors to seek her consent to posthumous publication of his work: knowing she'd shared his outrage when an old schoolfriend, Noel Hughes, wrote an article implying that their father had been a Nazi sympathiser, he trusted her to protect the Larkin brand. It wasn't her fault when it became toxic. But it wasn't surprising either, given some of his comments about women – including those on Kitty herself.

Perhaps it's no coincidence that only two of her letters to

him survive, when he kept the many hundreds from his parents ('To destroy letters is repugnant to me,' he said, 'it's like destroying a bit of life'). It's as if he thought her letters weren't worth the bother of preserving. Only when she argued with him about their duty to Eva did she become unignorable. For the rest of the time – as many a brother has done – he seems to have regarded his sister as a nonentity.

At least Kitty had no ambitions to write. Harriet Martineau did, which annoyed the hell out of her brother James. He'd been her mentor in their early life but came to resent her intellectual independence. When she published *Letters on the Laws of Man's Nature and Development*, co-written with Henry Atkinson, he published a damning review, mocking its mysticism: 'The authors appear to live exclusively among people who see through brick walls'. He saw no reason why his hatchet job should cause a rift but, as she told her friend Fanny Wedgwood, Harriet took it badly: 'The truth is that James has been injuring and wounding me in every possible way since my illness in 1839 (you know, he never went to see me all those years) . . . he despises my books, knows none of my friends, or my habits, and very few of my opinions, and has never seen me for 20 years without insulting me.'

Branwell Brontë wasn't as unkind as James Martineau but he too falls into the bad brother category. As a young man, with great things expected of him, he was accorded privileges denied to Charlotte, Emily and Anne: 'My poor Father naturally thought more of his only *Son* than of his daughters', Charlotte said. But whatever his gifts, he wasted them. 'I have been in truth too much petted through life,' he wrote in a rare moment of self-knowledge. 'I shall never be able to realize the too sanguine

190

hopes of my friends.' Before alcohol and opium addiction finished him off at the age of thirty-one, he caused misery to his sisters. The drunken, abusive Arthur Huntingdon in Anne's *The Tenant of Wildfell Hall* is a husband not a brother, but his behaviour is based on Branwell's.

It's not known whether he saw through his sisters' disguise when they published their novels under the names Currer, Ellis and Acton Bell or if he did see through it how he reacted. But it's safe to assume he'd not have felt good about their success (such recognition should have been his!) and that they chose to use pseudonyms partly to protect him. As Charlotte put it, 'We could not tell him of our efforts for fear of causing him too deep a pang of remorse for his own time misspent, and talents misapplied.'

For every well-behaved brother in fiction, the kind who would make a perfect husband if only allowed to marry his sister, there's a villainous one – squandering the family money, pushing his sister into marriage in order to further his own interests, or behaving violently towards her. In Trollope's *Can You Forgive Her?*, George Vavasor threatens his sister Kate – 'Say that you will do as I desire you, or I will be the death of you' – and breaks her arm. Then there's John Dashwood in Jane Austen's *Sense and Sensibility*: urged by his dying father to take care of his half-sisters, he's too mean and avaricious to provide for them. Young Tom Gradgrind in *Hard Times* is less obviously malevolent: in childhood he and his sister Louisa form a pact against their repressive father. But Tom later exploits Louisa's love for him ('She would do anything for me') by urging her to marry his odious employer Mr Bounderby, who's fifty to her twenty, in order to make his own life more comfortable. Later, 'a dissipate, extravagant idler', he extracts large sums from her in order to pay off gambling debts and when she can no longer oblige him is forced to rob a bank.

Even these fictional brothers pale in comparison to James Harlowe in Samuel Richardson's *Clarissa*, whose sis-dissing culminates in death. 'Grasping', 'arrogant', hot-tempered and cruel, he tries to bully Clarissa into marriage with a man she doesn't love but from whose fortune he and the family will benefit. Though Clarissa challenges his right to interfere, he's instrumental in turning the family against her. He has the excuse of acting as her protector against the rakish Lovelace. But his objection to Lovelace isn't moral but the result of a personal grudge (Lovelace wounded him in a fight which James provoked). And far from protecting Clarissa, his campaign to marry her off forces her into the arms of Lovelace, who abducts, rapes, drugs and destroys her. After her death, James takes the brunt of blame as 'the person who had kept up the general resentment against so sweet a creature'. But it's not he who avenges her death. That's left to a cousin, Colonel Morden.

Felix Mendelssohn joked to his sister that he belonged to 'the savage tribe of brothers'. But he wasn't as savage as this lot.*

David Greenglass, brother of Ethel Rosenberg, deserves a mention too: it was largely thanks to him that she and her husband Julius were sent to the electric chair in 1953. Greenglass was already a Communist sympathiser when he began work on

---

* Sisters can be savage too, of course, or have savage intentions: 'I wanted to kill him – my elder brother, I wanted to kill him, to get the better of him for once, just once, and see him die. I wanted to do it to remove from my mother's sight the object of her love, that son of hers, to punish her for loving him so much, so badly . . .' (Marguerite Duras, *The Lover*)

the US Atomic programme, the Manhattan Project, in 1944, and was 'glad' to help Julius pass nuclear secrets to the Soviet Union. Arrested by the FBI in 1950, he initially denied that his sister had been involved but later changed his testimony and said that she had typed up his notes. By co-operating with the authorities, he escaped the death sentence she was given for espionage. Years later, after serving a prison sentence, he admitted to having lied under oath about Ethel's involvement – his wife Ruth had been the one who did the typing. Asked if he'd have acted differently given the chance, he replied, 'Never . . . My wife is more important to me than my sister . . . My wife is my wife. I mean, I don't sleep with my sister.' To him, blood was thinner than water.

Greenglass didn't personally murder his sister but some brothers have done so, from Caligula, who according to Suetonius killed his sister Drusilla after learning that she was pregnant with his child (more probably she died of a fever), to another Roman emperor, Commodus, who ordered his older sister Lucilla to be put to death after she was implicated in a plot against him, to the Italian Renaissance poet Isabella di Morra, killed by her brothers for a suspected affair with a married nobleman (who they killed too), to the sixteen-year-old in the US in 2020 who put his older sister in a fatal chokehold after they'd rowed over a wi-fi password. Sororicide: the word may be less well known than fratricide or parricide, but the act is more common. Web-trawling one day I came across a listing for 'Most Popular Brother Murders Sister Films and TV Shows' (which for clarity's sake, since the popularity of the brother isn't the issue, might benefit from a couple of inverted commas). There were twenty-six items to choose from, including *Hallowe'en*.

*

The baddest brother in contemporary memoir is Shawn, in Tara Westover's *Educated*, who repeatedly threatens to kill her. And the baddest brother in contemporary fiction is Alan Sheridan, tormentor of Marianne in Sally Rooney's *Normal People*. 'Are you happy that you don't have friends?' he taunts her, adding that no one would miss her if she died: 'You're fucking pathetic, so you are.' Angry that she's cleverer than he is, he bullies her, pushes her about, spits at her and makes her swear not to tell their mother about it. Finally, after breaking down the door of her bedroom, he leaves her with blood streaming from a broken nose. Confronted by her lover Connell ('If you ever touch Marianne again, I'll kill you'), he wilts and weeps – a classic coward.

I seem to be saying that I wasn't as bad a brother as Philip Larkin, James Martineau, Branwell Brontë, Alan Sheridan or the Emperor Commodus.

It isn't saying much.*

---

*Of the more amicable brother–sister relationships in fiction, the following deserve special mention:
Jem and Scout Finch in Harper Lee's *To Kill a Mockingbird*
Freddy and Lucy Honeychurch in E. M. Forster's *A Room with a View*
Nicholas and Kate Nickleby in Dickens's *Nicholas Nickleby*
Ben and Lois Trotter in Jonathan Coe's *The Rotters' Club* and its sequels

20

Gill would sometimes call people late at night to share her woes. Beaty was one of them: they had never lost touch. Beaty would then ring or write to me, to say how worried she was about Gill: 'I am always scared she will top herself,' she said in one letter. It was good of her to be concerned since she had more than enough troubles of her own. At six months Josie's second child, a son, had been diagnosed with a rare form of cancer ('a schwannoma tumour', she wrote to tell me, a word I had to look up). He got through it but she and Josie had a horrible time before he did. And then there was Beaty's own cancer: eight years on, of the five women from her village who'd had mastectomies round the time she did, only she was still alive – and the risk of secondaries remained. She referred to this in passing ('not to worry, I am still here, God keeps sending me back'), as if her secondaries came second and Gill was her prime concern. 'She crucified your parents,' she said but, reluctant to criticise, attributed Gill's problems to an inferiority complex and a depression gene she shared with Mum and Auntie Sheila. She'd been saying prayers for Gill and hoped I'd do the same. Her faith in God, or the Virgin Mary, reassured her all would be well.

*

Beaty's buoyancy amazed me – as did the fact we were talking at all. She'd been so important to Dad, and cast such a large shadow over my childhood, that when I came to write a memoir after his death it seemed only right to make her part of the story. Though I changed her name, and Sam and Josie's names, to protect their privacy, I hadn't told her about the book; she'd moved away some years before, to Scotland, and I imagined she'd not get to hear about it. When she did, she asked me to send her a copy – and wasn't best pleased with the contents. 'I'm returning the book,' she told me over the phone a few days later, then changed her mind. The book never arrived.

For a time she fell silent, then began sending me letters – friendly letters, which omitted all mention of the memoir. Mum was still alive at this point and as her health declined the letters became more regular. Some were a touch messianic: Beaty's Catholicism went deeper than Mum's; she even sent me a little pamphlet, *How to Pray the Rosary* by Fr Jerome Bertram, published by the Catholic Truth Society: 'please read this' she scrawled on the cover. Since Dad's death she'd been phoning Mum twice a week, entertaining her with gossip and mimicry. She sometimes stayed with her, too, and was there for Mum's eightieth, a small party we held three months before she died. Embarrassed by all the weight she'd put on since cancer treatment, she joked to Mum about being pregnant. 'I didn't mind delivering Josie,' Mum said, 'but I'm not delivering this one'.

Beaty would often assure me of her love for Mum and admit how possessive it was. In one letter she complained of a neighbour who barged in and 'took over' when the two of them wanted some quiet time together. And in the last letter before Mum died she spoke of how she wanted to 'cradle her in my arms when the coughing racks her and gently stroke her brow.' Her hope was 'to be like a mother to her when the "child" in her can't take any more' – the mistress as mother to the woman she cuckolded.*

Were these professions of love for Mum atonement for the wrong Beaty had done decades earlier? Maybe, a little. But they did love each other. Life is less rational – less predictable, less programmed, less plausible – than fiction.

In a letter she sent me a month after Mum's death, Beaty almost owned up to the affair. Though she wouldn't admit to sleeping with Dad, she said she regretted the damage to Mum: 'I did not realise the extent of my "hurt" to someone I love.' She described a conversation they'd had after Dad's death. 'You two had a long affair, didn't you?' Mum asked her, a question Beaty wasn't prepared for: 'I nearly fell off the kitchen chair.'

If Beaty is to be trusted, Mum had never confronted her till then, either about the affair or about Josie – had kept her suspicions to herself and only at that point dared to voice them. I suppose it's possible. That Mum guessed the truth but till then had said nothing – perhaps not even to Dad. But I can't really believe Beaty. She was too wedded to denial. And she continued to deny Josie's paternity. That's what most upset her about my memoir – a passage where I speculated that Josie might be my sister. For me to think it was unthinkable, she said.

Did Sam also read the memoir? Beaty can't easily have kept it hidden from him and her distress on first reading it might not have gone unnoticed. But if he did read it, and saw through

---

*The term 'cuckold', derived from 'cuckoo' (a bird renowned for laying its eggs in other birds' nests), is usually reserved for the male sex. But if a man can make a cuckold of his lover's husband, surely a woman can make a cuckold of her lover's wife.

the disguise, any anger gradually receded. So I deduced from a phone call some years later. He was managing a caravan site in Scotland, with wooden lodges. One of the lodges was owned by a Morrison, who had fixed a sign with the surname over the door. When the lodge was sold, Sam called me: would I like the sign? It was a kind thought; I'd have felt ungracious saying no. He took it down, wrapped it up and put it in the post – at no small effort and expense, I imagine, since the sign was an awkward shape and measured two feet across. I put the sign over a wooden shed in the garden and thought of Sam whenever I passed it: the heavy brow, the pent-up violence, the kindness.

And Josie? Had she read the book? I knew Beaty wouldn't have drawn it to her attention. And that she was busy raising two small children. And that any time she might have free for reading wouldn't be given to books like mine. She had good friends and neighbours in the village where she lived and her diabetes was under control since she'd been given an insulin pump, which saved her having to inject herself. In short, things were going well for her. I rather hoped she *hadn't* read the book, in case – despite my changing her name and other identifying details – she recognised herself and it upset her.

When she wrote to tell me that Beaty had died, I might have seized the moment – called her up, reminisced a little then steeled myself to put the question: 'Do you think we're related?' But it didn't occur to me. I was no longer desperate to know. I'd come to accept I never would know. I already had a sister. One was enough.

21

At some point in the mid-90s, Gill's eyesight, already poor, got dramatically worse. As she told it, the change happened overnight. At 1 a.m. she laid a large-print library book on her bedside table and turned out the light; at 7 a.m. she woke with a map of Australia in front of her eyes, a landmass obscuring all but the edges of her vision. Her two eye conditions (night blindness and retinitis pigmentosa) had seemingly stabilised, until this improbably abrupt deterioration – from light to darkness during the hours between darkness and light. She could no longer see anything directly in front of her, only faint shapes across a room. She consoled herself that she could still see *something* – including, most importantly, her children – even if 'see' meant dimly perceive not clearly make out. The horror was the prospect of further deterioration. And of the speed at which that might happen. She came to dread going to bed at night, fearing she might wake to total blackness.

To begin with, she played down the extent of her 'handicap' – even now I can imagine her flinching at that word. All she'd own up to was peripheral vision. Peripheral vision sounded better than having to say she was partially sighted. Only later, when she was officially registered as a blind person, did she acknowledge how bad things were – how from seeing very little she now saw almost nothing at all.

After Mum's death, she and Wynn sold Arley House and moved into Windyridge. She knew the layout from all the time she'd spent there with Mum and Dad or, later, on her own. Even when less than sober, she moved around the rooms so confidently that it was hard – impossible – to believe she couldn't see. No one said 'she's putting it on' but it occasionally crossed their minds. One year it crossed the minds of the DSS, or DWP as it became, which disputed the extent of her sight problem and proposed to reduce her state benefit. The letter from her eye consultant wasn't enough to dissuade them. Nor was I allowed to testify on her behalf. We had to enlist the help of the RNIB to fight her case; a feisty worker called Sharon came up from London and spoke for Gill at the hearing in Leeds. Thanks to Sharon, Gill won her appeal.

Even Sharon, watching Gill nimbly negotiating her kitchen cupboards, might have questioned the accuracy of the medical evidence. It was only when she left the house, with increasing reluctance, that her dependency became apparent. She would cling tightly to your arm, and move her feet warily over the ground, in case of obstacles. ('Hidden obstacles' I was going to write, but to Gill everything was hidden.) She'd ask you where she was standing and what she was looking at. Once Kathy and I took her to Boundary Mill, in Colne, to buy her a Christmas present. She wanted a pink blouse, in silk or cotton, and as she stood by the racks would take the material between her fingers, feeling the texture, checking the buttons, testing the length of the sleeves, absorbing the design in her head. She asked us to describe the colour. I found it a challenge. Flamingo, peach, fuchsia, coral? The names for different shades of pink didn't spring to mind. Kathy was better at it. Eventually we found a blouse that felt all right to Gill and looked all right to us, and out we went, triumphant, with her on my arm.

Sometimes I'd peer hard into her eyes as though by doing so I'd see what was wrong with them. They weren't bloodshot or yellow, just glazed over – the eyes not only unseeing but themselves a blind spot or black hole, not to be fathomed.

Unseeing. Yet she saw so much – heard, sensed, understood what was going on around her.

Over time she developed a further condition, nystagmus, which causes the eyes to make involuntary, repetitive movements. They would dance from side to side, unable to settle, as though she was watching a tennis rally at Wimbledon, back and forth, back and forth. Observing her was like reading small print in a moving car; it made you nauseous. She'd sometimes complain of feeling dizzy herself, or of losing her sense of balance. I tried researching nystagmus, to see if it had developed from her previous conditions, but it seemed not. She'd just been unlucky, the victim of a malicious conjunction. Nystagmus often begins in childhood, but she'd had late onset. I noted down the causes, underlining the last: a stroke, multiple sclerosis, diabetic neuropathy, head injuries, trauma, certain drugs, excessive alcohol. Now when I looked in Gill's eyes they weren't glazed over so much as manic, febrile, all over the place.

From time to time, newspapers would carry some piece about a breakthrough in the cure of eye conditions previously considered incurable. After reading it I'd call her up, and sometimes she'd discuss it with her optician. But she was never suitable for treatment. One of her eye conditions, so she said, meant the optic nerves at the back of the retina had atrophied or shrivelled up – and nothing could restore them. The perfect storm affecting her vision meant that a cure, or even alleviation, was impossible.

Too late for it to be helpful, I began reading books about blindness, as if to enter her world or at least form an idea of it – to see what she saw or to share her not-seeing. Wearing a blindfold gave a sense of sensory deprivation but nothing of the emotional and psychological impact. A blindfold could always come off.

I read Helen Keller, who became both blind and deaf as an infant, and whose tone was relentlessly upbeat: 'It is not for me to say whether we see best with the hand or the eye. I only know that the world I see with my fingers is alive . . . Touch brings the blind many sweet certainties which our more fortunate fellows miss, because their sense of touch is uncultivated.'

I read Ved Mehta, who went blind after having meningitis at the age of four and who describes how hearing sounds told him what was happening around him – how if his mother 'had neglected to wash her hair, it crackled' and how 'her voice sounded one way when she was smiling, another way when she was pouting, and still another way when she was scowling'.

I read Candia McWilliam, who was for a time both blind and alcoholic, and whose memoir *What to Look for in Winter* describes her experience of blepharospasm, a condition where the eyelids refuse to open ('my eyes work quite well but my brain has decided that they must be shut'). She was cured eventually but not before a rude, psychologically inclined specialist ventured that she had 'taken refuge in blindness' because her life was such a mess that she couldn't face it.

I read John M. Hull's *Touching the Rock: An Experience of Blindness*, which compares blindness to 'a huge vacuum cleaner which comes down upon your life, sucking almost everything away. Your past memories, your interests, your perception of time and how you will spend it, place itself, even the world, everything is sucked out. Your consciousness is evacuated, and you are left to reconstruct it.'

I read *On Blindness*, a published exchange of letters between the philosophers Bryan Magee and Martin Milligan (the latter lost his sight to retinal cancer at the age of eighteen months).

I read *Planet of the Blind* and *Eavesdropping* by Stephen Kuusisto, who has been partially sighted from birth, suffers from nystagmus ('my eyes . . . went in all directions like the seeds of thistles'), and describes blindness 'not as an either/or condition' but as 'a series of veils: I stare at the world through smeared and broken windowpanes . . . It's like living inside an immense abstract painting.'

I also read fiction about blindness. There's H. G. Wells's story 'The Country of the Blind', for instance, in which a man called Nunez falls from the mountains into a remote valley where blindness has been passed down through fourteen generations, to the point where none of the inhabitants understand the concept of sight; when Nunez, a kind of coloniser among hapless natives, tries to explain it to them, they dismiss him as idiotic, childish, destructive and mad. The unbridgeable gap between seeing and unseeing is also a theme of José Saramago's great novel *Blindness*, though its real subject is the consequences of a coronavirus-like pandemic: as infection spreads, and vast numbers of people go blind, civilisation collapses and squalor, hunger and violence ensue. The novel is a primarily political allegory but also includes some telling aphorisms about sight loss.

No matter how interesting or well written these books were, my literature review did little to help me understand Gill. There was no consensus, no template. Those who wrote about their experiences spoke only for themselves. Some, like Ved Mehta, dismissed efforts like mine as a waste of time: 'People who can see . . . have an elemental fear associated with the loss of sight that they cannot easily overcome . . . The sighted go from one extreme to the other – from assuming that the blind are virtually cut off from all perception to endowing them with extrasensory perception.'

Still, some accounts seemed more pertinent to Gill's case than others. John Hull was especially astute in conveying how going blind can make you feel like a non-person:

> Because I cannot see, I cannot be seen. I can be ignored, treated as if I did not exist, spoken about in the third person . . . Being invisible to others, I become invisible to myself. I lack self-knowledge. I become unconscious . . .
>
> Occasionally I feel depressed and this is worst when I am frustrated in playing with the children. I feel as if I have become nothing . . . unable to survey, to admire, or exercise jurisdiction of discrimination. I have a strange feeling of being dead. My response is to go even further inwards, into a deeper deadness. I sink into quietness and passivity . . . I become the cipher my blindness tells me I am.
>
> In these states of depression I feel as if I am on the borders of conscious life . . . as if I want to stop thinking, stop experiencing.

I have a strange feeling of being dead. That hit home. Was Gill's blindness a rehearsal for mortality, a kind of death-come-early? A character in Saramago's novel says something similar: 'This must be what it means to be a ghost, being certain that life exists, because your four senses say so, but unable to see it . . . It's like a cemetery'. Being a mum gave Gill reasons to keep going. But her children were growing up and had less need of her. She'd always known about 'states of depression'. But this other know-ledge was new – how lack of vision made her invisible.

Stephen Kuusisto was also instructive, in relating how desperately some blind people hide their blindness: 'O Lord, let me never be seen with a white cane . . . Let no one find me out! This is my lacerating tune.' His denial went on for thirty years, and only changed when he went to study in Iowa, where a blind man called Barry urged him to stop pretending: 'You're afraid to be seen as a disabled person even though you have a huge vision impairment. I can understand that. All disabled people can. Hell, FDR had an agreement with the press that they wouldn't photograph him in his wheelchair. He thought disa-bility would screw up his image as a strong leader.' Using a cane came as a huge relief to Kuusisto: 'I'm walking in safety at last. The cane makes a pleasant *tacka-tacka*. I kind of like it.'

Gill had no such conversion. She had a white stick and we encouraged her to use it but she hardly ever did. Her great dread was to be noticed – to be categorised, patronised, marked out.

After discovering the advantages of a cane, Stephen Kuusisto went on to get a guide dog called Corky, who transformed his life.

Why did Gill not get a guide dog? She loved dogs and had grown up with Labradors, the most popular guide dog breed. There'd have been weeks of training. It wouldn't have been easy. Still, that wasn't the reason she avoided it. In her mind, a guide dog would have been as much a stigma as a cane.

She was sparing with aids around the house. Every Christmas or birthday, I'd consult the RNIB's online shop. There were magnifiers, big-button phones, scales that spoke your weight, audible liquid level indicators, vibrating clocks, adjustable bread slicers, tactile measuring jugs, talking kitchen scales, ratchet tin openers, daylight floor lamps, anti-spill suction mugs, automatic needle-threaders and tactile dominoes with raised spots. I'd read out various items to her over the phone and she'd occasionally settle on something. But mostly she rejected all options. She had no need of aids, she said, preferring to muddle through.

Unlike me, an occasional visitor, Louise and Liam lived with Gill's blindness on a daily basis. They were so used to it, they almost ceased to notice – which is what she wanted, for everyone to carry on as normal; as if being blind and having to feel your way around the house *was* normal. But sometimes her condition proved unignorable. Decorating the living room one Christmas, she blew up three balloons, two round, one long, and hung them up together. Seeing the phallic shape they made, Louise and Liam started giggling. 'What's wrong with you?' she said, affronted. 'I'm just putting up bloody balloons.' They were laughing too much to explain at first. Even when they did, she was still cross with them. Only later did her sense of humour return. It wasn't her they'd been laughing at. That was all right then.

She showed no interest in learning braille or in using a computer. When her sight became too poor even for large-print books, she turned to audiobooks. I signed her up for a loan scheme with the RNIB, but something went wrong, after which I bought her CDs instead. Romantic novels were her favourite. She also liked 'classics', meaning books she'd read in childhood. The aural versions were better than nothing, but only just: as Candia McWilliam puts it, 'I have listened to books. This is very far from reading them.'

*

206

Gill was watchful – through her ears.
She observed – aurally.
She bore witness – without using her eyes.

Her memory was extraordinary. For instance, after Mum died, when we were discussing who to call with news of her death, she reeled off the eleven-digit phone numbers of various friends – even one who was staying in Bath and had a temporary phone number which Gill can't have called more than twice. Was this some internal memorising process to compensate for lack of sight? Or was it that Gill had always been (as she said herself) the elephant in the family: archivist, memorialist, dutiful keeper of names, dates and numbers? The same instinct to preserve made her hang on to family heirlooms (toys, paintings and bric-a-brac) even though she couldn't see them. She found order and comfort through meticulous recall of the past.*

The blind are sometimes approached by people offering to pray for them. With no cane Gill was a less obvious target than some. And she rarely went out alone. Still, she'd have responded politely if accosted. She didn't believe that prayer could cure her but there was no call to be rude. The people who *did* annoy

---

* Charles Lamb on his sister Mary: 'Her memory is unusually strong; and from ages past, if we may call the earliest records of our poor life, she fetches thousands of names and things that never would have dawned on me again, and thousands from the ten years she lived before me. What took place from early girlhood to her coming of age principally lives again (every important thing and every trifle) in her brain with the vividness of real presence. For twelve hours incessantly she will pour out without intermission all her past life, forgetting nothing, pouring out name after name . . .'

her were those – whether disability activists or religious hard-liners – who urged her to see blindness as a gift. You what? This wasn't a gift she'd asked for. Nor could she regift it. Just fuck off.

The more she drank to forget about her poor vision, the poorer it became. She was blind and often blind drunk. 'She's unwell,' Liam or Louise would say when I phoned, covering for her but not really, since they knew I knew what they meant. 'She's out of it,' my parents used to say in earlier years, though she was really more in than out – cocooned in a world of woozy comfort, unlike the unkind and difficult outer world she had to negotiate with failing sight.

The born-blind are more accepting of their condition than the gone-blind: they don't know what they've lost. Over time, Gill became more accepting, too. I don't remember her being angry. And only when she'd drunk too much was she self-pitying. 'Who'd want a blind woman like me?'

For the most part, Wynn did still want her. She was a great mum, for a start. The prim and stuffy might think her incapable, but she was brilliant with Liam and Louise – not a pushy tiger mother but a mum who made them feel supported, listened to, guided, adored. She was a good mate, too: he'd stood by her through some difficult times not just for the kids' sake but for himself. When sober, Gill was nice to be around, compliant and companionable. But her binges were getting worse. He felt ground down by them. He'd a terror of the kids coming home one day and finding her dead. All the more reason for him to stick it out, of course. But it was exhausting.

*

For a time, he had a girlfriend. Young as she was, barely a couple of years older than Louise, Wynn was a kind of father figure to her, not an abusive one like her dad had been but somebody she could turn to when feeling low. That was how they first got talking in the pub, she pouring out her problems to him. She had an on-off relationship with a violent boyfriend and there were gaps Wynn was invited to fill. He admired her spirit; what she lacked in beauty, she made up for in zest. She was reckless, like Gill, but young-reckless not drunk-reckless. Some nights he didn't come home. He'd been given use of a caravan near Gisburn and the girlfriend would join him.

Late one night, pushing his luck, he smuggled her into the house; he'd created a teenage games room for Liam and Louise, and with Gill asleep or 'out of it' the risk of her finding them there seemed minimal. But Gill woke up, walked in and was furious: screamed, blasphemed, ordered him to take his dirty slut and get the hell out. Mum might have tolerated her husband having an affair under her nose but she, Gill, wouldn't stand for it. Did he think because she was blind that she couldn't see what was going on? That she was a doormat? That she deserved to be treated like shit?

The girlfriend didn't appear at Windyridge again.

My visits home became less frequent after Mum died. I would aim to see Gill if I was up in Yorkshire but any plan was likely to be scuppered. Typical was a trip to Lumb Bank, for an overnight stay at the Arvon Centre. We spoke on the phone several times to finalise details. As arranged, Wynn was waiting in the car at Keighley station. As not arranged, he was on his own. Gill had hit the bottle the night before, as she often did when looking forward to meeting friends or family.

We drove to Hebden Bridge and sat in a pub before he dropped me at the lane-end to Lumb Bank. As I walked towards it, I thought how habituated I'd become to Gill's alcoholism. The normalising of the unimaginable. The little girl with curly hair I used to run around the garden with was unable, at forty-eight, to meet me, because she was pissed out of her head.

Whether Wynn had given up the girlfriend made no difference to Gill. She'd other long-standing grudges and resented his efforts to control her – if she wanted to drink herself to death, what was that to do with him? When drunk, she saw him as a monster; when sober, as the cold-hearted witness to her woes. Either way, her mind was made up. Low though she'd sunk, she took the high ground. As the injured party, she wanted out.

It wasn't just his infidelity. Even before that she'd stopped loving him, she said, and thought she would be better off living on her own. It might *look* as if they got on. But she'd had enough of him. She wanted a divorce.

Divorce didn't appeal to Wynn. He was fond of Windyridge and took pride in looking after the place, doing repairs, cutting the grass, tinkering with his motorbike in the barn. He was fond of Gill, too, when she was herself, the woman he'd married not the one catatonic on the sofa. The kids were old enough for divorce not to be traumatic and were remarkably successful and resilient: Louise, initially reluctant to go to university, went on to graduate with a first, and Liam (a talented musician as well as a film student) looked set for a career in the arts. Still, no one but Gill was keen on the idea of divorce. A lawyer would cost money. Moreover, even at his most grumpy and disaffected, Wynn was protective of Gill. Who would look after her when they separated?

*

When Wynn accepted that Gill couldn't be dissuaded, after receiving a letter from her solicitor, he belatedly hired his own solicitor, who negotiated a better deal for him. Under its terms, she agreed to pay him £140,000 as his half-share of the house. She questioned the justice of this: it had been her parents' house and the ownership was now in her name. But he'd helped to build the place and had looked after it ever since. And he was understanding when she said she couldn't afford to pay him in full. The deal was that he'd get half the money straight away and the other half in seven years' time.

Of the £70,000, he spent £55,000* on a camper van (a Hymer, like the one Mum and Dad had owned), less to travel than to live in; he couldn't afford a house or flat and didn't want to rent. Occasionally, now the kids were no longer at home, he'd head off somewhere (mostly to a campsite in the Lakes) but for local excursions he used his car or motorbike, leaving the Hymer in the drive outside Gill's house. Soon it became a fixture; though divorced from her, he was living just feet away. From time to time she'd complain: why couldn't he park it somewhere else? Why should she have to put up with an eyesore? But she couldn't see the eyesore, and it was useful to have Wynn close at hand. For his part, it meant he could keep an eye on Gill. Every morning he'd come in and make them both tea.

After a while, she began to return his visits; if something needed doing, she'd go out to his camper van and ask for help. To make it easier, he bought a long blue rope and strung it from the handle on the side-door of his Hymer to the knob on the front door of her house. Like someone negotiating an improvised bamboo bridge across a torrent, she would hold the rope

---

*Or so Gill told me. Wynn said it was £32,000.

while tentatively edging across the ten feet of driveway that divided them.

On the face of it, they got on better than when they'd been married. If I came to visit, and Gill wasn't bingeing, he would pick me up from Skipton station and drive to the house, where she would offer me lunch. And if I was up for work of some kind, in Ilkley or Halifax, he would drive her over, and we'd have a meal or coffee together. Their keynote was an affectionate, mock-griping banter.

I knew that some of this was for show – that once we parted, there'd be tensions again; that they were no less enmeshed than before; that they brought out each other's faults – her dependency, his impatience; her jealousy, his insensitivity. Both felt betrayed, Gill because she didn't feel loved, Wynn because she'd become unlovable. But they couldn't escape each other. They'd divorced but were inseparable. For good or ill, the rope between them still held.

22

One Saturday, eleven years after my book about Dad came out, Josie phoned. I was in the kitchen, clearing up after breakfast. We'd not spoken since Mum's funeral but I recognised her voice at once: high-octave and high-strung, but eager to sound calm and sociable, as if jollying herself out of strong emotion. Did I have a minute to talk, she wondered. She'd just got round to reading my memoir.

I swallowed hard, expecting trouble. Let me turn the radio down, I said.

You've changed the name, she said, but I'm Josephine, aren't I?

It was hard to judge her tone. Indignation? Affront?

Yes, I said, Josephine's you. I expect you're angry with me.

Angry? she said. No. I've always had the same suspicions. I remember looking at Uncle Arthur's ribcage, when I was about seven, and thinking how big it was and how it looked just like mine. I once asked Mum if I was his. She denied it. And denied it again before she died. Dad denies it, too. But I've been wondering about a DNA test. What do you think? Not that I'd tell Dad. It might upset him. But I'd like to know.

Josie followed the phone call with a letter, saying she was grateful to have 'shared my lifelong thoughts and suspicions. I have to admit I have an awful lot of unhappy memories from when I lived with Mum and Dad. There were so, *so* many arguments and even at the best of times there was always tension between them – certainly not a relaxed or fun atmosphere to be growing up in.' Not that she didn't love them: she felt closer to Beaty once she had children of her own, she said, and closer to Sam after Beaty died. 'I've learnt a lot more about them both (warts 'n' all) so can understand and sympathise with both sides of their volatile relationship. In the end it was obvious how much they loved each other – it's so very sad that they couldn't have worked things out years and years ago. Their marriage was peppered with sadness for nearly 46 years.'

As to a DNA test, her GP had warned her how expensive it would be and 'tried to persuade me to wait another five years or so when it could be more easily available via the NHS.' All the same, she was keen to give it a go: 'In my heart I feel I already know the answer, but the uncertainties do torment my emotions and have plagued me all my life.'

Spurred on, I made enquiries. Though Dad was dead, which made the process more complex, tissue samples would establish whether we were related. I wrote to Josie offering to go halves on the £400 fee, if she was sure she wanted to proceed; she wrote back with a £200 cheque, saying yes, she was sure, she really did want to know. The Institute of Cell and Molecular Science Centre for Haematology, at St Bart's Hospital in London, instructed us how to go about it. I went to my GP and opened wide while she scraped tissue from the inside of my cheek, just as I'd recently seen happen with Saddam Hussein after his capture. My DNA samples, and Josie's, went off to Bart's – testing would take five to ten days to complete, we were told, after which a report would be sent to us by first-class post. A letter came a month later, apologising for the delay – initial results suggested that we were five times more likely than not to be related, but they were now carrying out further tests, to arrive at a more conclusive result. In time a second letter came, with results which showed that it was *fifteen* times more likely than not. A high ratio; there could be no real doubt.

It's odd, Josie said, when she called a few days later, but I don't feel any different. At some level I've always known. Yes, there's scientific proof now but it's as if the emotional proof has always been there.

It was true. I felt the same. There was a sense of anti-climax, though we agreed that if we'd been told we *weren't* related that would have been disappointing. So there we were, officially half-siblings at last. We didn't know what to do with that knowledge or how it might change things, but it felt good, an enlargement of possibility, one more person in the world to feel a special kinship with, though the kinship had to stay secret, because of Sam.

I said nothing to Gill, either. I wasn't sure how she would react. It would have to be in person, when the time felt right. For now I kept the knowledge to myself, like a smooth pebble I could rub for comfort. Mum and Dad might be dead but the family felt less depleted now.

I had all my sisters with me. Well, both of them.

Eight months later, on a cold day in early January, a young woman called from my publishers. 'It's a bit odd,' she said. 'A PC Lockhart just phoned, wanting to get in touch with you. He said it was something to do with a missing person. A woman. Someone in your family but perhaps not immediate family – I couldn't make it out. Here's the number. He said to call him as soon as poss.' I put the phone down with a sense of dread and, unwilled, a flicker of excitement. My first thought was Gill: could it be her? But when I'd spoken to her a few days before she'd seemed fine. Besides, Gill *was* immediate family. My second thought was Josie. Perhaps to PC Lockhart a half-sibling didn't count as immediate family. But how would he know about her being my half-sister? Even we hadn't known till recently. And aside from our partners, no one else had been told.

I remember thinking all this as I sat by the living-room window and looked out at the frost-glazed lawn. A magpie flew down and perched on the empty bird-feeder. Grey mist hung in the trees.

Kathy came into the room. Who was that?

I explained about the message, playing for time – 'collecting myself' – before I made the phone call.

It's not something to do with Kela? she said.

Kela, my cousin, just sixty-one, had died suddenly a few days before. Suddenly but not unexpectedly: she'd been frail for some time. No one really knew what the problem was – whether all those heavy childhood doses of cortisone, to cure her skin problems, had blasted her internal organs, or whether her spirit had weakened in the wake of so many family deaths: her granny's, her mother's, her stepfather's, my parents' (to whom she'd been close), and behind all these, way back in 1943, three weeks before her birth, the father she'd never known, an RAF pilot, shot down over France. All these deaths, and then her own, just days ago – I too felt the weight of them, in the living room.

Yes, Kela was now a missing person. But the call couldn't be about her. Had I been mistaken for someone else? Could whoever it was be a victim of the recent tsunami in south-east Asia – one of the holidaymakers swept away? Or a casualty of the storms that had been ravaging Britain? If I phoned PC

Lockhart, he'd tell me straight away. But I sat in suspense for a few minutes more. Why rush? Whatever the news, it was bound to be bad.

Finally – in reality it was just five minutes, but hours seemed to have passed – I dialled the number. PC Lockhart thanked me for getting in touch, and said he didn't want to alarm me, but Josie had been missing for twenty-eight hours. She had left home the previous day after packing her two children off to school; neighbours saw her get in the car with just a coat over a nightie, and her mobile phone had been switched off ever since. I was one of several people on a list with whom it was thought, or hoped, she might have been in touch.

I'm sorry, I said; no, I haven't heard from her.

That's what we expected, PC Lockhart said. No one else has heard from her either, but if she gets in touch will you please let me know at once – or let her husband know. It's he who gave us your name, by the way. He said you and his wife are related in some way.

Yes, I said, that's true.

Putting the phone down, I remembered the call Josie had made back in November. Her husband, she'd told me, was in love with another woman. A doctor, she added, just like your mum and dad – *our* dad. Ironic, eh? Josie had begun looking for work, in case her husband left home and she had to support herself, but how could she get a job when she'd lost the ability to smile, socialise, *perform*? She spoke in a voice – high, light, almost giggly – that belied her sadness. But there was a note of desperation in it, too. I urged her to hang in there – lots of people had affairs, no one knew that more than we two did, but that didn't mean they'd stopped loving their partners or that their marriages were over, and if her husband was still living at home, which he was, and planning to spend Christmas with her, maybe things weren't as bleak as they looked. Whatever happens, I said, you'll be all right. It was a bland and avuncular thing to say, hollow cheer to a miserable and demoralised woman, I knew that even as I said it, but by the time we ended the call she did seem brighter.

I'd meant to phone her before Christmas but then school broke up and I knew it would be awkward – how could she talk in front of her kids? A lame excuse, it seemed to me now, after what I'd just been told.

I called Josie's husband the next day. There was still no news, he said, but the police were treating her disappearance as high-risk, since she was diabetic, and there'd been a couple of suspicious 'accidents' with her insulin pump in recent weeks. He speculated about the places she might have fled to – the Yorkshire Dales, where we both grew up; Cornwall, where they'd spent holidays; Scotland, where Sam lived. Meanwhile the police had been at the house all day, taking statements and combing the house and garden, as though he were a murderer and had hidden the body.

I gave the police your name because of the DNA tests, he said. I hope you don't mind.

Of course not, I said.

Sam still doesn't know about them, he added.

No, I said, I realise that.

Now I wondered if the DNA tests might have affected Josie's state of mind. I dug out a letter she'd written, back in the spring, the one confirming she'd like to go ahead with the tests. What was forgiving in the letter – forgiving of me now, as I read it, wired with anxiety – was its upbeatness, the sheer *normality*, the sense of her being surrounded by good friends. 'I love my life,' it said. On the other hand, in retrospect, weren't there certain alarm signals in the letter, the passing reference to medical problems ('I suffer from autoimmune/endocrine disorders – have done for years') and something over-determinedly cheerful in her tone, a sort of whistling in the dark? Now she'd gone missing I berated myself for not phoning back before Christmas and, worse, for agreeing to the DNA tests. She'd hoped they would provide a sense of belonging or closure but perhaps they had made things worse. Her birth father hadn't acknowledged her as his. She'd been brought up on a lie. The DNA result was proof of that. But what if she'd wanted more than she thought? Not just truth but redress?

Something else would have added to my worries if I'd known about it at the time. After he retired from Yorkshire Water and was divorced from Gill, Wynn briefly worked behind the bar of the Royal Oak in Skipton. And one day that spring, Josie walked in. Skipton was a long way from home for her and he was struck by how lost she seemed. Why had she come, he wondered – out of nostalgia or on some kind of quest? The pub was busy, which left him no time to talk to her and next thing she was gone. Later, Liam arrived. He was taking GCSE exams at the time and sometimes called in afterwards to tell his dad how he'd got on. That dated Josie's visit to May or June. A couple of months after the DNA results.

Had the knowledge that Dad was her birth father destabilised her? Her husband said not: he brought it up when we spoke on the phone, saying the results had helped by ending decades of uncertainty. No doubt her fear that her husband would leave her was a bigger factor. I couldn't raise that with him; he didn't know I knew; and I didn't know the facts – only that Josie had told me he was having the kind of relationship that had produced her.

Anxious though I was, I consoled myself that Josie loved her life too much to leave it. She had her own home; two children; good friends; and was in close touch with her dad (the one who'd raised her). Why lose all that?

There was no sign of Josie in the press next day. The big story was of a student who had gone missing in the early hours of New Year's Day, after a party in Cambridge; her identical twin had been helping the search by posing in similar clothes, hoping to jog someone's memory. Two other people had gone missing in Cumbria, after severe storms and floods – it was feared they'd been swept away in a swollen river. A search for a man lost in the River Aire had been called off. A man in his sixties was killed when a barn blew down on his caravan. A pregnant thirty-one-year-old mother of five had been stabbed to death. Grim stuff – but nothing compared to the tsunami that had struck Sri Lanka and Indonesia on Boxing Day, with thousands dead and missing.

I scanned the news obsessively over the next few days. The case of the missing student ended as badly as feared: a body was found in woodland and the soldier wanted for questioning jumped to his death from a seventh-floor window. If Josie had still been missing, such stories would have been ominous. But by then the time for omens had passed. I already knew the worst.

PC Lockhart was sorry to be the one to tell me. And sorry – since he'd been off duty – that I hadn't been informed the day before.

When Josie had left her house, she'd driven straight to a hotel less than half an hour away and taken a room there. When a cleaner came in next morning and saw two feet at the end of the bed, she assumed the person was asleep and shouldn't be disturbed. Perhaps Josie was alive then, that wouldn't be clear until the inquest, but more likely she'd taken an overdose, or tampered with her insulin pump, and had already been dead for several hours. In any case, by the time the cleaner returned the next day, the body was cold. Two children had lost their mum. A husband had lost his wife. And (a small matter in comparison) I had lost the half-sister I'd only discovered *was* my half-sister eight months before.

She'd been half-aunt to my children, I realised. And I was – still – half-uncle to hers.

The weather had been bitter the day she left her house and continued to be: heavy snowfalls were predicted. I thought of Sylvia Plath taking her life in the cold February of 1963 – an errant husband, two small children, despair. And I thought of Primo Levi, who'd survived the horrors of Auschwitz but then killed himself decades later. Josie had coped with the threat that her son might die of cancer, had 'been there for him', and experienced the joy and relief of knowing he was OK – only to die in despair a few years later. The parallels didn't amount to much. And when Josie went to that hotel she can't have been in her right mind. But the act was calculated even if irrational. Premeditation and illogicality are compatible. To quote Voltaire, 'Generally one does not kill oneself in a rush of reasonableness.'

Would it have happened if her mum had been alive? Or if Dad – my, her, *our* dad – had been? If she'd called him, would he have done more to help than I did? Diagnosed the problem and kept her going, as he had when she'd been low before?* Or

---

*On an old tape recording I turned up the other day, made when she was about five, she pretends to be dead, after a baddie has shot her with a gun, then tells me she's alive again because 'Dr Morrison came and made me better'.

was she too set on ending her life? Did she think her husband and the kids would have a better life with her (depressed and useless) out of the way? 'I might as well top myself: everyone will be better off without me,' Gill sometimes said, in her cups.*
Gill had stuck it out but the insulin pump was an exit route for Josie. It was like turning up the volume till your hearing goes, with no pain involved, as there would be with guns, razors, pills, ropes, fires or leaps from high buildings. Diabetics – one study suggests – are twice as likely to kill themselves as the rest of us. In the weeks before, Josie had flirted with death; this time she gave herself completely. She booked that hotel room because it was private and she wouldn't be disturbed – not till it was too late.

'An act like this is prepared within the silence of the heart, as is a great work of art.' (Camus, *The Myth of Sisyphus*)

A couple of years after Josie died, two of her friends got in touch with me. She had told them we were related and they wanted me to know how hard they'd tried to keep her alive. She was much loved, they said, and had many friends (her husband told me the same: that compared to his address book hers was like the *Yellow Pages*). But in the autumn before she died she made no secret of her despair. Several mums in the village formed a kind of protective circle round her. Someone would phone or call in or take her out, to alleviate the risk of her 'doing something stupid' while alone. In the run-up to Christmas, it had worked well, and when the kids finished school, and her husband

---

*Virginia Woolf's suicide note to Leonard: 'I know that I shall never get over this: & I am wasting your life . . . Nothing anyone says can persuade me. You can work, & you will be much better without me.'

was off work during the holidays, they'd relaxed a little, knowing she'd be OK. They were due to resume their safeguarding once the kids went back to school; the aim was to enlist professional help and see her through to spring, by which time she'd surely feel better. But she had outwitted them. The moment the kids went off to school that first morning of the new term, she left the house and drove away.

They made no secret of their anger with her husband, who had since, they said, married the woman with whom he'd been involved. The word blame didn't come up – they just wanted to set the record straight, they said – but it hovered there. Holding him responsible made them feel less guilty. But none of us was responsible. Only Josie. The choice had been hers. Or the part of her that wanted to die.

'No amount of love from other people – and there was a lot – could help . . . Nothing alive and warm could make its way through my carapace. I knew my life to be a shambles and I believed – incontestably – that my family, friends, and patients would be better off without me. There wasn't much of me left anymore, anyway, and I thought my death would free up the wasted energies and well-meant efforts that were being spent on a fool's errand.' (Kay Redfield Jamison, *Night Falls Fast*)

I drove Gill to the funeral, our second in barely a week: first Kela, now Josie, one in her early sixties, the other in her mid-forties. It was a long way, through sleet, and we talked about Josie as I drove – the holidays she'd joined us on, her smile, the blonde curls she'd had, like Gill's. I'd told Gill about the DNA results a few days earlier. She hadn't reacted much then and didn't now.

Did you never feel sidelined? I asked.

Why sidelined?

Dad seemed to delight in Josie more than in us, I said (though really by 'us' I meant 'you' – I'd been a boy, not to be delighted in but toughened up).

Did he? I never noticed, Gill said.

And it never occurred to you that Josie was our half-sister?

No.

Not till I told you?

No.

All these years I'd been angry with Dad on Gill's behalf. I might have blamed Beaty, as the cuckoo who'd invaded the nest and laid an egg there. But it was him I held to account. A waste, that now seemed, if Gill hadn't even noticed. I sneaked a look at her face as I drove: was she lying, in pious memory of Dad? Had she repressed the memory of his face lighting up whenever he saw Josie? Or was it me whose memory was false?

I remember Beaty being kind to us, Gill said. She sometimes looked after us or took us out places when Mum and Dad were working – remember when she drove us to Morecambe?

Yes, I said, not adding that I remembered Beaty snapping at me that day and how indignant I felt – I wasn't her child; only parents and teachers were allowed to be cross with me.

And remember how Dad drew up plans for Beaty and Sam to carry out refurbishments at the pub? And virtually acted as foreman when the work began? And probably paid for half of it?

It made sense of course. His daughter was growing up there and he wanted her to live in a nice place.

And that time Josie came to Abersoch in her teens, she said, you probably weren't there, but we'd been looking forward to spending time with Nicola and Sally [two sisters they were friends with], but they both had boyfriends and couldn't meet up. It really upset Josie.

It must have upset Gill, too, but her sympathies were with Josie. This wasn't the tone of someone who held grudges. Or who felt that Josie had displaced her. Perhaps I'd imagined it all.

It took us a while to find the village. Even to those who knew it the place must have looked unfamiliar, its paths and verges whitened by fresh snow. The air was dark, though it was barely afternoon. I parked down the hill from the church, in the first space I could find – we were early but the lane was already packed with cars. I took Gill's arm; I might have anyway, because the ground was slippery, but there was no choice: not only was she blind but in recent years she'd developed back problems and a lopsided gait; her torso was bent and tilted to one side – her GP, she told me (and they must have had a good relationship for her GP to get away with it), called her 'Mrs Banana'. Frost glittered on the toecaps of my black shoes. We took a place at the back of the church, feeling like gatecrashers; the mystery mourners whose right to be there was known only to Josie's husband. But no one was looking. All heads were bowed, all eyes averted. The coffin was already standing there, under yellow flowers. The scent was familiar: whitewash, candle smoke, damp flagstones. But the age of the mourners was not. Only Sam and his new partner – he heavy on a stick, she holding his free arm – were over sixty. Most there were in their forties, Josie's age. And there were children, friends of Josie's children.

We're here to say goodbye to our dear departed sister, the vicar said, wresting the word 'sister' from Gill and me. He read out tributes from friends: they spoke of Josie's warmth, 'bubbliness', sense of humour, beautiful blue eyes, and how she lit up a room when she entered. Routine funereal hagiography perhaps but it was true that Josie had had an excess of vitality, till her highs gave way to lows. From tact or an old taboo (funerals for those who take their own lives used to be prohibited in Christian churches) or because children were present, nothing was said about the manner of her death. The service was short: after the eulogies came prayers, one of them about the man who, looking back on his life, sees two sets of footprints in the sand, his and God's, except for stretches where he sees only one set. Why did you abandon me in my hour of need? he accuses God; I didn't, God replies, those were the points when I was carrying you. It was a parable Josie knew from Beaty, who'd once sent me a postcard with it printed on the front. Beaty had faith. Perhaps Josie did too. I didn't, never more so than that afternoon. When Josie felt abandoned, God hadn't carried her to safety.

After the final hymn, 'You Make Me Feel Brand New' by Simply Red was played, a favourite of Josie's, the brand-newness of whose absence was dreadful. There weren't the sighs you hear at some funerals (*what a mercy that's done with*) but gasps and sobs. Gill and I stayed behind in our pew while the chief mourners filed out, Sam among them, who gave us the briefest of nods, whose face I searched for evidence that our presence was a surprise to him, unpleasant or otherwise, but which revealed nothing beyond weariness – his daughter might have left this world ahead of him but it wouldn't be long before he joined her, for what greater grief is there than for the child you raised to predecease you and what appeasement other than to follow her.

Sam didn't go back to Josie's house. I did, at her husband's invitation, steering Gill across the snow and ice into the living room, where Josie's kids, through the worst (or the worst that day), settled down to a game of Uno: ordinariness reasserting itself, or trying to. We didn't stay long. It felt intrusive. We weren't family, only half-family, and that a secret.

Back home I re-examined the little service booklet. There

was a picture of Josie on the back, smiling with her husband and two kids, and on the front her birthdate, 25 October, the day after Mum and Dad's wedding anniversary. They'd have gone out to celebrate the evening before, then next day Mum drove to Cawder Ghyll hospital to deliver her husband's child, and that same evening Gill and I were taken to see the new baby, which a nurse held up at the window to show to us, Dad beside her beaming like a proud father, though neither his pride nor paternity could be acknowledged while he lived. How much the deception affected Josie couldn't be measured: very little, since she'd always seen through it; a great deal, since she'd grown up in the shadow of a lie. Either way this wasn't the time to go blaming people. It never would be the time. Dad, Mum, Beaty, Sam – they'd only been trying to do their best.

23

No brother has been more affected by a sister's suicide than J. R. (Joe) Ackerley. It was only an *attempted* suicide but Nancy was fortunate to survive. He was fortunate, too, since he'd precipitated the attempt by being (as he saw it) 'persistently cruel to her' and 'driving her out of her mind.' Worse still, he had deliberately ignored the note she left telling him what she planned to do.

'Tiresome woman' or even 'dreadful woman' Joe used to say about Nancy to friends. During his twenty-four years as literary editor of the *Listener*, he kept her at bay despite (or because of) her nervous breakdowns and pleas for attention. He much preferred the company of his Alsatian, Queenie; 'bitch' was a term he reserved for Nancy. Only in old age, when he retired and they lived together, did he soften. 'Charles and Mary Lamb,' a novelist friend muttered on seeing them walk home from their local pub, Joe pulling her along with one hand while in the other he held a bottle. Francis King described the relationship as 'a ghastly caricature of the kind of marriage, devoid of sex, that is held together merely by feelings of obligation, pity and guilt' until 'the two participants, exhausted by their conflicts, eventually reached an undemanding and even mutually helpful *modus vivendi*'.

Nancy was three years younger than Joe and died over a decade after him. She was an attractive woman, as photos and a Don Bachardy drawing show. But she made a disastrous marriage, had a difficult relationship with her only child, a son, and was thought 'cruel' by her mother and aunt. A career might have provided an outlet but according to Joe there was no job 'that a woman so uneducated, uninterested, vain, self-centred, hypochondriac, idle-minded, irresponsible, left-handed, ignorant and untalented could hold for a week'. By her late forties, she was pressurising Joe to let her move in with him. 'Once she had youth, beauty, money, husband, child, a home of her own,' he wrote in his diary. 'Now, a woman nearing fifty, she lives quite alone, absolutely friendless, in poky bedsitting rooms at 35s. a week, cooking on a hotplate and washing up her dishes in her bedroom in a tin basin.' He felt sorry for her but worried that if she moved in he would have no life of his own. Besides, their elderly Aunt Bunny was living with him and the flat didn't have room for three.

The crisis came one winter. In the build-up to Christmas, he met Nancy on neutral ground in Haywards Heath. Already overwrought, she got worse once they started drinking: 'I hate you, I hate you, you're horrible, horrible, cruel, beastly, I shall kill myself and I shall haunt you, I shall haunt you,' she shouted as they walked the streets. She accused him of being in league against her with their Aunt Bunny. And his offers to put her up in a hotel near his flat, or to start looking for a house with room for the three of them, didn't placate her. Nothing less than him ejecting Bunny would do.

Over Christmas he settled on a compromise – to ask Bunny to stay with a friend while Nancy moved in for three weeks round the time of her fiftieth birthday. But before he could suggest it to her, Nancy wrote returning the £50 cheque he'd sent her as a present and telling him not to contact her again. Guilt-struck, he set off to see her in Worthing, writing a letter of 'capitulation' that he planned to leave if he didn't see her: 'I said that she was my only sister and I her only brother and that, in spite of wrangles and rows and disagreements, she and I were knit together inseparably and that I needed her as she needed me and that I knew in the end we should live together.' He even thought she could be 'of immense service' to him – if only she would stop emotionally blackmailing him. In the event, when he called her from a phone box near her lodgings, she was 'awfully sweet', invited him round and showed him a pullover she'd knitted for him. They reached a fragile peace – and made a plan for him to come down again, and stay overnight, on 2 January.

He arrived in the early evening and they spent most of it in Nancy's room, where she'd laid out salads, cheese, fruit and a bottle of Algerian wine. First, though, they made their way through a half-bottle of gin. By the time they began to eat Nancy was airing old grievances and complaining that he wasn't serious about her coming to live with him. By 10.30 he'd had enough and went to bed in the downstairs room he'd booked for the night. Interrupted when Nancy brought in a large piece of cheese and put it on the mantelpiece, he was woken again at 6.30 a.m. by a knock at the door. She'd pushed a note under it which accused him of abandoning her: 'I can't stand it any longer . . . I have wanted to die for a long time.' He'd had similar letters from her, 'in various degrees of jealous hysterics', for several months and despite a moment the night before when she'd pointed to her gas fire, with its flexible pipe extension, he read the note only perfunctorily. Rather than go upstairs to talk to her ('Oh, hell, I thought, why bother') he slipped out of the house and caught an early train back to London.

At 1 p.m., he had a phone message from the police. Nancy was seriously ill in hospital with gas poisoning. Weirdly, on arrival in Worthing, he was first made to go to the police station where he was interrogated by a youngish constable and a moralising sergeant ('Do you think it a proper thing to have left your sister down here with no one to look after her, knowing her state of mind?'). He was told there'd be a court hearing where 'she would have to swear not to do it again, and I would have to undertake care of her'. At the hospital he found Nancy out of danger but unconscious. He got the train back to London but immediately regretted it, reproaching himself for not being at her bedside when she woke.

The entry for this episode in his book *My Sister and Myself*, a selection of his diaries published in 1982, fifteen years after his death and three after Nancy's, runs for nearly fifty pages, far longer than any other entry, and includes a twenty-page section recounting Nancy's life history and dissecting her personality. It's a compelling piece of writing, self-lacerating yet self-exculpatory, panic-stricken yet calmly analytical, lachrymose (he wept when he returned to hospital and found her awake) yet self-serving. The examples of Nancy's past behaviour – threatening Aunt Bunny with a knife, say, or tearing off her clothes during a row and running naked into the street – certainly show her to have been unstable, and after she recovered from her suicide attempt she spent several months in a psychiatric hospital. But Joe's account of her should be treated with caution. He was a misogynist as well as a misanthrope, believing that 'Women are naturally vain and self-centred.'

There's no denying his remorse over Nancy: 'I had my chance to help her and I botched it, I lost contact, I withdrew the prop . . . My sister has preferred death to my care, in which she no longer believes.' Then again, he tells himself, 'She was my sister only, my only sister, but my sister only, and her assault upon me was more the assault of a lover, a wife. Was I to give up everything for her, my independence, my life, my own character? As lover, indeed I see I failed her. But as a brother did I do so badly?' He's conscious of rushing to help when she's ill but of the shutters coming down once she's better. Had he been married with children, or moved abroad, there'd have been no question of her living with him or being his responsibility: 'I am only her brother, her only brother, but only that.'*

In mid-April, three and a half months after her suicide attempt, on her release from the psychiatric hospital where she was given ECT, he brought her home to live with him in Putney. Within a week, tensions arose. She wanted to join him on his morning walks with Queenie, which he preferred to take alone. She complained of him feeding Queenie fresh eggs. She objected to him asking friends round for meals. She rejected invitations to go to restaurants with him but then made him feel guilty if he went without her. Things went from bad to worse. She was bored. Hated Putney. Longed to be in the countryside (despite previous failures at living there). His patience ran out: 'I hated her all over again. The bitch, I thought, destroyer of other people's lives, out of jealousy and envy and conceit.' He placated her with awkward endearments ('Old girl') but cursed her under his breath and in his journal: 'What an awful woman! . . . Horrible, horrible woman . . . What a pity she did not die.' By September that year, he was comparing her to a tapeworm that had been living inside him for thirty-five years: 'It is stubborn,

---

*There's an echo here of what the eponymous Clarissa tells her brother in Samuel Richardson's novel: 'I would be glad sir, said I, to understand that you are my *brother* – and that *you* would understand that you are *only* my brother.'

resisting all efforts to get rid of it; even if you manage to get rid of the main body, the head remains and soon grows a new one'.

The remaining diary entries in *My Sister and Myself* are sparser and less anguished – the last dates from 1957, two years before Joe left his job at the *Listener* and ten before he died. 'Joe's friends, many of them women-haters, would often say that Nancy had ruined his life,' Francis King writes in the introduction, 'but it could be said with no more injustice that, kind only to be cruel, he had subtly ruined hers.' Unstated in the diary is that he wanted the freedom to pursue his sex life, without her interfering. What Nancy thought of him being gay isn't recorded. But his friendships made her jealous. According to E. M. Forster (a good friend of Joe) she was in love with him. And looked up to him like a god. Her god and hers alone.

Perhaps the most revealing aspect of his account of Nancy's suicide attempt has to do with the note she left him. Having failed to disclose its existence to the police when they questioned him, he panicked about what to do next. What if the note came to light? Would the police hold him responsible? And what to tell Nancy – that he'd read it but ignored it? Or that he'd failed to see it? In which case, should he smuggle it back into her room while she was in hospital? Or would it be safer simply to destroy it? His worries about being implicated outweigh his distress about the suicide attempt itself.

In the end, he simply lied. When Nancy, still in hospital, asked him whether he'd read the note she left him he told her that she must have been drunk or delusional to think she'd written one. For good measure he told the policewoman in attendance at the hospital the same thing. It's a blatant case of gaslighting. Rather than tell the truth, he let Nancy believe she was mad.

24

Round the time that Josie died, I heard from Jill again – my first real girlfriend, the one who'd left for Australia when I was fifteen. She missed the Old Country, her email said, and was coming over to visit relatives. If time allowed, maybe she could see Gill and me as well. She'd not met Wynn but knew all about him: his sister Joan had been her best friend at school.

I invited Jill to an event I was doing in Hebden Bridge and had dinner with her afterwards. My jealous fantasies about her joyous teenage years in Australia couldn't have been more wrong. She'd quit school early, worked as a hairdresser and often been miserable. Later – six kids and two marriages later – she'd re-invented herself: gone to university, had a successful career in business, moved into social work, and was now about to do a PhD. When the last of her kids had grown up, she planned to move back to Yorkshire.

Next morning we drove over to see Gill, who'd been looking forward to the visit. I knew what that sometimes meant and, sure enough, when we arrived, I found her in Dad's old study, shredded newspapers all over the floor, her hands pressed against the French window. Where's Liam, she kept saying, he must be at Nut Tree Cottage (a place I'd never heard of). Jill was waiting in the kitchen. I'd not mentioned Gill's drink problem, hoping she need never know, but now there was no hiding it. I took Gill by the arm, holding her steady while she muttered about Liam and Nut Tree Cottage, and walked her to the kitchen, where Jill sprang into action. She needs rehydrating, she said, and took over, sitting Gill down, forcing her to drink water from a pint glass while I made black coffee. Was she used to dealing with alcoholics? Had she been a nurse at one point? Either way, she was amazing. They'd not seen each other for almost forty years, but quickly hit it off; Gill responded to Jill's ministrations far more readily than to mine.

Together, we made an appointment for Gill to see her GP later that day and to attend an AA session that evening. I knew she might not get to either but she was sober enough to exchange phone numbers with Jill before we left that afternoon. Jill and I said goodbye at the local station. I'll make sure to call on Gill next time I'm over, she said.

True to her word, she made a point of seeing Gill whenever she visited the UK. If they didn't go out somewhere, they'd sit in the living room poring over old photographs – from memory, knowing where they'd been put in the album, Gill would describe where each photo was taken and who the subjects were. Jill was struck by Gill's tenacity and how well she navigated her disability; if she stayed over, for example, Gill would treat her to tea in bed (blindly filling the kettle from the tap, pouring boiling water into the cup without burning herself, adding milk to the right level and carrying the cup upstairs). Keen to revisit Dales beauty spots, Jill would hire a car and they'd set off for Bolton Abbey, say, or Malham Tarn – a difficult feat since Jill had no sense of direction and Gill couldn't read maps or road signs. Sometimes they'd have to backtrack from some cowpat dead end, but mostly Gill would get them where they wanted to be.

On one of their days out, they went for tea and cakes in Kettlewell. Belatedly realising they'd have to descend more than twenty steep steps to the café they'd chosen, which Gill's blindness and a limping gait made tricky, they hobbled to the Blue Bell Inn instead. 'I haven't been in a pub in years,' Gill said, as they sat by the fire. Oh God, what have I done, Jill thought, but let it slide. They stuck to lemonade and didn't speak about Gill's drinking problem. Why spoil a good day out?

They felt like sisters to each other: Gill didn't have one (even her half-sister was dead) and Jill wasn't close to hers (there were two, both younger). While they hung out together, they reminisced about their time at the high school, which neither had much enjoyed; talked about their children, who they considered their greatest achievement; and laughed a lot. Yes, laughter was the key to their sorority. Where others thought Gill unhappy, a sad case, Jill found her fun.

So did Gill's friend from primary school days, Christine. If Wynn declined to take Gill shopping (as a punishment for bingeing), she sometimes stepped in. At Boundary Mill one day they were looking for a pair of shoes, to which an extra heel could later be fitted to correct Gill's lopsided posture. The shoes have to be stylish, Gill said, make sure you find me a suitable pair. Christine presented her with various options, describing their look while Gill appraised their features (soles, uppers, laces, buckles, etc) then tried them on. They finally hit on a pair she liked. But something wasn't quite right. My left foot's uncomfortable, she complained. And no wonder. Christine had handed her two right shoes.

They joked about it later: remember that time when . . . That was the thing, Christine said – you could have a good laugh with Gill.

Wynn said the same; Louise and Liam too. I hadn't seen the fun side of Gill since childhood. The failing was mine, not hers.

In 2012 she turned sixty. I came up to mark the occasion, meeting her and Louise (who'd driven her there) in the Rhubarb Restaurant of the Herriots Hotel in Skipton. We chose a table by the window, in the light, so she could make out at least a little of what she was eating. It was a weekday lunchtime, and we had the place to ourselves, which helped. She ordered a veggie burger, which Louise cut up into quarters for her. The burger was splodgy, oozing ketchup from each side, but she handled it adeptly, the French fries too. Her blouse and cardigan stayed pristine. She used paper napkins to clean her bloodied hands.

Here's to you, Gill, I said, raising a glass of water, I can't believe you're sixty. And I couldn't: the plump pink infant with golden curls, the ballet dancer, pony girl, blazered schoolkid, Bee Gees fan, sun-seeker, wife, mother of two small kids was now a greying woman with a white stick (albeit a stick hidden on the floor beside her feet). It felt sad, not a celebration, a marker of all the years that had gone and all the people taken with them. Back in London, I could keep the sadness at bay but there with Gill it rushed in. I felt embarrassed that Louise might spot me welling up. At least I could hide it from Gill.

Before I left, I handed her three novels – two romances and a thriller – in audio versions. Then I paid the bill, kissed them both on the cheek and crossed the road to the station. I was going north for a change, to Lancaster, and the stations were like stop-offs from childhood: Gargrave, Hellifield, Long Preston, Clapham, all those places up the Dales we used to visit.

The fields by the track had been tilled by moles and blue-daubed sheep scattered in panic as we passed. Water had pooled in tractor ruts and when the sun broke through the pools it blazed like phosphorus. My eyes welled up again.

After Gill's sixtieth we reached a kind of accord. Meetings were infrequent but phone calls a weekly routine. We'd ask after each other's health and grown-up children. I'd tease her about her elephant-memory; she'd tease me about my always being away somewhere; we'd tease each other about our inability to think of suitable Christmas or birthday presents. It wasn't an intense, we-two-against-the-world relationship. But it was cordial, reassuring, good enough. 'A strengthener of love, this,' Jane Austen writes in *Mansfield Park*, 'in which even the conjugal tie is beneath the fraternal. Children of the same family, the same blood, with the same first associations and habits, have some means of enjoyment in their power, which no subsequent connexions can supply.' For us the enjoyment lay in reminiscence – what we shared before partners and children came along. There was comfort in it too: as Austen puts it, 'all the evil and good of [our] earliest years could be gone over again, and every former united pain and pleasure retraced with the fondest recollection'. Though I'm itching to edit the lazy repeat of 'provides' and 'siblings' in the passage below from Judy Dunn's *Sisters and Brothers*, the sentiments strike a chord: 'Contact with siblings in late adulthood provides not necessarily deep intimacy but a sense of belonging, security, attachment to a family. The tie between siblings provides an important buffer against the insecurity of ageing and the loss of parents.'

If Gill didn't call for a while or a meeting we'd planned fell through, she'd pretend it hadn't happened. Introspection was painful and any discussion of her drink problem unwelcome.

It was bad enough having to look inside herself without others poking around. Who knows what they'd find there? Better to say nothing – to keep herself to herself.

Whether to speak was an issue when the *Mail* approached Gill after my book about Mum came out. She phoned to tell me a journalist had been in touch, asking for an interview and offering a fee: what should she do? Perhaps if I'd encouraged her she'd have gone ahead. But we knew what the journalist was after. Sister enjoys book about mum written by her brother wouldn't be a story worth running. But if Gill went on record as hating the book or hating me, that might make a piece. It was up to her, I said, knowing she could do with the money but hoping she'd say no. She called back later that day, having turned the interview down. (Whenever I wonder if Gill secretly did hate me, I take comfort from that episode.)

Perhaps the journalist's motive was more innocent than I'm allowing – simple curiosity, not malice. People do sometimes ask me what Gill thought about my memoirs of Mum and Dad. The assumption is she must have disliked or felt exposed by them. But most of the book about Mum drew on letters predating our births and the book about Dad relied on stories we shared, to which Gill, as the family's chief memory-keeper, contributed.

The trouble about being a memory-keeper is that you can live too much in the past. Difficult though her relationship with them had been at times, Gill badly missed our parents, Mum especially. At some point in the 90s, Mum presented us with a list of her furniture and knick-knacks and asked us to take turns in picking out items we'd like – to place an advance order, so there'd be no confusion or squabbling after she'd gone. Gill was already losing her sight by then but had clear views of what she wanted. Among Mum's collectibles, for example, she chose Lladró figures, silver sugar tongs and thimbles. One of Mum's rings had been promised to Kathy but after her death Gill (who had it on her hand) couldn't bear to part with it – she offered Kathy, who'd no strong feelings about the matter (Mum wasn't *her* mum), a cheap brooch instead. It was ungenerous but easy to understand. As if by keeping all Mum's rings she could stay close to her. As if she could keep her alive.

In the summer of 2014 Gill moved house. She'd been stalling for years: the other half of the money she owed Wynn was long overdue. It was hard to leave Thornton where she'd spent all but the first few years of her life. And hard to leave Windyridge, with all its memories. Then again, some of those memories were bad: rows with Wynn; binges that had left her with bruises or broken limbs; the deaths of Mum and Dad. Besides, the house was bigger than she needed and she liked the idea of being nearer Louise, in Bradford or Leeds. Reluctantly, she began to look for suitable properties, or rather – given her blindness – to have Wynn or Louise take her round and tell her what they saw. Eventually she found a modern bungalow in Sutton-in-Craven. The property was nothing special but Sutton had shops, buses, a park and (more worryingly) plenty of pubs. Perhaps even the name was a comfort: from Thornton-in-Craven to Sutton-in-Craven you only had to go fifteen miles and change a few letters. Windyridge went on the market. An offer was made and accepted. The difference in price between the two properties allowed Gill to pay Wynn, give money to Louise and Liam and put £80,000 in the bank – not a fortune, but on top of her state pension and disability allowance, enough to see her through another decade or two.

The stuff she had no room for mostly went to an auction house in Harrogate but she kept back some items for me, including a dining table and a desk. I hired a van from Enterprise and drove up with Kathy in late July. Gill was well away when we arrived, giggling at all we said. A half-empty bottle of pink Cava was hidden behind the living-room door.* I'd guessed from recent phone calls that she would be like this. The prospect of the move made her nervous and upset. Trouble was, the triggers for drinking were becoming more numerous. Now the addiction had tightened its hold, there was always a reason. Or to put it less kindly, any excuse would do.

With Gill wobbly beside us, we wandered from room to room, inspecting what was left for me to take. I felt like a scavenging nineteenth-century Egyptologist, about to make off with valuables from a looted pyramid; or like the male heir who thinks it his duty or entitlement to retain the family heirlooms. In the end I took more than I'd planned but less than I could have with a larger van. Not that this one was small – it stuck out two feet from the parking space at the B&B where we were staying. Still, it hadn't the space to accommodate everything of sentimental value. And sentiment was the point – as if by surrounding myself with the furniture of childhood I could turn the clock back and everything would be as it once was, the hard stuff of adulthood still to come.

We agreed a sum – since Gill could have sold what I was taking, it was only fair for me to pay her – and when Wynn got back from a supermarket trip I loaded the van with him while she fell asleep on the sofa.

---

*Liebfraumilch was her usual tipple. Or any cheap German white. In a box not a bottle. Medium-dry preferably. Though sweet would do too. Or fizzy. Anything really, once she'd started.

Wynn grumbled about her as he worked. His plan was to stay with her for the first six weeks at the new place, after which he'd park his Hymer on a caravan site. I can't take any more, he said. I've had thirty-two years of it. I could have walked out a decade ago when we divorced. I know she's your sister and I'm sorry. But I want some me-time. I know men in their seventies who go to Spain and have a fine old time. Still it's hard leaving the place. Not just the house, the garden and all.

I surveyed the garden over the desk we were carrying: the York stone paths, raised beds, sundial, hedge, fruit bushes and lawn. He'd worked hard to keep it in order. The house too, though it had suffered from Gill's binges – the glass in the display cabinets had cracked and there were water stains on the dining table.

I ruined the views by planting that hedge, Wynn said, but it's been worth it. The wind used to blow out the pilot light on the Aga – now the hedge diverts it over the roof.

Gill appeared, having woken. I've got my head round it now, she said, about the move. I wanted to believe her but the more she asked what I thought of the bungalow, which I'd looked round with her a couple of months before, the more I doubted it. There was every chance she'd be unhappy there – and drink herself to death. I've got my head round it now, she said again.

The evening light was benign. With the van loaded, we sat on a bench looking west, men to the left, women to the right. I was angry with myself for being angry with her. So, she'd been drinking: get over it. I should be warmer to her. How terrible to be blind. And to feel you'd married the wrong man. And to be leaving the village where you've spent your adult life without the conviction that it was the right thing to do.

It will be more sociable in Sutton, Kathy said. You're isolated here.

Yes. But I'll miss Heather, in the big house, and Christine.

You can still see them, I said. You're not going far.

Mm, and I don't see a lot of them anyway. I'll be fine, I've got my head round it.

She wouldn't be taking any of Dad's stone troughs, she said, the ones with ferns and cacti. The largest of them, the shape and size of a coffin, was worth a lot: a man had offered £600 for it but Wynn had checked on eBay and its value was nearer £3,000. Trouble was, you'd need a crane to lift it. They had decided to leave it for the new owners.

Like most people, Gill was a mixture of generous and canny. She'd made sure to keep some of the most valuable items, including a painting by Howard Riley. She couldn't see it, and might not have room to hang it anywhere, but its value would increase. She'd been careful to keep some of Mum's collectibles too. They meant a lot. And she could always touch them.

As the sun went down, Kathy and I headed to the B&B in Skipton, our takeaways rattling in the back of the van. I'd no more room for them in my house than Gill had in hers. But they'd replace other stuff. Or just sit there. Like Gill, I was too wedded to the past to let go. We made a sad pair: curators of the museum of our childhood.

In Thornton, visual memory had helped her move about the house: she knew where everything was; she could even describe the views from the window. But as John Hull says, 'For the blind person, the house is only there because of the past'. There was no past in the Sutton house and living there was a challenge: she had to learn afresh where the doors were, the sharp edges, the number of steps down to the garden.

I like to think she could still remember our faces. Though what she remembered would have been out of date, based on last sightings or old photos. In her mind we must have looked at least a decade younger than we were.

Loss of sight sharpens the other senses, and Gill's hearing was acute. Touch, too: her fingers appraising blouses that time at Boundary Mill. Taste and smell I'm less sure about. Perhaps to appreciate food you have to see it. Gill's appetite was modest to start with. And a fear of spilling things and messing her clothes made it more modest still.

In Sutton, she began to live less in the world and more in her body. She had always loved the sun and now she sunbathed at every opportunity, not just for the warmth pouring down but because its rays dimly broke through the darkness. Making new friends had never been easy (John Hull: 'One of the most difficult aspects of blindness is the way it tends to make you passive in getting to know people.'). Now she was blind, and living in a new village, it became impossible. She hugged her family closer – aurally, by phone.

She'd stay up late, a nocturnal animal by default. Why bother with daylight when she lived in a permanent dusk? At least she had a little peripheral vision; it wasn't like dwelling in deepest dark. Still, time was a problem, dragging its heels when she was alone. As the space she occupied grew smaller, so time expanded.

I didn't forget what Dad had said – that after his death, I would have to assume responsibility for Gill. It sat there like a toad on my conscience. But in the end – so I told myself, with sound reason or lazy indifference – the only person responsible for Gill was Gill. That she rarely asked for my help made it easier to believe.

I was being self-protective too. To see how bad things were was painful. The worst time was a trip to Sutton six months or so after she'd moved: Kathy hadn't been to the bungalow and Gill kept urging us to come. We were wary – too often in the past she'd not shown up to meetings or not shown up as her – and took the precaution of booking a nearby hotel rather than staying with her. I was hopeful, nonetheless; she sounded happy, settled, keen to see us and be taken out somewhere. No one answered when we rang the bell. I tried the door: unlocked. Gill, I called, before finding her, a tiny figure, alive but unarousable under a duvet. We tidied up, put a glass of water by the bed, went for a walk, returned, failed to wake her, went for a drive, phoned, got no answer, went to the hotel, phoned again, got no answer, went to bed. When we returned the next morning, a taxi driver was delivering wine boxes; she must have woken at dawn and ordered them. Sheepish, he promised to stop delivering in future. We knew it was futile; there were other taxi drivers, even if this one kept his promise. Draining the wine boxes was futile too; she'd order more. We put them on a high shelf. In the bedroom, she was sound asleep, in the same position as the afternoon before.

She'd wanted us to see the house. But she didn't want to see us. Or the drink didn't want her to see us. The drink demanded her full concentration. The reward for which was stupor. I'm stupid, she used to say. And as she lay there, 'eyes settled in a stupid peace' (Dryden), she was: insensible, deadened, lost to the world. Had she found a better world? Maybe. But not a world with room for others.

For years, she'd had a pattern. Something would give and she'd be off down a hole, beyond help, beyond our control, beyond her own control. Then she'd come back as herself, her better self, as if she'd never been away.

In Sutton, as we all feared, the pattern grew worse.

Binge. Dry out. Lapse. Binge. Dry out.
Lapse. Binge. Dry out. Lapse.
Binge. Dry out. Lapse.
Binge, Dry out.
Lapse.
Binge.
Binge.
Binge.

Whatever state she was in, she never failed to notice our parents' birthdays. She'd call me up, in case I'd forgotten. Sometimes she'd call on their death-days too: 'Today Dad would have been . . .' – eighty, ninety, a hundred, whatever. Anniversaries mattered too. Once she phoned as Kathy and I were standing in the foyer of a theatre, about to see a play. 'Celebrating, are you?' she said. It was our wedding anniversary. We'd forgotten. She had not.

She talked about Dad more often than about Mum. That seems to be the way with children, or grown-up children. When I've worked with students who're writing memoirs, fathers are invariably the focus, because absent, alcoholic, violent, criminal or dead, whereas mothers – present, dependable, nurturing, *nicer* – stay in the shadows. The dads are at the wheel, driving the narrative, while the mums take a back seat. It's a reflection of how power used to be apportioned within marriage, still is mostly, with women the primary carers and men enjoying greater freedom – a freedom which, in these memoirs at least, they abuse.

Dad sometimes abused his power, as both husband and parent, but Gill didn't hold it against him. Not that she said. Only when drunk did she suggest that he'd mistreated her – in the same breath as saying how much she missed him.

*

In February 2018, Wynn asked if he could move in with her. The lease on his flat in Sutton was due for renewal and the rent was being upped dramatically, by £200 a month. He was spending half his time round her place anyway.

What did you say? I asked her on the phone.

I said no way.

He could keep an eye on you.

And drive me mad.

Where will he go if not?

I told him I'd think about it.

So he *will* move in with you?

I feel sorry for him. And I've a spare bedroom. If he's more co-operative about driving me places, I don't mind giving it a go.

I remembered the summer evening I'd drunk beer with Wynn outside Windyridge, before her move, when he'd talked of wanting me-time: six weeks of settling her into the new house, then he'd be gone. Instead of which, for the last two and a half years, he'd been renting a flat just round the corner. Whatever the hassle, he felt responsible for her. And she for him: twice before when he'd had hospital treatment – first for his heart, then for throat cancer – she'd let him stay. The rope that used to stretch between them at Windyridge was still there They were tied together till death.

For the Christmas before her sixty-sixth birthday, she asked me for talking-book versions of *Winnie the Pooh*, *The Secret Garden*, *Heidi*, *Black Beauty* and *Little Women*. I went ahead and ordered all five. She called in late March, three months after the Amazon delivery, to say that something had gone wrong with the order: one of the CDs was a musical version of the book, another was in German, a third was for an MP player – could I bear to order again? Of course, I said, wondering if she was pissed and the story a fantasy: could I really have screwed up so badly? Later I checked my original order, and found she was absolutely right.

'It's only me,' she'd say whenever leaving a voice message, as if she wasn't of much consequence and I needn't bother to call back. She'd a knack of phoning at inconvenient moments, as certain people always seem to: when you're putting the food on the table or sitting on the toilet or having sex. Perhaps it's always the wrong moment when the caller is someone to whom you don't want to talk. I *did* want to talk to Gill, but (knowing what it meant when she didn't pick up) I usually left it to her to call me. Our conversations tended to be short. She didn't dwell on her troubles but if pushed she'd own up to back pains or a cough that had lasted all winter. She was twice in hospital with fractures after falling over. Discharged, she'd resolve to stop drinking then relapse.

For her last Christmas, I bought her (at her request) audiobook versions of *Jane Eyre* and *Rebecca*.

For her last birthday, audiobooks of several Danielle Steel novels.

25

I'm in Suffolk, outside in the sun reading Ian Sansom's book about Auden's poem 'September 1, 1939', unaware that today's date, 2 August 2019, will be one I'll always remember. My mobile phone is indoors so I miss the calls from Liam and Louise. When I see them, I know it's trouble. Bad trouble, if they've both tried to call me. It's Louise who tells me, though it's only later that afternoon I get the details from Wynn.

He'd gone down to a party in the Midlands the previous weekend and decided to have a few days' holiday on the east coast afterwards. His absences gave Gill greater freedom to drink so he usually kept them short, but this time he was away for nearly a week – 'I feel guilty about that,' he'll later tell me, more than once. He got back round 4 p.m. on the Thursday to find her lying on the floor of his bedroom, in the narrow gap between the bed and the radiator, scrunched up in a kind of kneeling position, as if she were hiding something (a wine box?) under her body. When he asked if she was OK she murmured that she was and didn't want to be moved. It was the sort of stupor he was used to finding her in; no cause for alarm. He left her where she was and cleared the place up, removing all the wine boxes, and checked on her at various points during the evening, the last time at 3 a.m., when after watching late-night television he went to sleep on the conservatory sofa. Didn't he think to get her up onto his bed? Didn't the fact she hadn't moved worry him? The questions would nag away at me afterwards. But to ask might have sounded like an accusation. And he was used to her crashing out.

When he checked again at 8 a.m. the next day she still hadn't moved but she was breathing.

At 10 a.m. the cleaner, Denise, came in. Wynn asked her to have a look at Gill and see how she was. Denise felt Gill's hands. They were cold – frozen – and she didn't seem to be breathing. She thought they should call an ambulance. While the ambulance was on its way, the 999 operator talked Wynn and Denise through what to do – get Gill up on the bed and try CPR. The paramedics tried it too, on arrival. Gill's body was still warm but her hands were like ice. She looked a little yellow in the face but it could have been suntan. Wynn asked the paramedics why they weren't trying electrical shocks to restart Gill's heart. No point, they said, too late.

She must have died between 8 and 10 a.m.

On a bike ride that morning, Kathy had asked me 'How's Gill? Have you spoken to her lately?' I said that she'd tried to call me earlier in the week. I checked my phone: the call had come at 18.06 on the Tuesday. She hadn't left her usual message – 'It's only me' – and she'd phoned at a time when she knew I'd be playing tennis. Perhaps that's why I didn't call her back, because I guessed she was probably drinking and would either not pick up or not make sense. Or perhaps it was because I was rushing – I'd finished tennis early to join Kathy at The Bridge theatre, to see *A Midsummer Night's Dream*. Now I berated myself for not calling her from the train. Or later that night. Or next morning. What if she'd still been sober? What if it had only been afterwards, feeling neglected, that she'd called the taxi to fetch a stash of wine boxes? More likely – 99 per cent likely – she'd begun drinking when Wynn departed, or had been drinking for weeks before, and it would have made no difference. Still, I felt guilty and bereft. There wouldn't be another chance to speak to her.

I haven't cried yet, Wynn told me on the phone. I hadn't either. Liam – who I got hold of as he was catching a train at King's Cross – said something similar, that it hadn't sunk in. Only Louise cried, though we all would later. Louise and I are sitting here with a glass of whisky each, Wynn said that afternoon. Drinking to cope with the death of an alcoholic. By 6 p.m. I'd be doing the same.

Meanwhile Albinoni was playing on the radio – the same piece I'd chosen for Dad's funeral. And I cracked a cryptic crossword clue. 19 down, 6 letters, 'Hang around, girl, we say, in a period of inactivity.' Stasis was the answer. As in, Stay sis. Which mine – now forever inactive – hadn't.

Everything conspired to be relevant. I remembered this from Mum and Dad's deaths. Omens which, if you were writing fiction, would seem contrived. Truths you couldn't make up.

In the call to Liam, I told him how much his mum had been looking forward to him moving north again, to Leeds, and how pleased she was whenever he came up to visit. Yes, he said, she was like that, excited, but it hadn't stopped her getting drunk and making a spectacle of herself on his thirtieth birthday. That's how it used to go: animation for a glass or ten before she became maudlin, after which she'd knock herself out and sleep. Wake. Drink. Sleep. Wake again. Drink again. Sleep again.

Sleep for good.

The drink always came first. The drink always won on points. There'd been countdowns before – cuts, bruises and fractures from falls she took – but she always got up for another round. This time drink had landed a knockout.

The consolation for Liam was remembering her last words to him and his to her: I love you. Gill's phone calls with her kids always ended that way. She would say it three or four times – not as a reflex, commonplace sign-off, 'love-yer', but needily, fervently, as if she could never say it often enough. I love you, she'd go, repeatedly, and they'd say it back.

That Friday evening in Suffolk two friends came for the weekend. One of them talked about his difficult relationship with his sister, who'd been packed off to boarding school at eight, whereas he remained at home and went to the local school till thirteen. It had been a source of conflict between them ever since, he said.

All these complications with siblings, I said to his wife, to bring her into the conversation, whereas you're an only child.

So are you now, she said.

The next day – the second day of Gill being dead – it was the village fete, with a raffle, stalls, games and two donkeys to stroke. I didn't stroke them, but all weekend felt acutely aware of what it means to be sentient. The sensation of soft sand between my toes on Covehithe beach (and the colder, harder, wetter sand when I burrowed down). The slap of seawater on my head and shoulders. The sound of wood pigeons calling from trees or of a curlew in the marshes. The music of Mozart's clarinet quintet, which we heard at Snape. The taste of nectarines and greengages. The smell of sausages on a barbecue. I don't include sight, only the other four senses, heightened for Gill by the loss of the fifth. The pleasures of existence. The displeasures, too: no one enjoys going to the dentist but the pain when you're having your teeth drilled is proof you're alive. What a waste to surrender sensation, when there's nothing – only nothingness – to take its place.

On the other hand . . . oblivion. No more depression or distress. No struggle for Gill to feel her way round the house. No self-loathing. No anger or sense of neglect. Peace. And a peaceful death, 'in her sleep'. And 'by a sleep to say we end/ The heart-ache, and the thousand natural shocks/That flesh is heir to; 'tis a consummation/Devoutly to be wished.' (*Hamlet*) Tranquillity, despite the ugliness and indignity, her body in a half-kneeling position in the narrow strip between bed and radiator.

Virginia Woolf: 'To be nothing – is that not, after all, the most satisfactory fact in the whole world?'

It turned out that Gill had made a funeral plan. Perhaps one of her fractures spurred her on. Or a kindly social worker at the hospital did, or health visitor, or someone from social services. The plan didn't amount to much – nothing beyond an opting for cremation. No request for certain poems, hymns or songs. Just burn me.

Did she make the plan from a sense of foreboding? She'd been told many times, by all of us close to her and by health workers, that if she went on like this she would kill herself. But part of us didn't believe it and maybe she didn't believe it either: she'd survived several close shaves, a cat with nine lives; why not go on doing so forever?

She misjudged things and crossed a line, that was all.

Put it another way: she'd been killed by a disease, as she might have been by cancer or TB or Covid-19.

The word 'disease' was one I heard many times when people offered condolences over the next few days. And I was grateful.

The word let us all off the hook: there was nothing that Gill (a helpless victim) or we (helpless bystanders) could have done. But a nasty voice in my head wasn't having it: 'Disease? She brought it on, she had agency, she cosied up to death when she could have kept her distance. She abandoned those who loved her and threw away her future.' The voice was angry and vindictive. But unreasonable too. Whatever her agency, addiction was stronger. Drink filled a need. It overwhelmed what she most valued. It trumped even her love for her kids.

When dependency tops your dependents, what's that if not a disease?

Three days after Gill, Toni Morrison died. Another Morrison gone. I used to joke we were related – Aunt Toni – poor cousins of the supermarket Morrisons.

The image of Gill half kneeling between bed and radiator continued to haunt me. The word 'squalid' would also surface despite my efforts to hold it down. Her house was often a mess because she couldn't see the spilled food and 'accidents', and when she drank she couldn't give a fuck. But there was no mess on the floor where she died. She curled herself up and slept.

There was another word I couldn't push away. Two, in fact: mental illness. Had it been a factor in her drinking? And a characteristic that drinking then made worse? A friend said that she recognised in my account of Gill the traits and symptoms of Borderline Personality Disorder, including fear of abandonment, trauma (e.g. from being locked in the cellar), self-harm, emotional instability, chronic feelings of emptiness and stress-related paranoia. It was hard to deny that she had personality problems. But she could also be kind, loving, patient, sensitive, humorous, etc, and thereby 'normal'. Aren't we all on the spectrum anyway? I argued with myself, defensive on her behalf.

I felt defensive in relation to Wynn too, though he'd left her lying there for eighteen hours. Hadn't Kathy and I left her lying there, in bed, that time we came up to see the bungalow? Wynn could be hard on her, adopting cruel-to-be-kind methods that made things worse. But he'd bailed her out on countless occasions, at no small humiliation to himself. She might have died years earlier but for him.*

After the paramedics removed the body, two policemen came round to interview him – standard procedure with an unexplained death. They took notes while they listened and let him know as they left that no further enquiries would be necessary. Blood and tissue samples had been sent to a toxicologist; the coroner had yet to establish the official cause. Despite that, the death could now be registered and funeral arrangements go ahead.

The body was available for viewing at the undertakers. Louise didn't want to see it but wondered whether I might. I'd seen Mum and Dad's dead bodies. But that was because I was with them when they died – before they became fully mature (hah) corpses. What would be achieved by going to see Gill when she was several days gone? Certainly not – that absurd, overused word – closure.

Each day I woke with a refrain in my head.

My sister's dead.

My sister's dead.

My sister's dead.

---

*A twenty-year study conducted in Scandinavia and published in 2015 found that people with 'alcohol use disorder' have an average life expectancy of 47–53 years (men) and 50–58 years (women) and die 24–28 years earlier than people in the general population.

Hear it enough times and I might start to believe it.

After Dad died, I was consumed by grief.

After Mum died, less so – I loved her as much or more but I was prepared.

With Gill, I didn't know what to feel – shock, obviously, but also a lack of surprise.

Is that why I couldn't mourn her in the way I mourned them? Or because I'm older and more able to cope? To lose a sibling brings a different kind of grief, perhaps. You owe your existence to your parents. Your tie to a sibling isn't foundational. However much you love them, they didn't create you. They weren't the ones who fed you, changed your nappies, bought your clothes, put you to bed, taught you to be good, punished you for being bad. And when they die, it's the death of a peer, an equal, someone from your own generation. It's terrible but less primal.

Gill should have died hereafter. Then again, she might have died so much earlier. Martin Amis's sister Sally, born two years after Gill, had an addiction problem and only made it to forty-six. Gill had two more decades.

A week after she died, I phoned Wynn again. 'I seem to have lost my purpose in life,' he said. Which was to prevent her drinking herself to death.

Liver failure seemed the obvious cause. But an article I read on SUDAM – Sudden Unexplained Death in Alcohol Misuse – suggested that deaths due to an arrhythmic heart condition often go undiagnosed and don't show up in a post-mortem. There is 'an immediately higher cardiovascular risk following any alcohol consumption but by twenty-four hours only heavy alcohol intake confers continued risk'.

It was alluring to think that Gill might have died painlessly.

Less alluring was the article's suggestion that SUDAM has implications for close relatives, since arrhythmia is often genetic.

Kathy and I drove up the day before the funeral, leaving early and arriving in Sutton by midday. Wynn welled up on seeing us, saying he still hadn't cried properly while wiping his eyes with a kitchen towel. As he made us tea, I went into his bedroom to look at the gap between bed and radiator. There was nothing to see but the narrow strip of carpet – what had I expected?

In the wardrobe of her bedroom Gill's clothes were immaculately lined up, as though on a rack in a boutique – you'd never have guessed the woman who'd hung them there was blind. High on a shelf was a plastic bag full of old photos, newspaper cuttings about Mum and Dad's retirement, aerial shots of Windyridge, and an Irish family tree I'd sent her. It must have been years since she'd been able to see them.

Back in the kitchen Wynn opened a tub of margarine to show me. Can you see? he said. She'd left her handprint on the surface. In her last binge, unable to find anything else to eat, she must have clawed some marge into her mouth.

The print was tiny – her tiny frozen hand.

I thought of a glass plaque with my handprint that had been made at some literary festival and which I kept on my windowsill at home. Would Wynn keep Gill's handprint as a memento? The margarine would go mouldy in time. He'd have to take a photo.

Liam and Louise arrived with fish and chips. Liam showed us the photos he'd compiled for the wake – over a hundred. Louise talked about the Christmas present they'd bought Gill, an Alexa. At which point, hearing her name spoken, Alexa came alive on the sideboard, and we all laughed. Louise had used Alexa to replay the last tracks Gill ever listened to – a sad thought. But our mood wasn't mournful. Wynn told us about a time he'd been angry with Gill for drinking and threatened that if she didn't stop he'd put her over his knee and give her a good spanking. Mmm, she purred, what would you like me to wear?

Outside the conservatory he'd built a ramp across the drop between the house and the lawn. It was covered in Astroturf and had a rope Gill could hold when feeling her way along. The lawn stretched away, below a high hedge. The rope went all around the hedge but at a lower level, so she could use her stick to check where she was. She didn't mind using the stick when no one could see her.

Liam's photos included two taken recently. She looked tiny. The hair against her tanned skin was white. She reminded me of Mrs Tiggy-Winkle.

Later I sent Liam some childhood photos of Gill to add to his collection. They were a revelation to him. Her eyes were clear. You could look into them. They hadn't clouded over.

That evening we picked up our youngest, Gabriel, from Skipton station and drove him to Thornton. We parked by the church, walked past the almshouses and stopped at Morrisons' Meadow, the field Gill and I donated to the village in memory of Mum and Dad. It was meant to be a playing field for children but the grass looked too long for ball games. Next to it was the house where our godparents used to live, Uncle Gordon and Auntie Edna. Behind the hedge, a woman was mowing the lawn. She'll have known Gill, I thought – I'll let her know about the funeral. The driveway gate had an entry code. And when I waved and shouted over the hedge, her head was down and the mower too noisy for her to hear. The symbolism was so obvious it seemed trite. There I stood, waving to the village where we'd grown up, unable to get its attention.

At the hotel we'd booked in Skipton, the Rendezvous, I noticed a giant poster advertising a nationwide tour by a psychic called Alicia Bickett: 'I SEE and TALK to the loved ones you think you have lost.' *Think* you have lost? I was tempted to take down the details, to arrange a rendezvous with Gill on the other side. But I didn't believe in the other side and nor, as far as I knew, did Gill. So either the rendezvous wouldn't work or if it did we would sabotage it rather than admit we'd been wrong.

Later I googled Alicia and found she was available for private readings or on FaceTime and Skype at $300 an hour. It wasn't just the dead she had access to but 'your future lovers, your future babies, your miscarried babies . . . I can help with court cases, bringing in abundances, healthy scans and healing.' For £25 I could buy her book, *It's All About Love*, with its 'beautiful client stories' and descriptions of spirits, all of them 'busting to speak'. She sounded to be off her trolley but talked with total self-belief.

I slept badly, preoccupied by the eulogy I was due to give. Whether from writerly narcissism or sensitivity to those who'd be listening, I was anxious how it would come across. It felt indecent to fret so much, as if I should be having new thoughts about Gill, not revisiting those I'd drafted on paper. How to balance respect with honesty? The sentence about drink not defining Gill had to go: it was less than honest, an untruth too far; she'd had a drink problem for over thirty years. But nor could I dwell on the addiction. 'The times when she was less than herself shouldn't eclipse the times when she was fully herself,' I wrote and left it at that. Anything I said would be gone in a minute and insufficient to the occasion. But it mattered to strike the right note; to speak, adapting Claudio in *Much Ado About Nothing*, 'as a brother to a sister' with 'bashful sincerity and comely love'.

The celebrant, Sandra, had sent me her choice of poem, which was naff but upbeat, a poem about remembering the good times. I'd have liked to slip an elegy into my eulogy, ideally one written by a brother for his sister, but all I could think of was Oscar Wilde's 'Requiescat', which was unseasonal for August ('Tread lightly, she is near/Under the snow') and composed for a sister who had died aged twelve ('All her bright golden hair/Tarnished with rust,/She that was young and fair/Fallen to dust'). A truer expression of how I was feeling was a Seamus Heaney sonnet comparing bereavement to walking round and round the empty space where a tree has been felled – but that was a poem about the loss of a mother. Where were my brother writers when I needed them?

I swam in the hotel pool before leaving for the crem. Was I guilty of frivolity and lack of feeling, I wondered, thinking of Meursault in *L'étranger* and how he went swimming the day after his mother's funeral and how this was used against him in court to bring about his murder conviction. Back in the room, I put on my black suit, white shirt, black shoes, blue socks and black tie.

It was raining, as it had to, and continued to rain as we sat in the car waiting for the previous ceremony to wind up. Bafflingly, when we got out, I couldn't lock the car – then realised I'd left the ignition on. Earlier, pulling out from the hotel, I'd failed to see a car approaching. Later, heading for an empty parking space, I almost knocked down one of the hotel staff. Mental lapses and eyesight failures. As apt as the rain.

*

We entered the crem to Tchaikovsky and left with Fleetwood Mac; in between came Elton John's 'Your Song', a lyric which mimics the struggle to articulate strong emotion, to find the words for what you think and feel. Did my eulogy seem the opposite: written out, rehearsed and therefore insincere? My hands shook as I read it. Afterwards, when the people behind us were filing out, I stood by the coffin with Wynn, Liam and Louise, and we stroked the wooden lid, as if to commune with Gill or magic her back.

'The sting of death is less sharp for the person who dies than it is for the bereaved survivor . . . There are two parties to the suffering that death inflicts; and, in the apportionment of this suffering, the survivor takes the brunt.' (Arnold Toynbee, *Man's Concern with Death*)

The wake was back at the Rendezvous, in the same room where we'd had breakfast, its floor-to-ceiling windows overlooking the Leeds–Liverpool canal. Beyond the glass, tourist barges passed just feet away. Their passengers sat below deck, sheltering from the rain and waving to us as they went – with our drinks and sandwiches, they must have thought we were having a jolly time. And we were – a less mournful one anyway. The nasty bit was over. The thirty people at the crem had all come back: family, neighbours and a few old schoolfriends, including Christine from across the road and Stephen from primary school and Jill, who if she'd not already been in England for the summer would have flown from Australia to be there. Gill's favourite tracks floated from a loudspeaker at the far end of the room. Next to it, on a screen, a slideshow of her years went by: Gill as an infant, teenager, wife and mum. Over the water, green hayfields rose to distant moor, while joggers and cyclists crowded the towpath and a barge-boy ran ahead to push the swing bridge open. The barges might have been hired specially for the occasion – a ceremonial slide-past, wooden coffins slowly borne past us out of sight.

In the evening, Kathy and I walked into Skipton along the canal, under soft rain, leaving the towpath when we reached the middle of town. In a restaurant off the High Street, Wynn's sister Joan was eating with Jill. They beckoned us to join them, but we'd no appetite and continued up the High Street, struck by how deserted it was, till we turned the corner opposite the church, and saw a crowded bar with people standing outside smoking cigarettes. The name of the bar was somehow inevitable: Two Sisters.*

---

*It's a common title. Picasso, Derain, Gauguin, Mary Cassatt, Fragonard and Auguste Renoir all have paintings with that name. It's also the title of a non-fiction book by Åsne Seierstadt (about a father and his two daughters' journey into the heart of Syria) and novels by Mary Hogan and Gore Vidal. Further back, there's H. E. Bates's debut novel *The Two Sisters*, published in 1926, a plodding and melodramatic tale of two sisters in love with the same man. To be fair, Bates was only twenty-one when it came out. To be fairer still, I read it in the A&E ward of Lewisham Hospital, while waiting to be seen after a piece of food had got stuck in my oesophagus – one of several times this happened in the three months after Gill's death but the only one that ended in an endoscopy. A&E wards aren't ideal for reading, least of all in the middle of the night when you can't swallow, but I doubt that having a second go at *The Two Sisters* would make me like it better. At any rate I'm not going to try.

26

Did both my sisters kill themselves? It's possible. Different circumstances, different methods and with different levels of conscious intent but both used substances (insulin, alcohol) to achieve oblivion. You could say that the balance of their minds was disturbed or they'd not have acted as they did. But they resemble each other in their self-destructiveness, in leaving two children behind, and in having me as a brother. It doesn't make me Ted Hughes. Still . . .

Still.

No, I don't feel like Ted Hughes must have done when Assia Wevill killed herself six years after Sylvia Plath (lightning striking twice). But I do feel a little like Thomas Hardy after Emma died, as if I should have made more effort towards Gill and Josie, rather than taking their presence for granted. In all the reading I did afterwards, it was a sentence in Jane Austen's *Mansfield Park* – 'Fraternal love, sometimes almost everything, is at others worse than nothing' – that hit me hardest.

To lose one sister may be regarded as a misfortune, to lose two looks like carelessness.

*

The guilt is hard to shake off. It's not the Catholic guilt I inherited from Mum but the offshoot of an *if only* game, a fantasy of preventability, where everyone behaves differently and the worst doesn't come to pass. But self-blame and self-exoneration serve no purpose. Nor should I think of my sisters as victims or of their lives as bleak. They died before their time but used the time they had – gave and received love, enjoyed their children and friends, knew happiness. I think of Alice James's reproach to her brother William: 'when I am gone, pray don't think of me simply as a creature who might have been something else . . . I have always had a significance for myself.'

I tell people who didn't know her that Gill's death was unexpected, which is both true and a lie.

We always expected it would happen, given the risks she ran.

We also thought the day would never come.

'Of course you're sad,' a friend says. 'You've lost your kid sister.' It was true. Yet the words didn't fit. I'd never thought of her as my kid sister. She was my coeval.

The image of conjoined twins keeps coming. We weren't conjoined, and our twinship was only Irish, but we grew together. Later we went our separate ways – but never fell out or lost contact.

We weren't close.

We were never not close.

In the morning, when I sit in bed and look out the window, it's like peering through a series of veils.

The steam rising from my mug of tea.

The condensation on the window.

The smoke drifting from the condenser boiler.
The early-morning mist.
The contrails of planes bound for Heathrow.
The clouds on the horizon.

I'd love to tear through the veils to penetrate the mystery of my sisters – what made them who they were; what made them so careless of life. But revelation's not at hand. The 'deep blue air' (to quote Larkin) 'shows/Nothing, and is nowhere, and is endless.'

At night I lie awake, newly conscious of my heart – with its aches and beats – and worried it will give out. You start to feel mortal after your parents die, when you realise you're next in line; now Gill's death that has brought mine closer still. Her body packed up because she abused it. But was there also a genetic weakness? She was sixty-seven; at the same age Dad had a pacemaker fitted; at sixty-eight *his* dad died of a coronary. Are the Morrisons not only susceptible to bowel cancer (which I knew) but dodgy hearts?

My heartbeat is steady – boum, boum, boum, boum. But it bothers me that I'm hearing it at all. I never used to hear it. And the possibility of it stopping is all too clear. Why should it continue? What motivates it to make the effort? Wouldn't it be easier to stop?

The worry is exacerbated by my dentist, who tells me about the link between gum disease and heart disease – 'the nasties that get in the bloodstream', as he puts it, the bacteria narrowing the arteries. I work hard at my teeth, with flossing and interdental brushes as well as an electric toothbrush. But the gums keep bleeding. The white washbasin is sometimes crimson.

*

In bed I keep stroking Kathy's skin – arms, back, shoulders, breasts – to feel what a living body is and shut out the image of Gill's coldness: the frozen hands the cleaner touched; the prints in the margarine tub.

Was Gill always a black sheep, long before drink and blindness took over? On the edge of things, the shy one half hidden in family photos. An outsider and (academically at least) an under-achiever, and in that respect like Kela, as though an early death was the penalty for being on the fringes.

On holiday in early September I lie in the dunes of a sandy beach and think of Abersoch and childhood holidays and how Gill and I would shelter in the sand hollows above the Warren and listen to the waves crashing and watch the marram grass blowing, which I thought of as time passing, and here's the marram grass blowing today but she's gone (Mum and Dad too) and I'm the only one left to see it.

'They're all gone now. And there isn't anything more the sea can do to me.' (J. M. Synge, *Riders to the Sea*)

A walk in the Trossachs takes me upwards to a dam. It's open to the public to walk across the top, with nothing to stop you from jumping into the reservoir on one side or throwing your-self to the ground on the other. I gaze down the steep concrete wall and wonder if I could throw myself far enough out to land on the grass or if I'd hit concrete first. It's a long way down, fifty metres maybe. I've felt the urge before, at the top of cliffs or bell towers or skyscrapers, the thrill of knowing how easy it would be – which isn't the thrill of skydiving or bungee-jumping or riding on a rollercoaster where, barring a freak accident, you'll be safe, but a death-wish.

My fellow dam-walkers are busy taking photos of the view across the water, the autumn colours, the far hills. If they knew what I was thinking, they'd frogmarch me back down. I feel ashamed and selfish: imagine the trauma for them of seeing me – of seeing anyone – leap to their death. But it's not that which stops me from jumping. It's not even cowardice. Depressed though I am because of Gill, I don't want to join her. I'm too addicted to life.

A month after her death I finally dream about her. She emerges from our kitchen, neatly dressed in a green blouse and brown skirt and with piercing blue eyes. She's slightly taller than I remember and walks straight towards me, unimpeded by blindness or a lopsided gait. She's not smiling but nor does she look sad or worried; on the contrary, she radiates calm. I'm shocked to see her – relieved to see her reliving. Some enormous mistake has occurred. She's supposed to be dead yet here she is. What trick did she pull to deceive us? I'm dying to hear her explain it. But before I can ask, she evaporates.

The dream is like a snatch of film. It lasts about three seconds. Perhaps in reality only a millisecond.

It's seven weeks before the post-mortem results come through. Louise calls me after the coroner has phoned her. Two undetected heart conditions are given as the cause of death: 1) myocardial fibrosis, 2) ischemic heart disease. In effect, damage to the heart muscle and clogging of the arteries. We await a written report but it's clear, from a little googling, that alcoholism contributed: 'heavy drinking weakens the heart muscle, which means the heart can't pump blood as efficiently. It's known as cardiomyopathy and can cause death, usually through heart failure'. Moreover, 'clinical studies strongly suggest that fibrosis has a central role in the genesis of arrhythmia'.

In the event, we don't get a written report: when I call the coroner, a couple of weeks later, she tells me that such reports are available to relatives only when a death is suspicious, which this one wasn't. Sorry not to help, she says, sounding not sorry in the least.

I do some more googling and come across the term Holiday Heart Syndrome, first coined in 1978. It's a condition that follows episodes of bingeing, when at least seven and a half pints of beer or a bottle and a half of wine are consumed in a twenty-four-hour period. Irregular heartbeats ensue (supraventricular tachyarrhythmias) causing breathlessness and the risk of a coronary. It's not only heavy drinkers who present with HHS; light drinkers who've been on the piss can get it too.

The syndrome doesn't apply to Gill. By the end, drinking was no holiday for her. It was a full-time job.

Would I feel better if I knew why she drank – if I'd unearthed a Definitive Answer? Maybe. But all I've found are some tentative *becauses*.

Because of a genetic predisposition.

Because she felt rejected as a child.

Because marriage proved a disappointment.

Because her eyesight failed.

Because of multiple traumas – boarding school, the cellar, the car accident in Spain.

Because she felt lonely.

Because drink granted oblivion.

Because drink was the demon that banished all these other demons.

At other times I decide there's no answer.
Because? There is no because.

I keep thinking about all she's missing. Not so much the news (Brexit, Boris), in which she'd take little interest except perhaps to express a *Mail*-like impatience with Westminster politicians ('Why don't they just get on with it?') but the ordinary stuff of life: the chittering of swallows, the rush of a beck, a kettle coming to the boil, the taste of scrambled egg, the feel of a woolly sweater, the squeak-rumble-oomph as a car slows down for a speed-bump then pulls away. Then again, there's all the stuff she was missing already: green fells upside down in a lake, the glint of cutlery, red brake lights, purple heather, a clump of bracken flexing in the wind. How depressed did blindness make her? At best she was remarkably free of self-pity, until the effort of stoicism became too much. The only images she had were in her head and drink made them woozier and kinder. Not that *she* was kind if anyone tried to prevent her from drinking. But left alone, she found a kind of peace – the balm of self-forgetfulness.

Should she have been prescribed anti-depressants? But that would have meant admitting she was depressed. She was too proud and feared the exposure involved, the risk of being referred to a counsellor. She hated talking about herself. That was the good thing about drink. It stopped the talk. Sure, at first it makes you more voluble. But get beyond that and the words dry up.

Mary Cregan writes in *The Scar*, a memoir that's insightful about depression: 'The profoundly depressed person can't see that her thinking is distorted and, after a certain point in the downward spiral, can't hear or comprehend the people who argue that she has a life ahead if she can just hold on.' We did all urge Gill to believe she had a life ahead. At best she listened and her own voice told her the same. But it wasn't enough to save her.

Nor Josie.

Cregan quotes Robert Burton in *The Anatomy of Melancholy*: 'So sweet, so dear, so precious above all other things in this world is life'. But everyone at some point has felt the opposite: so bitter, so futile, so painful above all other things is life. Even the knowledge that it's all we have – as the overused axiom has it, that life is not a rehearsal – might not be enough in a moment of despair.

Traditional religion claims your body belongs to God and only He has the right to take it. But edicts have no weight when you lose hope. If you can't go on, you can't go on.

I find in an old notebook that I was writing about Gill this time last year. Was I already writing elegies for her a year ahead? I don't credit myself with foresight. Death was a more likely outcome for her than for most people her age. And perhaps at some level I've *always* been writing about her. Still, it does feel a little eerie.

What are you writing these days? a friend asks. No surprises there then, he says when I tell him. Ah yes, to complete the trilogy, someone else says, more cynically still. Predictability isn't the worst of it. In a creative-writing workshop, we look at Kathryn Harrison's memoir *The Kiss*, about her incestuous relationship with her father – a couple of the students find its confessionalism distasteful. That's the accusation any memoir writer has to face: that to publicise difficult family stuff is mercenary, opportunistic and, worst of all, un-literary.* The

---

*Miss Lavish in E. M. Forster's *A Room with a View* confirms such suspicions: 'We literary hacks are shameless creatures. I believe there's no secret

accusation will be fiercer if you do it more than once. Here I am, a serial offender.

Another friend is discouraging for a different reason. As we're swimming up and down a pool together, he asks me about the book I'm writing. I'm not sure if it's a book, I tell him, but alcoholism, suicide, blindness, depression and grief are among the themes. Jesus, he says, who'll want to read *that*?

It's a fair question. And I do sometimes ask myself: why are you writing this? (At other times, defeated, I'm not writing this.) It's a sad story. And it will upset Louise and Liam to read it. Why bother? And what if it's no more than a misery memoir, that most despicable of genres? Then I think: if my parents' stories were worth telling, why not Gill's? Aren't all lives, however damaged, of importance? Besides, what else would I write? For now it's all I can think about. You don't choose your subjects (or obsessions), they choose you.

Still, it's a sad story, as Josie's is too, and I wonder why I'm so drawn to sad stories. Murder, death, grief: haven't I had my fill? And what more is there to say? As Amy Clampitt puts it in a poem, 'The Dakota': 'Grief/is original, but it/repeats itself: there's nothing/more original that it can do.' I like to think I'm a positive person. But darkness always seeps in. I'm like the poet James Thomson, setting out to write something cheerful but succumbing to the music of grief: 'Striving to sing glad songs, but I attain/Wild discords sadder than Grief's saddest tune…/My mirth can laugh and talk but cannot sing./My grief finds harmonies in everything.' .

*

of the human heart into which we wouldn't pry.' But I prefer what Annie Ernaux says about one of her memoirs: 'This book can be seen as a literary venture as its purpose is to find out the truth . . . And yet, in a sense, I would like to remain a cut below literature.' (*A Woman's Story*)

Reading Michèle Roberts's memoir *Negative Capability*, I feel a pang when she describes a recent trip to the opera with her twin sister. Not that I'm greatly into opera but I'm struck, yet again, by how few common interests Gill and I had in adult life.

She didn't go to plays,* even when her eyesight was good.

She didn't go to exhibitions, ditto.

She didn't go to concerts.

Some of this was to do with her living in a village. But even people who live in villages go to the city occasionally – London, Manchester, Leeds, Birmingham – to see plays or listen to concerts and visit exhibitions.

It was no big deal. There was plenty other stuff we could share. Still, most of what we shared went back to childhood. As Louise Glück says, 'We look at the world once, in childhood./ The rest is memory.'

I feel a similar pang, more jealousy than regret, when reading Miriam Toews's novel *All My Puny Sorrows*, which describes the relationship between two sisters, the gifted concert pianist Elfrieda (Elf for short) and her younger sister Yolandi, from whose point of view the novel is told. It's a painful story: Elf is bipolar and suicidal. The joy of it is the intimacy between the two sisters: Yolandi banters with Elf, cuddles up to her in hospital, and tells her how much she loves her.

---

*She did, though, come to at least one of the plays I adapted for the Northern Broadsides theatre company. In a diary entry from 1996, about the first preview of *The Cracked Pot* at West Yorkshire Playhouse, I wrote: 'Plenty people in audience including my mother, sister and Wynn – who come in late for the second half, their seats conspicuously empty as Barrie Rutter winds up to sing 'From Hull and Hell and Halifax'. He tells me later he thought of halting proceedings and saying, 'We can't start without t'author's mum'. Gill's vision was already going at this point: how much of the play did she see and not just hear?

Yolandi can't save Elf. I envy their closeness all the same.*

I think back to all those conversations I had with Gill about the past: whenever we spoke, we'd share some childhood memory. Was that because we found adult life difficult? Or because our childhood was so powerful and we so weak that we couldn't let it go? Or because our *childhoods*, plural, diverged and we were searching for common ground? I'm stuck in the past, Kathy sometimes tells me, as though affronted that the first twenty years of my life, before I met her, matter more than the decades we've spent together since. It's not that they matter more, I say. And I don't think I'm stuck. The point about revisiting the past is that you find new things each time you go there – things you missed or didn't understand or failed to see the significance of, which as you get older you begin to grasp.

If I'm addicted to the past, I tell her, it's because it hasn't passed. I'm still there, still working things out.

Old photos help the process – the sheer number of them, zealously commemorating our childhood years. I understand now why I struggled to leave home. It's a normal part of growing up to separate yourself from your family – your *first* family – but some parents try to thwart you. Dad was desperate to keep his children close, to each other as well as to him. The pressure was there even after he died. That letter of his: 'I must remind you that when I am gone it will be your job to see to the welfare of your sister and her children as long as you live.' My job. My responsibility. No wonder I feel guilty. And there are other kinds of guilt. Survivor's guilt – the Irish

---

*The novel has an autobiographical basis – Miriam Toews's sister Marjorie committed suicide in 2010.

twin who lived on. The guilt of being the lucky one. Of having the larger share.

While looking at the photos I come across one I've never noticed before. It comes from a sheet Beaty sent after Mum died and shows Gill, Josie and me lying on a rug. It's black and white but lush with the heat of high summer. Gill is lying on her side in a swimsuit, supporting herself on one arm. Josie, to the right, aged about five, is sitting up, naked from the waist upwards, her dress around her navel. I'm wearing shorts and lying on my front between them, face turned round to the camera. A transistor radio sits on the grass.

Where were we? I don't recognise the setting. Beaty must have taken it, not Dad. Gill and I look like moody adolescents and Josie isn't smiling either. But there we are, a little girl and her two half-siblings. It's the only photo I've ever seen with just the three of us.

Gill has named me as co-executor of her will along with a Skipton solicitor. Another solicitor at the same firm offers to act on my behalf. He means well, to spare me work I'm unused to and he's not, but I feel obliged to play a part – less to honour Gill's wishes than to do my best by Liam and Louise, her beneficiaries. Which I guess *is* honouring her wishes (and Dad's too).

As executor, I'm meant to have access to her bank statements. I want to check what happened to her investments, in case some remain for Liam and Louise. It's a huge palaver before I get access but a quick perusal confirms they were all cashed in. At least there's something left in her deposit account. There's also the bungalow, which Wynn will live in for now but which Liam and Louise can sell one day.

Curiosity is my other reason for studying the bank statements. The last two weeks make bleak reading: every day from 19 July there are withdrawals of between £40 and £60 – sometimes two withdrawals on the same day. She'd call the cab firm; a driver would collect her debit card and go to the cashpoint outside Costcutter or the Co-op; the card would be returned to her, along with the wine boxes purchased at the till. The last two withdrawals were on Tuesday 30, both for £50. Nothing after that: the 31 and 1 are blank; Friday 2 as well, of course. Did she sink into a comatose state on the Wednesday, the day after she tried to call me, the day before Wynn found her on the bedroom floor? It seems she must have, despite her seeming to respond when he offered to move her. Why else would she have lapsed from her daily routine?

Two months to the day after Gill died I meet Jill at King's Cross station. It's my birthday in a week's time, the first that Gill won't be around to remember for me. (Actually, she'd want to correct me, the second; she was still in the womb when I turned one.) Jill's in London on a shopping trip before flying back to Australia: first stop will be the Disney Store, for presents for her grandchildren. We sit in a café near the Eurostar check-in. A waiter with a smile and broken teeth comes to take our order. Just a coffee for me, Jill says, I already ate on the train. I order a toasted sandwich, the cheapest thing on the menu. Very Yorkshire, she laughs, in solidarity not mockery, and tells me how she's given up trying to buy a flat in Yorkshire: one she looked at in a converted mill seemed affordable till she saw what the service charges were.

The waiter brings our order. The coffee cups have no handles – a designer innovation mistakenly premised on the coffee being so tepid that you won't burn your fingers holding the cup.

Soon enough we start talking about Gill; that's why we're here. Jill's not surprised by the post-mortem result. She used to enjoy seeing Gill when she was over but the last two years had been a write-off: she'd phone to arrange a visit and Wynn would tell her Gill was too pissed. At least they'd had a good fifteen years before that. Plus those weeks back in our teens, when I was dating her – Dad's efforts to catch us up to no good and Gill's help in frustrating him. She and Gill used to joke about the sex-policing. It's why we got on so well, Jill says: we laughed a lot.

The toasted sandwich is greasy; I push it aside.

I can't remember when it was, she says, but Gill was talking to me once, about your mum and dad or how you'd written books about them, and she said: 'I wonder if Blake will write a book about me one day.' I left it a while, Jill adds, then I asked her how she'd feel about it. 'Why not,' she said. 'I think I might like it.'

We talk about alcoholism and how, in Jill's experience as a social worker, most of those as addicted as Gill die in their forties not their sixties. Maybe Wynn's monitoring gave her an extra twenty years. Then again, if her problems had been addressed at an earlier point maybe she'd still be alive today. The literature Jill has read on alcoholism isn't much use, she says. A good book on the subject would be helpful. Maybe you should write it, she adds – I'll be your research assistant, if you like. I couldn't, I say, laughing, I'm not a doctor or a psychiatrist. I'll send you some links on epigenetics, she says. I've never heard of epigenetics, I say. It's about how external factors – environment and so on – can modify DNA, she says.

We tip the waiter and leave. As we walk to the Tube, she talks some more about the research she's read. I'm struck by how bright she is, and how unusual her life has been, the girl who left school at fifteen, worked as a hairdresser, had six kids, pursued a business career, retrained in social work, and now spends half of every year travelling in Europe. Maybe it was that intelligence and adventurousness that drew me to her as a teenager rather than the sex we never had.

Any minute she'll be off into the underground – like Eurydice, I think, or (since she'll be back in six months) Persephone. But for the moment we're still talking: about our children, and grandchildren, and how siblings can take such different paths in life, and whether every adult is defined by the childhood they've had or do adults shape their future for themselves. Then we hug goodbye at the ticket machines and she disappears.

Acknowledgements

My thanks, first and foremost, to my niece Louise and nephew Liam, who read and corrected the draft of this book along with their father Wynn. Though there were things in it that shocked and upset all three of them, they didn't ask for anything of substance to be omitted. 'It's all stuff that happened', they said.

I'm also grateful to Josie's husband. We agreed that I'd keep the name I'd given her in a previous memoir; a couple of other identifying details have also been changed.

Jill Ross and Jennifer Potter were invaluable in helping me to fill gaps in Gill's life. My wife Kathy had her own special insights into Gill, some of them stimulatingly different from mine.

Others who have contributed, sometimes without realising it, are Maureen Freely, Maura Dooley, Alan Downie, Sean French, Nicci Gerrard, Ardashir Vakil, Howard Colyer, Pamela Todd, Liz Oxley, Pat Sunter, Richard MacSween, Christine Rawlinson and Stephen Ormrod.

My agent Sarah Ballard had some astute suggestions to make fter reading an earlier draft. My thanks also to Eli Keren and arles Walker at United Agents.

m hugely indebted to my editor, Ann Bissell at Borough who – through her own experience of how alcoholism can impact on a family – could see what the book was trying to do and had some great ideas about the structure and much besides. I'd also like to thank Amber Burlinson for her copy-editing, Ellie Game for the cover design and Emilie Chambeyron for help with publicity. Thanks too to others in the team at Harper Collins, including Roger Cazalet, Kimberley Young, Suzie Dooré, Margot Gray, Ben Hurd, Sophie Waeland, Abbie Salter, Fliss Porter and Alice Gomer.